ON THE NEED FOR ECONOMIC DIVERSIFICATION

Economic diversification is a crucial subject for Kuwait and the other countries in the Gulf Cooperation Council. We need to step up efforts to diversify economic activities in order to reduce dependence on oil as the main source of output, exports, and public revenues, and to provide the high and growing number of newcomers into the labor market with productive jobs.

Kuwait's growth model has delivered substantial improvements in living standards over the past several decades. It has also ensured a sufficient level of infrastructure and high-quality public services. However, this growth model has incurred large costs. The public sector wage bill as a percentage of public spending is very high, and subsidizing basic goods is a heavy burden on our state budget. Non-oil public revenues were never an important part of total government revenue. The participation of national labor in the private sector is very low, and, above all, limited progress has been made on economic diversification.

Kuwait has initiated a number of steps to expand and enhance the business environment and to encourage the private sector to lead development and create jobs. As a matter of fact, one of the main goals of the economic development plan is for the private sector to lead the development of the economy. Public-private partnerships through the Partnership Technical Bureau and entrepreneurship through the National SME Fund are possible channels to spearhead development and diversification.

Yet, this is only the beginning of the process to diversify our economy. There is still a long way to go. While some of the reforms needed to promote private sector growth are complex and will take some time to pay off, we need to be persistent in our efforts, and make sure that the door is open to national and foreign private sector initiatives. We can learn from the experiences of other countries and apply the lessons to take the diversification agenda forward.

His Excellency Anas Al-Saleh
Minister of Finance
Kuwait

BREAKING THE OIL SPELL

THE GULF FALCONS' PATH TO DIVERSIFICATION

EDITORS
Reda Cherif
Fuad Hasanov
Min Zhu

*To Fred /
with best wishes
Reda Fuad
May 2016*

INTERNATIONAL MONETARY FUND

Cover design: IMF Multimedia Services Division
Cover image courtesy of Kuwait Petroleum Corporation.
Calligraphy by Mehveş Konuk. Used with permission.

Cataloging-in-Publication Data
Joint Bank-Fund Library

Names: Cherif, Reda. | Hasanov, Fuad, 1978– | Zhu, Min, 1951– |
    International Monetary Fund.
Title: Breaking the oil spell : the Gulf Falcons' path to diversification /
    editors: Reda Cherif, Fuad Hasanov, Min Zhu.
Other titles: Gulf Falcons' path to diversification
Description: Washington, DC : International Monetary Fund, 2016. |
    Includes bibliographical references and index.
Identifiers: ISBN 978-1-51353-786-3 (paper)
Subjects: LCSH: Petroleum industry and trade—Persian Gulf Region. |
    Economic development—Persian Gulf Region. | Natural resources—Persian
    Gulf Region. | Diversification in industry—Persian Gulf Region.
Classification: LCC HD9576.P352 B73 2016

Please send orders to

International Monetary Fund, Publication Services
P.O. Box 92780, Washington, DC 20090, U.S.A.
Tel.: (202) 623-7430   Fax: (202) 623-7201
E-mail: publications@imf.org
Internet: www.elibrary.imf.org
www.imfbookstore.org

Contents

Foreword

Natural-resource-rich economies face a peculiar development dichotomy. The natural resource wealth helps increase living standards, both directly and indirectly, in the latter case via the additional government revenues that are transferred to the population in the form of social and infrastructure services, while avoiding, at least in part, the tax levies that are needed to provide those services in other economies. At the same time, these economies face the adverse development effects highlighted in a now extensive literature on the "Dutch disease," giving rise to what has been called the "natural resource curse."

Some of the adverse effects are institutional in character: the strong reliance on the state for income and employment discourages the risk taking necessary to develop new activities, and rather promotes "rent-seeking" behavior by entrepreneurs who can benefit from overtly generous government contracts—and in the worst case, from corruption. Others are of a distributional nature, and relate to how natural resource assets (land, mines, and oil and gas wells) are distributed and/or how the opportunities to access the natural resource revenues captured by the state are distributed across different social groups.

This book underscores, however, the strictly economic issues highlighted in the Dutch disease literature, particularly those associated with the difficulties of diversifying the production base into new high-technology activities. I would add the interlinked problems posed by the adverse effects on domestic production structures of commodity price booms. These effects can be called the structural and the cyclical dimensions of the Dutch disease.

The *structural* problems are related to the fact that the high profitability of natural resource sectors in these economies reduces the incentives to invest in other tradable sectors, including high-technology manufactures and services that are the clue to economic growth at high-middle-income levels and, even more, at high-income levels. This problem is reflected, in particular, in de-industrialization, lack of industrialization and, more generally, the reduced opportunities to develop the non-natural resource tradable sectors, which is structural in character but is enhanced by commodity price booms. This problem, it can be added, is particularly severe in high-income oil- and gas-rich countries, such as the Gulf countries, on which this book focuses.

This aspect of the problem is frequently linked with a phenomenon that has received significant attention in development debates in recent years: the "middle-income trap," which in the case of the region this book looks at can be called the "resource-rich high-income trap." The basic problem in this case is the incapacity to develop the higher-technology tradable sectors that are essential to continue to increase productivity at higher levels of development. I would add that this problem is compounded by the challenges faced by "latecomers" into any activity; entering into new activities to diversify the production structure is made more difficult by the entry costs associated with technological learning and the need to capture markets from other firms, most probably sacrificing profit margins. Smallness is a further complication—and most of the Gulf countries are small by international standards—when activities are characterized by scale economies and/or the external economies provided by the development of complementary activities, a typical problem in manufacturing activities.

The structural challenges are formidable in very rich natural resource economies. This is why the "leading hand of the state"—the editors' terminology in this volume—is a *sine qua non* of any diversification strategy, and should focus on the development of "sophisticated tradables" that are critical for productivity growth at high-income levels. This involves an array of policy instruments, which, to quote from the concluding chapter of the volume, include "subsidies to support exporters and taxes on firms in the nontradables, access to financing and business support services through venture capital funds, development banks, and export promotion agencies, and the creation of special economic zones, industry clusters, research-and-development centers, and start-up incubators." This is an excellent summary, not only of the different authors' contribution to this volume, but of an extensive literature on industrial policies in emerging market and developing economies. This involves exploiting the forward and backward linkages of the commodity sectors, to use Albert Hirschman's terminology, but also developing entirely different activities, which are essential for a strong diversification— vertical and horizontal diversification, in the terminology of this book. Skills and human capital are essential but, as some chapters in this volume point out, they can be created through the diversification process, indeed as part of the broader learning that successful development of alternative economic activities require.

Let me also underscore the *cyclical* dimensions associated with the management of commodity price cycles, and particularly those cycles of longer duration, such as that experienced with the commodity boom of the 1970s (including, in the case of oil, the two oil shocks) and the collapse, first for non-oil commodities in the early 1980s and later for oil in 1986, which lasted for almost two decades. The new boom started in 2003–04, lasted for about a decade, and came to an end—sharply so in the case of oil. Indeed, as both cycles show, one of their major features has been the tendency for oil prices to experience stronger booms, but also stronger busts.

The management of these cycles requires extraordinary countercyclical policies to avoid an excessive expansion of aggregate demand during booms, which would tend to increase the relative prices of nontradables, generating a real exchange rate appreciation that would hurt non-resource-based tradable activities, either for export or competing with imports. If the latter effect is strong, firms active in those tradable activities may go bankrupt during commodity booms, with lasting effects on structural diversification and productivity, to the extent that the latter is associated with production experience (that is, learning). Furthermore, unless there are explicit policies to diversify production activity, the incentives to do so during commodity booms would be very limited. In either case, the economy would destroy or fail to create the sectors that are likely to provide the growth engines when commodity prices weaken.

This means that the management of commodity booms must count, first of all, on strong instruments to increase savings, and keep them abroad. This is what natural-resource-rich countries have learned to do with the creation of sovereign wealth funds and the accumulation of massive foreign exchange reserves. However, in the case of the Gulf countries, these countercyclical savings were insufficient during the boom of the 1970s and early 1980s, leading to what the editors of this book call the "Greatest Depression": the fact that per capita consumption fell by about 20 percent after the boom and did not recover to previous levels until the late 2000s. But, as pointed out in the previous paragraph, aside from savings there must be explicit policies to use the resources generated by the natural resource boom to promote new economic activities; otherwise the economy would lack growth engines when commodity prices collapse. Promoting new activities is, of course, a must during the periods of weak commodity prices, but the crisis conditions that then prevail and the reduced resources available may not be the best environment to promote new activities.

The Gulf economies, the focus of this book, have experienced these challenges in a remarkable way, as is reflected in the already mentioned "Greatest Depression" but also in the related fact that their per capita incomes relative to those of developed countries fell massively in the 1980s and 1990s before catching up only marginally during the recent commodity boom. Furthermore, efforts to diversify have only been partially successful in these economies. But the problem is broader, as the analysis of other regional experiences in this book indicates. The East Asian experience is the success story, as the review of the cases of Korea, Malaysia, and Singapore indicate, of which the latter two are more directly relevant to the Gulf countries, given that Malaysia is a commodity-rich country and Singapore is a small economy. As Chapter 6 describes, the Latin American experience is a less successful one, particularly during the era of market reforms that started in the 1980s (in the 1970s in a few countries), because the region has experienced "premature de-industrialization," that is, de-industrialization at lower per capita income levels than those at which it started to take place in developed countries. This is despite some success stories in terms of designing policy instruments, such as the development bank of Brazil (BNDES), as explained in Chapter 9.

I congratulate the editors and authors of this book for their contribution to the analysis of these issues, which have become even more important because of the major challenges that all commodity-dependent economies now face as a result of the end of the 2004–2013 super-cycle of commodity prices. It should inspire the design of new policy frameworks, difficult as it may be to implement them under crisis conditions.

José Antonio Ocampo
Professor, Columbia University
Formerly Under-Secretary General of the United Nations for
Economic and Social Affairs, Executive Secretary of the
Economic Commission for Latin America and the Caribbean,
and Minister of Finance and Minister of Agriculture of Colombia

Acknowledgments

This book would not have been possible without the support of the IMF's Middle East Center for Economics and Finance (CEF) in Kuwait. Indeed, the book is based on the high-level diversification conference[1] organized by the IMF and the Ministry of Finance of Kuwait. Hosted by the CEF, the conference took place on April 30–May 1, 2014—at the time when oil prices were still high and the topic was not as pressing—and was *the* forum for discussing ideas on how to shape the future of the region.

As shown throughout the book, the importance of investment in human capital to succeed in diversification cannot be overemphasized. In this respect, the establishment of the CEF has enabled the IMF to scale up the provision of training in the Arab region at a crucial juncture as many countries in the region undergo an economic transition. The Center works closely with the IMF, which provides technical assistance, and partners with other international organizations to strengthen policymaking institutions and capacity in the region. In the short period since its establishment, the CEF has become a center of intellectual leadership and has enriched the debate on the economic challenges of the region.

We would like to thank the government of Kuwait for its generous funding and tremendous support of the CEF, which plays an active role in disseminating high-quality training to the Arab region.

We are very grateful to His Excellency Anas Al Saleh, Minister of Finance of Kuwait, Badr Al Saad, Managing Director of the Kuwait Investment Authority, Ahmad Bastaki, the Executive Director of the Kuwait Investment Authority, His Excellency Muhammad Al Jasser, Minister of Economy and Planning of Saudi Arabia at the time of the conference and currently Minister at the Royal Court, and Fahad Alshathri, the IMF Executive Director for Saudi Arabia, for their generous support and contributions. Their participation and the support provided made the conference a success and paved the way for this book.

This book is also the product of tremendous support received from many IMF colleagues. In particular, we would like to thank Alfred Kammer, Deputy Director of the Strategy, Policy, and Review Department, and Tim Callen, Chief of the GCC Division of the Middle East and Central Asia Department (MCD), whose strong leadership, commitment to promote an open intellectual dialogue, and continuous support made the whole project possible. We are also indebted to Tarhan Feyzioglu, Advisor, Office of the Managing Director, for his strong support and help throughout the project.

We would also like to thank Sharmini Coorcy, Director of the Institute for Capacity Development (ICD), Masood Ahmed, Director (MCD), Alan MacArthur, Deputy Director (ICD), Ray Brooks, Division Chief (ICD), and Deputy Directors

---

[1] For more details, see http://www.imf.org/external/np/seminars/eng/2014/mcd/.

Aasim Husain (MCD), Andrew Berg (ICD), and Gerd Schwartz (ICD) for their strong support.

We are grateful to the staff of the CEF for their intellectual and organizational support. In particular, we would like to thank former Director Abdelhadi Yousef and former Acting Director Philippe Karam, as well as current Director Oussama Kanaan and Deputy Director Sami Ben Naceur. We would also like to express our gratitude to the conference coordinators Alia Al-Duaij and Muhannad Darwish at the CEF and Sara Knight in Washington, D.C., for their superb logistical support and outstanding effort.

We are greatly indebted to our colleagues in the Communications Department for their tremendous work in the publication of the book, in particular, Jeremy Clift, Joanne Creary Johnson, Linda Kean, and Linda Long. We are also grateful to Mehveş Konuk for the calligraphy of a falcon and to Kuwait Petroleum Corporation for allowing us to use the image of the historical Kuwait mural in their building for the book cover.

Lastly, we would like to thank our prominent contributors and speakers at the conference, who made this event lively, insightful, and stimulating, and without whom we would not have this volume: Philippe Aghion to Jose Miguel Benavente, Iftekhar Hasan, Clement Henry, Huck-ju Kwon, Mohamed Lahouel, Julio Ramundo, Ahmad Tajuddin, Meredith Woo, and Philip Yeo.

We hope that this collection of essays can serve as a starting point for policymakers to undertake diversification, one of the most challenging and pressing issues facing oil exporters.

Introduction

Tim Callen, Reda Cherif, and Fuad Hasanov

Creativity always comes as a surprise to us; therefore we can never count on it and we dare not believe in it until it has happened. In other words, we would not consciously engage upon tasks whose success clearly requires that creativity be forthcoming. Hence, the only way in which we can bring our creative resources fully into play is by misjudging the nature of the task, by presenting it to ourselves as more routine, simple, undemanding of genuine creativity than it will turn out to be.

Albert Hirschman, "The Principle of the Hiding Hand"

Economic development can be thought of as a chain of hard challenges, complex choices in the face of uncertainties, and creative solutions. Policymakers see high standards of living and sustainable and equitable growth as the ultimate goals of economic policy. Yet in pursuit of these goals, they probably do not consciously look for challenges. Rather, people are "apt to take on and plunge into new tasks because of the erroneously presumed *absence* of a challenge—because the task looks easier and more manageable than it will turn out to be" wrote Albert Hirschman in his famous essay "The Principle of the Hiding Hand." In Hirschman's formulation, the entrepreneur undertakes the project while perceiving the project as not risky—the hiding hand principle. As obstacles are discovered midway, without the possibility of turning back, the only way forward is to overcome them. So it is on the path to economic development and diversification. Economic development is a complex process, and policymakers may hesitate to plunge themselves into this challenging endeavor, especially in the presence of large oil revenues. However, as this book shows, the countries of the Cooperation Council for the Arab States of the Gulf (commonly referred to as the Gulf Cooperation Council or GCC) and most oil exporters cannot escape tackling these challenges.

The quest for the grail of economic development and growth is far from over. One of the major difficulties in identifying the factors contributing to development or the lack thereof is the wealth of historical experiences, institutional arrangements, and policies, making it hard to isolate the most important determinants. To paraphrase Leo Tolstoy, all developed economies are alike and each underdeveloped economy is underdeveloped in its own way.

In the universe of development experiences, oil exporters represent a particularly interesting group, lacking a diversified production base despite large oil income flows. Although oil revenues brought high living standards to many of these countries, even the high-income oil exporters are lagging technologically and are not economically diversified enough. Most of their export and fiscal revenues are coming from oil or oil-related products. Non-oil output consists overwhelmingly of nontradables, in particular of low-skilled services (such as restaurants, transportation, telecommunications), while most of the tradables are imported. Many oil exporters need to upgrade technologically and diversify their production base.

The decline of oil prices between the summer of 2014 and the fall of 2015 (while this book was being prepared) reinforced the importance and urgency of diversification for oil-exporting countries. During this period, oil prices fell by more than 50 percent and remained low, raising the specter of a return of the oil slump of the 1980s to 1990s. Citizens and policymakers from oil-exporting nations still remember the ordeal their countries went through at that time. The promise of easy and swift development brought by large oil revenues failed to materialize, resulting in unemployment, falling living standards, and heavy indebtedness. Oil exporters went through what can be described as the "Greatest Depression," which has lasted for about 30 years. Real consumption per capita on average fell by about 20 percent from 1980 and recovered to the same level only in the late 2000s as oil prices increased substantially. History does not repeat itself, but it should not be ignored.

Dealing with low oil prices in the current context of increased government spending and rising expectations about the provision of jobs and income transfers is even more challenging. Having learned from experience, many oil exporters accumulated large sovereign wealth funds during the years of high oil prices in the 2000s. Yet the funds only provide a temporary cushion. With a gathering momentum in investment in renewable energy, fuel efficiency, fracking and other technologies to exploit unconventional sources of oil and gas, and increasing use of electric cars, a secular decline in oil prices cannot be ruled out. Whether oil prices will stay low or rise again in the near future, it is high time to ask fundamental questions about the nature of oil-exporting economies. The key question is how to break the dependence on oil exports and pave the way for sustainable growth.

Despite the episodes of steep downturns in oil prices, many observers seem to consider that technological upgrade and economic diversification should not be a priority in high-income countries with long horizons of oil reserves. According to most of the recent literature, the main issues to tackle for resource-rich countries fall within three broad categories. In the first category, the main problem stems from a lack of redistribution, where wealth does not trickle down to all citizens. The argument goes that if such states were to relinquish their hold on revenues from natural resources and transfer rents directly to households, living standards would improve markedly. In the second category, the main issue facing natural resource exporters is the conduct of fiscal policy to manage volatility and provide for intergenerational equity.

In the third category, the missing ingredients of the standard recipe for growth represent the main challenge. The standard recipe includes, for example, financial deepening, openness to trade and capital flows, privatization, infrastructure development, flexibility in the labor market, and lifting legal and regulatory barriers to doing business. In short, market distortions, mostly due to the government, are preventing countries from taking off. The much-discussed topic of diversification in oil exporters is usually framed within this context, that of an enabling environment to support growth and private sector development.

In contrast, this book argues for placing diversification at the top of the policy agenda for oil exporters and traces the path to achieving it beyond the confines of the standard growth recipe. Although redistributing oil wealth and managing volatility and intergenerational equity are important, finding solutions for these problems would not prevent exporters from continuing the "secular decline" they have witnessed over the past several decades. Indeed, as shown in Chapter 1, the relative income of most oil exporters—and in particular the GCC countries—has fallen dramatically in the past 30 years, typically from above U.S. income per capita to a fraction of it. Even high oil prices would not counteract this decline. It is argued in the same chapter that the standard growth recipe is not sufficient, and the lack of sustainable growth is attributed to the lack of a dynamic tradable sector. This book focuses on the GCC countries, especially because their experience represents a quasi-natural experiment with important implications for development theory and practice. These countries have managed to achieve relatively high indicators along many standard dimensions of binding constraints on growth—for instance, availability of quality infrastructure, free mobility of capital and labor, including skilled labor, and low tariffs and taxes. Yet their productivity growth has been anemic and even negative for the past decades and the non-oil tradable sector has barely developed. Market failures are the main impediment to creating a dynamic export sector and, ultimately, sustainable growth. To correct these distortions, governments need to intervene, in particular to encourage the private sector to endeavor where it would not.

This book provides historic experiences and theoretical and empirical analyses of how different economies managed to spur long-term growth. It brings together the views of academics and policymakers. Chapters cover such regions as the Middle East, East Asia, and Latin America, and combine perspectives from various disciplines such as economics, history, political science, and social development. It is hoped that this interdisciplinary and interregional study can offer practical advice for the future while shedding new light on the past.

Part 1 discusses diversification attempts in the Middle East and North Africa region. Chapter 1 is an overview chapter presenting the case of the GCC countries to illustrate that policymakers need to consider the diversification of tradables as a policy priority. The GCC countries face the difficult task of refocusing their growth models toward creating more diversified economies, with less reliance on hydrocarbons to support growth as well as less reliance on the public sector to absorb new entrants in the job market. The chapter argues that a sustainable growth model requires a diversified tradable sector that is lacking in the GCC countries. It draws lessons from the diversification experiences of oil exporters, in particular from the few relatively successful ones—Indonesia, Malaysia, and Mexico. Success or failure appears to depend on implementing appropriate policies ahead of the fall in oil revenues.

Because export diversification takes a long time, it must start now. In contrast with the previous literature, the chapter argues that the standard policy advice—implementing structural reforms, improving institutions and the business environment, creating infrastructure, and reducing regulations—while necessary, is insufficient due to fundamental market failures stemming from Dutch disease; that is, the crowding out of the non-oil tradable sector by the income generated from oil exports. To overcome these barriers, the GCC countries need to change the incentive structure for workers and firms. The study of country experiences suggests that successful strategies mix vertical diversification (in specific sectors) to create linkages in existing industries and horizontal diversification (across sectors) beyond the comparative advantage, with an emphasis on exports and technological upgrading. Investment in skills and social development transforms the worker incentives.

Chapter 2 examines successes and failures in the Middle East and North Africa region, in particular Algeria and Saudi Arabia, the two countries that pushed most with industrialization in the 1970s. Through their experiences, the chapter discusses the mix of policies that might foster a sustainable diversification of the region's hydrocarbon-based economies. The human capital and education aspect is critical in developing a sophisticated export base. Attempts by the two most populous Arab oil states, Algeria and Saudi Arabia, to develop industry starting with limited resources of human capital is particularly instructive. Their experiences suggest that achieving a high human capital stock before industrialization is not a requirement or an obstacle.

Part 2 examines the experiences of East Asia and Latin America. Chapter 3 narrates the extraordinary transformation of Singapore since the mid-1960s from a poor port city to one of the richest countries in the world. Singapore's experience can be divided into five development phases, being labor intensive in the 1960s, skill intensive in the 1970s, capital intensive in the 1980s, technology intensive in the 1990s, and finally a knowledge and innovation economy since the 2000s. The chapter summarizes key policies that helped the transition from one phase to another as well the role of multinational corporations. In particular, it explores four different themes in the government's approach to developing its exports through the examples of four industries: electronics (creating value added), precision engineering (building around the value chain), chemicals (developing clusters), and biotechnology (focusing on research and development).

Chapter 4 studies the development path followed by Malaysia and the factors that contributed to its success. Malaysia is a particularly interesting case because it is one of the very few resource-rich developing economies that has managed to build a sizable and sophisticated manufacturing export base. The chapter provides an account of the country's social, political, and economic challenges and how they were overcome. The chapter further explains the rationale of the strategies devised to develop Malaysia's industrial and scientific capabilities that would take the country further down the development path in the decades to come.

Chapter 5 analyzes the experience of development in East Asian countries, with a particular emphasis on Korea. The chapter anchors the discussion in an historical context and helps explain how the general prescriptions suggested in Chapter 1 were pursued in Korea and how obstacles encountered along the way were overcome. The chapter offers an account of the actual constraints, relations with the private sector, incentives, and the real objective behind its industrialization strategy.

Chapter 6 explores the Latin American experience of diversification. The chapter argues that although many Latin American countries did well in the past decade or so, they rode the wave of a commodity boom. The stagnation of productivity in the region rings an alarm bell. The chapter discusses types of policies such as public inputs and market interventions along the horizontal or vertical dimensions of diversification. It concludes with the role of science, technology, and innovation in Latin American countries.

Part 3 explores some of the key policies to support diversification. Chapter 7 brings an important contribution to the theory of development in general and to natural resource exporters in particular. It tackles the key issue of how to overcome the middle-income trap. The chapter discusses potential determinants of productivity and productivity growth in firms. It also considers potential barriers to growth in the size of firms. The chapter revisits the role of vertical targeting (or sectoral policies) and proposes some elements of a new growth strategy for middle-income countries.

Chapter 8 studies the effect of diversification beyond the GDP measure, in particular poverty alleviation, technological innovation, capital flows, women's empowerment, and entrepreneurship. The results indicate that industrial diversification greatly improves the economy's output in all of these nonconventional measures. Illustrating the importance of diversification, the chapter then studies the different government programs used in Organisation for Economic Co-operation and Development countries to support innovation in certain industries. In particular, it provides evidence of the effectiveness of the U.S. Small Business Innovation Research Program and its equivalents in Europe.

Chapter 9 provides the practitioner's vision of industrial development in Brazil. It descends from a bird's-eye view of Brazil's industrialization toward the specifics of the role played by the Brazilian Development Bank in Brazil's growth over the past decades. It briefly provides an overview of the country's past industrial policies, their successes and failures, and the return of new industrial policies in the 2000s, followed by the discussion of policies and instruments that the bank has implemented as a development-oriented venture capitalist.

Chapter 10 examines the *Saemaul Undong* movement in Korea, arguing that it can provide a missing link between market- and state-oriented development policies. Saemaul Undong contributed to social and economic development in Korea not only as a self-help community movement but also as a mechanism of social inclusion. Its success was based on grassroots participation supported by the government and a social structure that was made more open to upward mobility by the land reform of the 1950s. For the Saemaul Undong "was in a sense, a movement for spiritual reform of Korean people, and has achieved a lot in this respect. It changed people's attitude from laziness to diligence, from dependence to self-reliance, and from individual selfishness to cooperation with others."[1]

---

[1] Choe, Chang Soo. 2005. "Key Factors to Successful Community Development: The Korean Experience." Discussion Paper 39, Institute of Developing Economies, Japan.

Chapter 11 takes a look at lessons for today and the way forward. The book concludes with the transcript of a conversation between His Excellency Muhammad Al Jasser, former Minister of Economy and Planning of Saudi Arabia and currently Minister at the Royal Court, and Min Zhu, Deputy Managing Director of the IMF, on the theme of diversification challenges in developing economies.

PART I

Diversification Attempts in the Middle East and North Africa

Soaring of the Gulf Falcons: Diversification in the GCC Oil Exporters in Seven Propositions

REDA CHERIF AND FUAD HASANOV

The countries of the Cooperation Council for the Arab States of the Gulf (GCC) face a difficult task in refocusing growth models to diversify their economies.[1] Yet doing so will reduce their reliance on hydrocarbons, allow the private sector to drive growth, and give people the skills needed to enter the high-value-added jobs those economies would create.

A key challenge is to find ways to develop non-oil tradable sectors, which should support sustainable private sector employment. Currently, however, most export and fiscal revenues in the GCC come from oil and gas sales, which affect economies through government spending, including public investment. The large amounts invested so far have not produced tradable sectors outside of oil and oil-derived products. These offer little export diversification and minimal linkage with the rest of the economy. In addition, the countries in the region cannot keep relying on their public sectors to absorb their own nationals newly entering the labor market. The GCC states also have many foreign workers, mostly low-skilled, and employed in the nontradable sectors rather than non-oil tradables.

Although all GCC countries do share this reliance on hydrocarbons, the difficulties they face in diversifying vary. For Bahrain and Oman, oil reserves could be depleted sooner than for the others, making it more urgent to find other sources of economic growth and export revenues. In Saudi Arabia, though oil reserves will be long-lasting, increasing the employment of nationals in the private sector is a key challenge. As in Saudi Arabia, nationals in Kuwait, Qatar, and the United Arab Emirates work predominantly in the public sector, with little incentive to work in the private sector and invest in developing their skills. Dubai's economy, by contrast, is more diversified, but its non-oil exports are concentrated in minerals, metals, tourism, and transportation services. That said, all GCC countries need to develop growth models that will allow citizens to continue to enjoy the fruits of development that have come with oil income.

We analyze, in seven propositions, the major economic challenges the GCC countries face. The prevailing oil-reliant growth model in the region has markedly

---

[1] The GCC is comprised of Bahrain, Kuwait, Oman, Qatar, Saudi Arabia, and the United Arab Emirates.

improved development indicators such as health, education, sanitation, and physical infrastructure. But it has also resulted in a decline in economic performance relative to other countries. We argue that a sustainable growth model requires a diversified tradable sector, which is now lacking. Because export diversification takes a long time, it must start now. In contrast with the previous literature, we argue that the standard policy advice—implementing structural reforms, improving institutions and the business environment, creating infrastructure, and reducing regulations—though necessary, will not be sufficient, because of fundamental market failures stemming from Dutch disease.[2]

To overcome these failures, other countries, including oil exporters, have gone beyond comparative-advantage sectors and targeted high-value-added industries such as manufacturing and innovation, with large productivity gains and spillovers to the rest of their economies. The state has often acted as a venture capitalist and fostered public-private collaboration to achieve sustainable and equitable growth.

We draw lessons from the experience of diversification in oil exporters; in particular, the few relatively successful ones—Indonesia, Malaysia, and Mexico. Success or failure appears to depend on implementing appropriate policies ahead of the fall in oil revenues. Our study of different diversification strategies suggests that a mix of vertical and horizontal diversification seems to be most successful. The former creates linkages in existing industries and the latter diversifies the economy beyond its comparative advantage, with an emphasis on exports and technological upgrading.

SEVEN PROPOSITIONS

Proposition One

The prevailing growth model achieved a large improvement in human development indicators, but also reduced relative economic performance.

Ever since oil was discovered in the GCC countries, it has been both a boon and a curse. The flow of oil revenues provided an opportunity to develop economies and improve standards of living. The GCC countries invested heavily in infrastructure and heavy industries, started developing services such as finance, logistics, trade, and tourism; spent considerably on education and health; and provided affordable food and energy to their populations. However, the decline of oil prices in the 1980s–1990s did not pave the way for export diversification—the concept that we argue is most relevant in the analysis of diversification and sustainable growth, as opposed to the share of non-oil GDP. The region's economies remain as dependent on oil as they were in the past.

The growth model in the GCC consists of extracting oil and producing oil-related products and nontradables while importing most of the tradable goods it

---

[2] Dutch disease here is broadly defined as the crowding-out of the non-oil tradable sector by the income generated from oil exports.

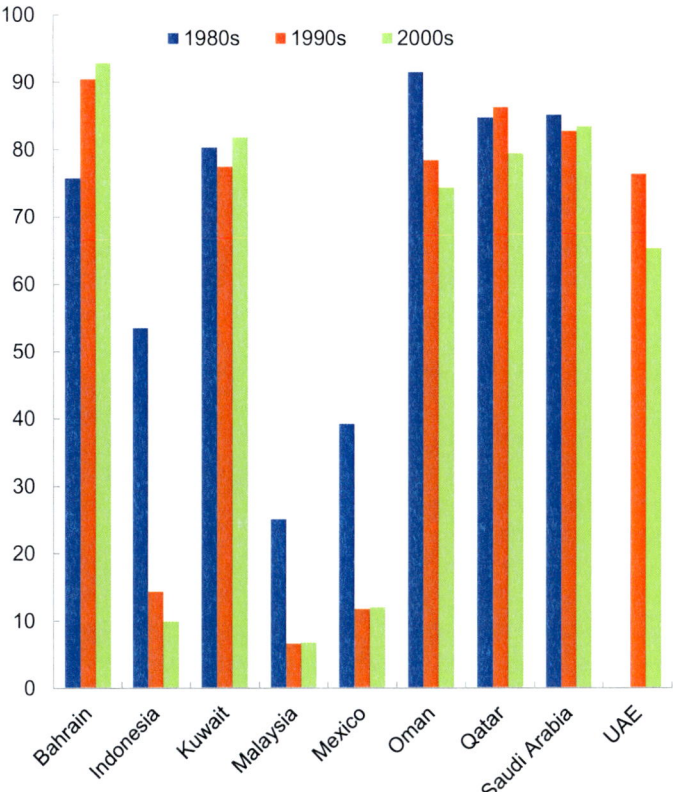

Figure 1.1 Average Oil Exports *(Percent of Total Exports)*
Source: IMF, World Economic Outlook database.
Note: UAE = United Arab Emirates. UAE goods and services exports exclude re-exports.

consumes.[3] Oil exports accounted for more than 60 percent of total exports of goods and services in the GCC in the 2000s, and this share either increased or has not fallen much since the 1980s (Figure 1.1). In contrast, oil export shares fell drastically in oil exporters such as Indonesia, Malaysia, and Mexico. In addition, oil revenues were more than 60 percent of total fiscal revenues in the GCC in 2013.

Output composition in the GCC countries varies, but they all share an export composition heavily concentrated in oil, chemicals, and metals such as aluminum. The share of mining/utilities output (in real terms) is above 30 percent in all but one GCC country; Bahrain's is about 15 percent, similar to Norway's. Manufacturing shares are smaller than in comparator oil exporters. Starting from a low base, non-oil exports grew about 13 percent per year on average during

---

[3] Annex Tables 1.1.1 and 1.1.2 list the main economic characteristics of the GCC countries and other oil exporters.

2000–10. Compared with the rest of the GCC, the United Arab Emirates has increased its non-oil exports substantially.

The state dominates the economy, receiving oil revenues and redistributing them through different channels. Fiscal policy acts as the main transmission channel of oil price fluctuations to non-oil output (Husain, Tazhibayeva, and Ter-Martirosyan 2008). Government spends a large part of the oil revenues directly and provides for citizens through transfers and jobs in the public sector, which employs the majority of nationals in most GCC countries (IMF 2013a). A part of revenues is invested in mega projects, especially infrastructure and real estate, while the rest is saved; for instance, in the sovereign wealth funds. In addition, most private sector jobs are held by expatriate labor, and most of those workers are employed in low-skilled and low-productivity activities.

The GCC has raised living standards hugely, and human development index scores have improved substantially. Infant mortality has fallen, expected years of schooling risen, and life expectancy increased (Figure 1.2). Even in comparison with oil exporters in the advanced countries, such as Canada and Norway, the GCC countries are performing relatively well.

In parallel, however, the GCC countries slid in international income rankings. GDP per worker (in purchasing power parity dollars) has fallen, except in Oman and Qatar; standards of living declined as oil prices dropped to their lowest levels in the 1980s–1990s and improved somewhat after oil prices started rising (Figure 1.3). In relative terms, overall performance was even more disappointing. The GCC countries fell substantially in relative income rankings, from about 1.5 to 4 times U.S.

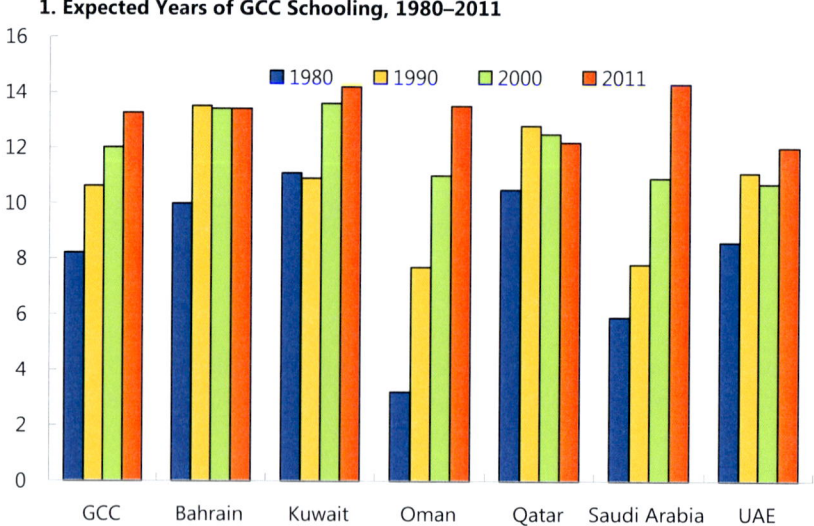

1. Expected Years of GCC Schooling, 1980–2011

Figure 1.2 Social Indicators

Sources: New York, Department for Economic and Social Affairs; UNESCO Institute for Statistics; United Nations Department of Economic and Social Affairs (2009); and United Nations Development Programme.
Note: GCC = Gulf Cooperation Council, UAE = United Arab Emirates.

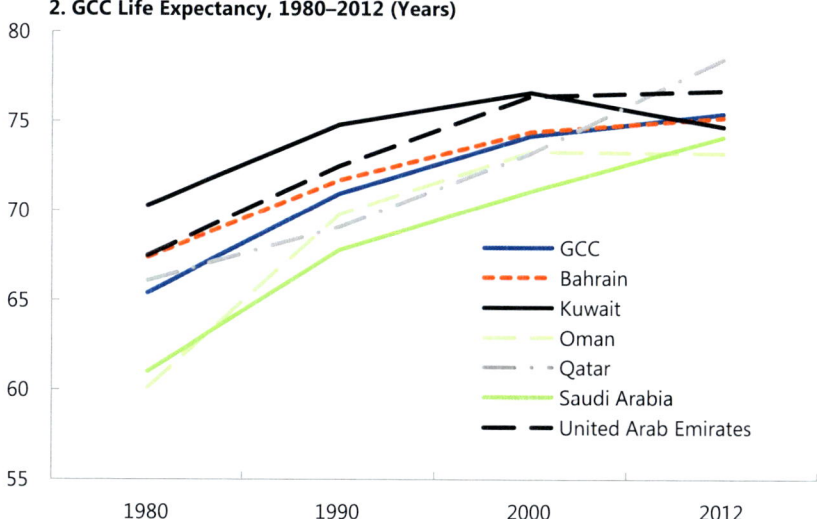

2. GCC Life Expectancy, 1980–2012 (Years)

Figure 1.2 (Continued)

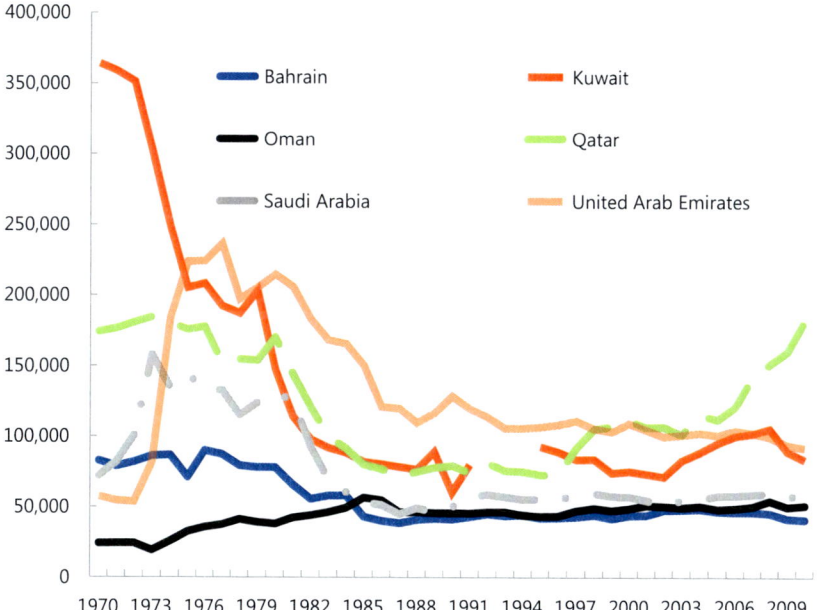

Figure 1.3 GDP per Worker, 1970–2010 (Purchasing power parity, 2005 constant dollars)
Source: Penn World Tables 7.1.

income per worker in 1980, for most, to U.S. levels or below in 2010.[4,5] Even Qatar, with large gas production and a small population, decreased from more than three times the U.S. level to only about double the U.S. income per worker. Bahrain and Saudi Arabia slid to the 43rd and 31st rank of income per worker relative to the U.S. level in 2010, respectively, from top-10 positions in 1980.

The fall in relative income was also accompanied by declining productivity, while real GDP growth was mostly driven by factor accumulation (Figure 1.4). High capital accumulation—including human capital—and population growth contributed to the high growth of output in the GCC, but was not accompanied by increasing relative performance on a per capita basis. Total factor productivity (TFP) declined in all GCC countries during the three decades through 2010.[6] TFP in Mexico has also declined, but it grew in Indonesia and Malaysia, increasing the gap between the GCC and other oil exporters. Large accumulations of physical capital contributed to growth in Indonesia and Malaysia and supported TFP growth (see Annex Figure 1.1.1 for other countries).

Proposition Two

A sustainable growth model requires a diversified tradable sector.

Sustainable growth is driven to a large extent by export diversification and the sophistication of the country. Hausmann, Hwang, and Rodrik (2007) and Cherif and Hasanov (forthcoming) show empirically that export sophistication is one of the major determinants of growth, accounting for initial conditions, institutions, financial development, and other growth factors. Jarreau and Poncet (2012), using regional Chinese data, reach the same conclusion, but emphasize that it is the domestic firms' export activities that have the largest effect on subsequent growth. Foreign firms mostly contribute to export upgrading. Papageorgiou and Spatafora (2012) also indicate that export diversification in low-income countries is one of the major determinants of growth and is associated with the decline in the volatility of GDP per capita in developing economies. Their study finds that quality upgrading, especially in manufacturing, is positively correlated with growth. Since export sophistication is crucial for growth, the manufacturing sector, with its high potential in this area, represents an important sector to focus on. Moreover, Rodrik (2011) shows that labor productivity in manufacturing industries converges across countries, independently of initial conditions.

To create sustainable growth, a country needs to constantly produce new goods and adopt and develop new technologies. Lucas (1993), in the seminal paper "Making a Miracle," argues that constantly introducing new goods, rather than only learning on a fixed set of goods, is needed to generate productivity gains for

---

[4] Although 1980 corresponds to the peak of the oil price boom that began in the 1970s, using it as a base year is valid as oil prices in real terms are about the same level in 2010 as in 1980–81. In addition, our results are still valid overall whether we use the 1970s or 1980 as a base year.
[5] The data on PPP GDP and employment come from the Penn World Tables 7.1 and could differ from other sources.
[6] IMF 2013a also finds declining TFP during 1990–2012 using national accounts data.

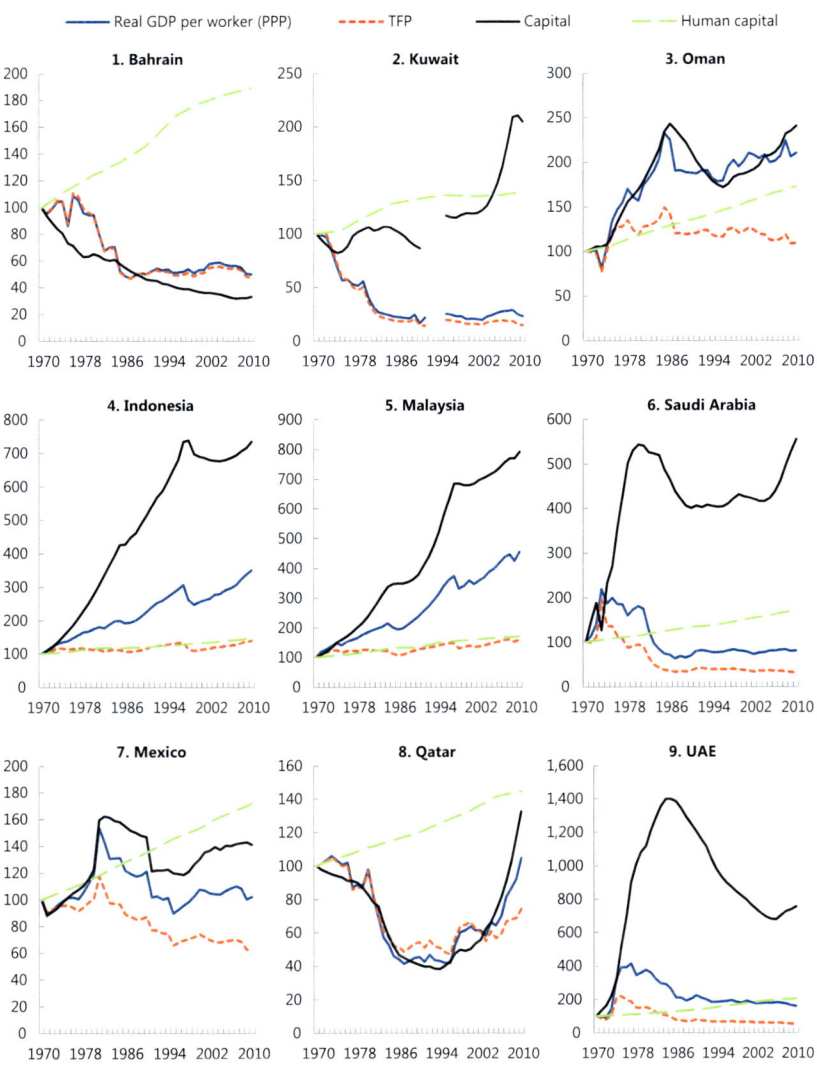

Figure 1.4   Growth Decomposition, 1970–2010 *(1970 = 100)*

Source: Penn World Tables 7.1.

Note: PPP = purchasing power parity; TFP = total factor productivity; UAE = United Arab Emirates.

a sustained growth miracle. Learning by doing (learning on the job) is one of the most important channels for accumulating knowledge and human capital in this process. Producing the same set of goods would rapidly lead to stagnation in productivity. In contrast, introducing new goods and tasks would allow managers and workers to continually learn and move up the "quality ladder."[7] To do this on a large scale, Lucas argues, the country must be a large exporter.

---

[7] See the seminal paper on creative destruction by Aghion and Howitt (1992).

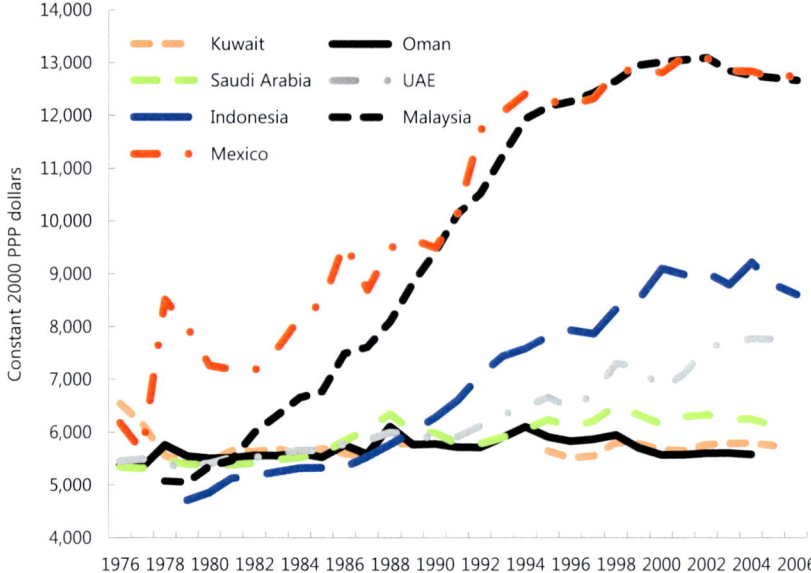

Figure 1.5 Goods Exports Sophistication, 1976–2006

Sources: Hausmann, Hwang, and Rodrik (2007); and World Bank.

Note: PPP = Purchasing Power Parity; UAE = United Arab Emirates.

Declining productivity and relative income stagnation in the GCC can be explained by the nondiversified export base and stagnating export sophistication. As the studies just mentioned show, sustainable growth depends importantly on export sophistication and new goods production. Compared to commodity exporters such as Indonesia, Malaysia, and Mexico, the GCC countries' export sophistication is low and has not improved much over the years (Figure 1.5).[8] Productivity gains were negative over the period.

The comparison of Bahrain and Singapore offers a stark example of the distinction between export diversification and output diversification. The output compositions of the two countries are comparable overall (Figure 1.6). Starting at comparable shares, the mining sector share increased in Bahrain from the 1990s relative to Singapore's. The manufacturing share in Bahrain is similar to that in Singapore, while the share of construction is slightly greater. In contrast, exports in Bahrain are almost exclusively concentrated in oil and metals (more than 95 percent), which is vastly different from the diversified export base of Singapore, where the manufacturing sector accounts for more than 60 percent of total goods'

---

[8] Export sophistication is measured according to Hausmann, Hwang, and Rodrik (2007). The measure, EXPY, is defined as the export-share weighted average of sophistication levels of the country's export basket. The sophistication of each good is measured as the weighted average of real GDP per capita—a proxy for the level of sophistication—of all countries that export that good.

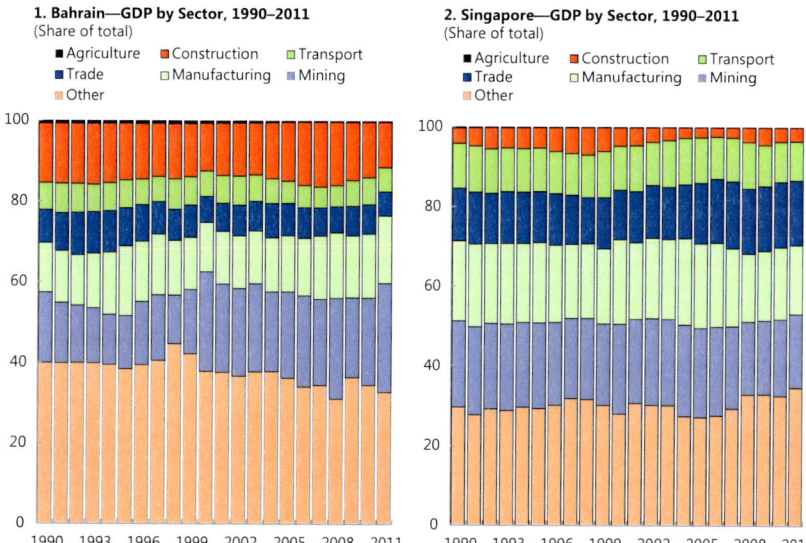

Figure 1.6 Bahrain and Singapore: Output Structure, 1990–2011

Sources: Country authorities; and United Nations Statistics Division database.

exports (Figure 1.7). In addition, manufacturing in Bahrain is mostly aluminum and other metals, which is not necessarily the most conducive to the introduction of new goods and tasks and moving up the quality ladders that Lucas (1993) advocated. Even when Bahrain's exports of services (transportation, travel, communication, and insurance) are taken into account, oil still represented more than one-half of total exports of goods and services in 2010.

In a similar vein, output diversification and non-oil growth are misleading indicators of diversification and sustainable growth. The example of Bahrain shows that a relatively diverse output composition does not necessarily imply export diversification. The export structure is a proxy for tradable production, the main source of productivity gains for sustainable growth. In fact, TFP declined in the GCC countries during 1980–2010, despite high non-oil growth over the same period, ranging from about 4 percent in Saudi Arabia to 10 percent in Qatar. This increase in non-oil GDP, however, is mostly due to oil revenues channeled to the economy through fiscal and related private spending. Non-oil GDP comprises energy-intensive and resource-related industries such as metals and petrochemicals, as well as construction and services, such as retail and restaurants, transport and communications, and social services. High non-oil growth in these economies is not an indicator that growth could be sustained in the long term, or, if oil prices were to fall, for a sustained period.

The literature on diversification in the GCC suggests that past attempts have yielded few benefits. Hvidt (2013), analyzing the national visions of the GCC governments, argues that the implementation of these plans is plagued with many

1. Bahrain, Top 50 Exports of Goods, 2008
(Percent of total exports of goods)

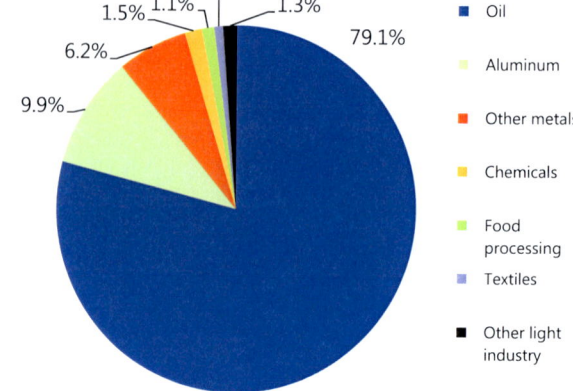

2. Singapore, Exports by Sector, 2008
(Percent of total exports of goods)

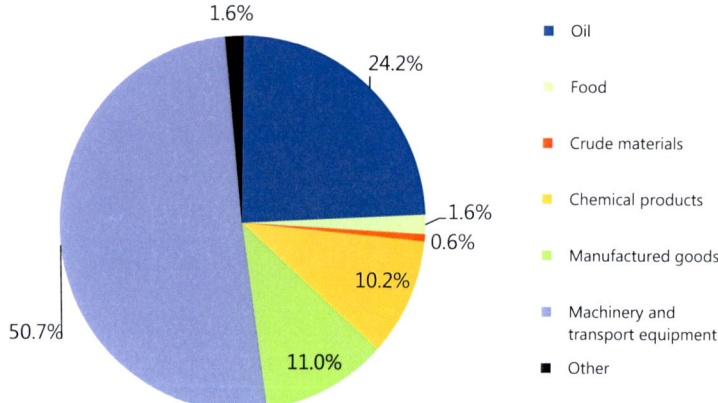

Figure 1.7 Bahrain and Singapore: Export Structure, 2008

Source: Country authorities.

obstacles. These include barriers to interregional trade, the duplication of economic activities across the GCC, and political environments in which governments tend to revert to patronage and increased government spending rather than follow through on tough reforms. Poor diversification in the GCC, according to Looney (1994), can be explained by the lack of an overall industrialization strategy, Dutch disease, the reliance on migrant labor, and inadequacies of incentives in production and exports. To fight the oil curse, Elbadawi (2009) suggests a stable macroeconomic environment, rules-based fiscal policy, and sound economic and political institutions for the management of oil rents. El Beblawi (2011) stresses that natural-resource-based industries and import substitution industries such as food processing and construction materials are not sustainable growth drivers. Nabli and others (2008) discuss the need to promote horizontal policies and improve governance.

Heavy industrialization strategies in the GCC, in chemicals and energy-intensive sectors such as aluminum, helped diversify production and exports, but had several shortcomings. These industries are capital intensive and have resulted in few linkages to the rest of the economy. Local sourcing of tradables in support of the heavy industries was not developed, and most of the complex technology is still imported. Although some technology was acquired (such as Saudi Basic Industries Corporation's 2007 acquisition of GE Plastics), there was not much technology transfer to the rest of the economy. The productivity gains and spillovers were limited. The employment opportunities available in these capital-intensive industries are small. In addition, the exports of oil derivatives such as petrochemicals are strongly correlated with oil prices, in turn hampering the reduction of high export income volatility. Recent attempts at creating industrial clusters, technology parks, and other manufacturing industries have yet to yield substantial results.

Service sector exports have grown strongly in a number of countries in the region, though the development of services may not be sufficient for sustainable growth. The GCC countries have developed tourism, logistics, transportation, and financial services. The development of services resulted in output diversification, but most of these services rely mainly on low-skilled labor (such as tourism and transportation) and would not attract nationals. Low-skilled activities such as restaurants and transportation are less conducive to sustained productivity gains, and cannot be the engine of a sustainable growth strategy for high-income countries such as the GCC. In addition, the amount exported is insufficient to cover imports. In the United Arab Emirates, exports of services barely covered a quarter of imports of services in 2011, and the net service balance has been negative since 1990, despite the growth of exports. In Bahrain, the net service balance is positive, but only covered about a third of goods imports in 2011.

The focus on such sectors is not sufficient for countries with larger populations to reduce their dependence on volatile oil prices and decrease unemployment. In theory, high-value-added sectors and the associated high-wage jobs exist in both the tradable and nontradable sectors. But for an economy to generate sufficient jobs in high-value-added nontradables (such as software or design), it needs to create a network of interlinked tradable and nontradable sectors. It is unlikely that existing high-value-added sectors such as finance, insurance, and managerial jobs can absorb the massive number of entrants projected. As Arezki and others (2009) show, specialization in tourism yields limited growth benefits. For instance, an increase in the tourism sector share of exports by 8 percent (one standard deviation in a sample of more than 80 countries over 1980–90) increases growth by only one-half percentage point a year. Nor would the sector help absorb a labor force of nationals with high reservation wages. Even the finance sector, paying high wages, is not enough to generate sufficient employment. Bahrain's finance sector, about 17 percent of GDP, directly employed less than 10 percent of nationals in 2012, similar to London's share of the finance and insurance sector.

Proposition Three

Both the initial technological gap and the size of oil revenues determine the chances of success or failure at diversification in oil-exporting countries, while policies adopted magnify or mitigate this effect.

During the past decades, oil exporters diversified their economies with different degrees of success. Countries such as Algeria, Congo, Gabon, the GCC countries, and Yemen have not developed many tradables, but Malaysia, Indonesia, Mexico and others have increased their export sophistication and developed manufacturing industries. We argue that the relative success or failure in diversification stemmed mainly from the manifestation of a crowding-out of the tradable sector, which could be described as a type of Dutch disease, while the policies that were pursued magnified or mitigated this effect. Broadly speaking, Dutch disease is the crowding out of the tradable sector as a result of oil revenues compared to the counterfactual of no oil revenues.[9] In the following we will use Dutch disease to describe this crowding out of the tradable sector, although not necessarily linked to real exchange rate movements.

The severity of the crowding out of the tradable sector depends both on the amount of the oil revenues and the initial technological gap or distance to the technology frontier (Cherif 2013).[10] Oil exporters can be classified along two dimensions shown in Figure 1.8, in which the real value (deflated by the U.S. consumer price index) of machinery and transport equipment exports per capita in 1970 is used as a proxy for the initial level of technology.[11] Four groups of oil exporters are distinguished: low tech (initially) and low revenues (such as Algeria, Angola, Republic of Congo, Ecuador, Indonesia, Malaysia, Mexico, Nigeria, and Venezuela), low tech and high revenues (Bahrain, Gabon, Kuwait, Libya, Oman, Qatar, Saudi Arabia, and UAE), high tech and low revenues (Canada), and high tech and high revenues (Norway).[12]

---

[9] When income increases as a result of oil revenues, and both tradable and nontradable goods are normal, the increased demand for nontradables is met by real exchange rate appreciation and a relocation of labor toward the nontradable sector (see, for example, Krugman 1987). Empirically, the real exchange rate in the GCC is unaffected by oil revenues, implying that traditional transmission of Dutch disease does not apply (Espinosa, Fayad, and Prasad 2013). However, as discussed in proposition five, the crowding-out of the tradable sector takes place in the GCC by the impact of oil revenues on incentives for exporting in these economies, given the distribution mechanisms of oil revenues to the rest of the economy.

[10] In the Cherif (2013) model, the relative wage depends on relative productivity in the tradable sector. The bigger the productivity gap, the bigger the relative wage, and thus an increase in oil revenues, when translated into domestic income, would have a bigger income effect than is the case with a lower productivity gap. This would result in greater crowding-out of the tradable sector. Empirical evidence supports this result.

[11] The data come from Feenstra and others (2005) (code 7 of the U.N. SITC classification). Jarreau and Poncet (2012) use a similar measure (share of high technology manufacture in total exports) as an alternative to EXPY, the export sophistication measure from Hausmann, Hwang, and Rodrik (2007). Both measures exclude services; however, it should not affect the results as the services share of exports is small for many countries.

[12] One could argue that instead of flows or revenues, the stock of oil reserves or oil wealth matters most through consumers' expectations. However, consumers might not internalize the ownership of reserves,

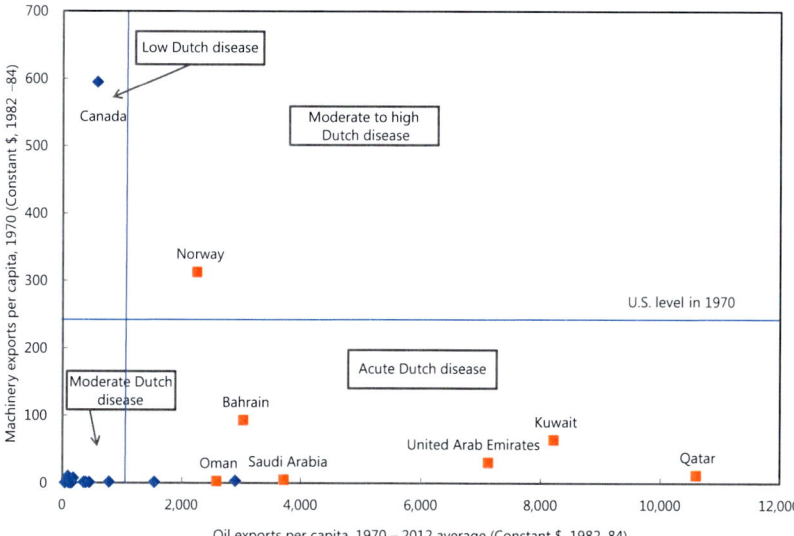

Figure 1.8   Initial Machinery Real Exports per Capita (1970) vs. Oil Revenues (1970–2012)

Sources: Feenstra and others (2005); and IMF, World Economic Outlook database.

Overall, the performance of oil exporters has followed this typology (see Figure 1.9):

- Canada, a high-tech/low-oil-revenue country, did well in increasing its technological development proxied by real machinery exports per capita.

- In contrast, Norway, which received large oil revenues and is technologically sophisticated, did not increase its exports per capita as much and actually fell from above the U.S. level in 1970 to below it in 2000.

- Low-tech countries with large oil revenues did not do as well. Out of nine countries, Oman and the United Arab Emirates increased their exports more than others, but only to about the 1970 U.S. level.

- Lastly, among low-tech/low-oil revenue countries Indonesia, Malaysia, and Mexico succeeded in diversification compared with Algeria, Nigeria, and Venezuela. Although Indonesia's machinery exports did not increase as much as Malaysia's and Mexico's, its export sophistication improved significantly. Both indicators improved substantially in Mexico. Malaysia stands out for its significant improvement both in export sophistication and machinery exports, reaching levels close to Canada's.

---

and even if they were to do so, either (1) credit constraints would prevent them from properly smoothing their consumption; or (2) the precautionary saving motive would be high as a result of the high level of uncertainty in the oil price (Cherif and Hasanov 2013). Empirically, most studies find evidence of Dutch disease based on flows to stocks (such as Cherif 2013 and Ismail 2010).

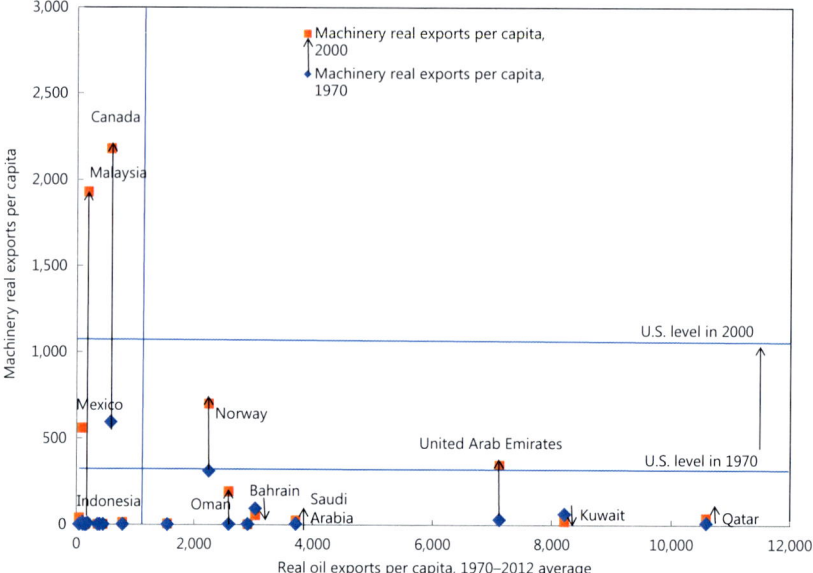

Figure 1.9 Machinery Real Exports per Capita (1970 vs. 2000) vs. Oil Revenues (1970–2000)
Sources: Feenstra and others (2005); and IMF, World Economic Outlook database.

To sum up, high-tech countries were better prepared for coping with Dutch disease and were already diversified before receiving oil revenues. However, as oil revenues increased, the odds of success were overwhelmingly against the low-tech countries, such as the GCC countries. In the low-tech/low-revenue quadrant, we contend that the policies pursued put these countries on different and diverging development paths.

One would think the high-tech countries such as Norway, with an already diversified export base, could escape Dutch disease. But as it received much bigger oil revenues than Canada, Norway fell prey to Dutch disease, despite its strict rules designed to sterilize most of the oil income. In 2012, manufacturing hourly wages were the highest in the world and about double those of the United States or Japan, according to the U.S. Bureau of Labor Statistics. Unit labor costs increased by 50 percent in the 2000s, whereas they declined in Germany and Sweden. In addition, Norway's annual average hours per worker declined to about 1,400 in 2012, down 600 hours since 1960, according to Norway's State Statistics Bureau, the third fewest hours worked in the Organisation for Economic Co-operation and Development.

Norway's export sophistication has been on a declining trend since the late 1970s, despite its relative increase in machinery exports per capita. The rapid decline coincided with the spike in oil prices in the late 1970s, but then export sophistication recovered slightly in the period of very low prices through to the mid-1980s. Since then, sophistication has been declining. One could argue that incorporating services in the measurement of export sophistication would mitigate the observed decline.

But the largest service export is maritime transport, the incorporation of which is unlikely to reverse the decline. In addition, neighboring Denmark witnessed a slight increase in sophistication during 1976–2006, despite starting with higher export sophistication. The gap with Norway widened substantially. Interestingly, Malaysia, which stood at about 45 percent of Norway's level in the mid-1970s, caught up by the late 1980s, and was about 65 percent higher by the mid-2000s.

It could be argued that the few success stories among oil exporters are in the group of countries where the size of oil revenues received was not large enough to crowd out their non-oil tradable sectors. In other words, they stood a fighting chance at diversifying their economies. As the performances within this group show, however, policies did matter. Norway's case suggests that at much earlier stages of development, the potential effect of large revenues is likely to be detrimental to the tradable sector, as observed in many Middle East and North African oil exporters.

The experience of oil exporters suggests that very few countries—Indonesia, Malaysia, and Mexico—successfully diversified (see Annex 1.2). These countries prepared the ground before the dwindling of oil revenues occurred. Although the three increased their export sophistication, they have yet to achieve the successes of Korea and Singapore, and remain dependent on natural resources, to a significant extent.

Malaysia, one of the earliest oil exporters to scale down its import substitution strategy in the 1970s, has relied on an export promotion policy (Jomo and others 1997). The country successfully expanded its export base as well as the sophistication of its manufacturing sector. Today, manufacturing represents more than a third of all its exports (and three-quarters if one includes refining and other natural-resource-related manufacturing). To achieve this goal, it used a multifaceted approach by (1) selectively encouraging foreign direct investment (FDI) in exports, especially in electronics; (2) relying on free trade zones; (3) offering lower taxes; and (4) providing a stable business environment and an educated workforce with competitive wages. The country has promoted specific strategic industries to achieve the maximum technological transfer possible. It relied on both horizontal and vertical development of industries and natural-resource-related industries (Yusof 2012; Jomo and others 1997). And it used active state intervention to spur growth in sectors it deemed important, in effect acting as a "venture capitalist." In parallel to rapid physical accumulation, human capital accumulation was very important. The Malaysian state also used public agencies to enforce a continuous retraining and skill upgrading of employees.

With the collapse of oil prices in the 1980s, Indonesia adopted a set of policies meant to attract foreign capital in export-oriented manufacturing. The main instruments of this policy were the creation of free trade zones, tax incentives, the easing of tariff restrictions and non-tariff barriers, as well as the largest exchange rate devaluation among developing nations in the 1980s (Jomo and others 1997). The result was substantial growth in labor-intensive manufacturing (textiles, footwear, electronics, and so on) because of the attractive level of wages. During the liberalization of the 1980s, the government performed a "strategic retreat" and retained several strategic projects, in particular in steel and the aircraft industry. Jomo and others (1997) note that Indonesia's experience also shows that, with government commitment, a complex technology industry was successfully started from scratch in what was a poor nation at the time. Indonesia today is part of a selected group of developing economies with clusters of aircraft maintenance and aircraft parts manufacturing. The creation of the national champion, albeit at a large cost, did facilitate the establishment of this cluster.

Like Indonesia, Mexico started with labor-intensive industries and moved to more sophisticated production. The country also relied on free trade zones focused mainly in labor-intensive industries (mostly foreign owned). It did help increase exports, but firms did not climb the value-added ladder and had weak linkage with the rest of the economy.

The upgrading of Mexico's industries is evident in the automobile industry over the past 15 years. In 2012, employment in the sector in Mexico surpassed that of the U.S. Midwest (40 percent of North American employment in Mexico versus 30 percent in the Midwest) and is expected to continue rapid growth. Obviously, the North American Free Trade Agreement and exchange rate depreciation in the 2000s helped propel FDI into the country from automotive companies planning to export to the United States. However, the policies adopted by different states in Mexico in pursuit of building manufacturing clusters and their performance in productivity and quality upgrading are important. In particular, the State of Guanajuato followed what can be described as a purpose-specific investment strategy in parallel with strong incentives to attract firms. In infrastructure, the state built a 2,600-acre interior port, customs facilities, a railroad depot, and link to the local airport (Cave 2013). Nearby, there is also a polytechnic university to supply engineers, and the state gives incentives to firms to send workers for training abroad. The state has attracted foreign firms by providing tax incentives, but, more interestingly, by acting as an active consultant.

In summary, the main policy lessons from the diversification experiences of relatively successful oil exporters are as follows:

- Import substitution strategies created mostly inefficient firms because they were not encouraged to compete on international markets. Instead, they relied on a captive domestic market and imported inputs and technology. A focus on competing on international markets and an emphasis on technological upgrading and climbing the value-added ladder are crucial.

- Malaysia's policy mix, involving investment in higher-value-added, comparative-advantage industries (such as natural-resource-related manufacturing) and going beyond comparative advantage (electronics) was the most successful.

- Comparing the experience of Malaysia to that of other oil exporters shows that it is more important for the state to actively encourage the supply of inputs in target industries (such as skilled labor, infrastructure, consulting) than to impose price distortions to protect an industry (tariffs and price controls).

- Indonesia and Mexico show that relying mostly on low wages and labor-intensive manufacturing eventually leads to limited productivity gains. Mexico's experience shows that efforts to attract FDI need to be directed toward the creation of industrial clusters.

Proposition Four

Export diversification must start now.

The GCC countries enjoy high standards of living and very long horizons of oil reserves, so one could argue there is no urgency to start diversifying economies. However, we contend that implementation of a true diversification strategy is urgently needed.

It would take 20 to 30 years to achieve high export sophistication. The few successful oil exporters prepared their non-oil export base for decades before they could take off when oil revenues dwindled. Malaysia started its export-oriented strategy in the early 1970s, for example, and experienced rapid growth in export sophistication in the 1980s–1990s. Despite the rapid pace, it took more than 20 years to reach a level of sophistication comparable to some advanced economies.

The experience that oil exporters went through in the 1980s–1990s is a cautionary tale of reduced spending, falling standards of living, and increased debt levels. The oil exporters went through a long recessionary cycle—measured by consumption per capita developments—that lasted 30 years. Consumption per capita on average fell about 20 percent from the 1980 peak, returning to this level only in the late 2000s as oil prices recovered (Figure 1.10). Continuing with the implementation of the same model (extracting oil, saving part of it in a sovereign wealth fund, and investing mostly in infrastructure without focusing on tradables) is likely to be suboptimal for social welfare. Even if the GCC countries tackled subsidy and tax reforms and managed to create more fiscal space, this would not be sufficient to diversify the tradable sector, which is crucial for sustainable growth (see proposition five).

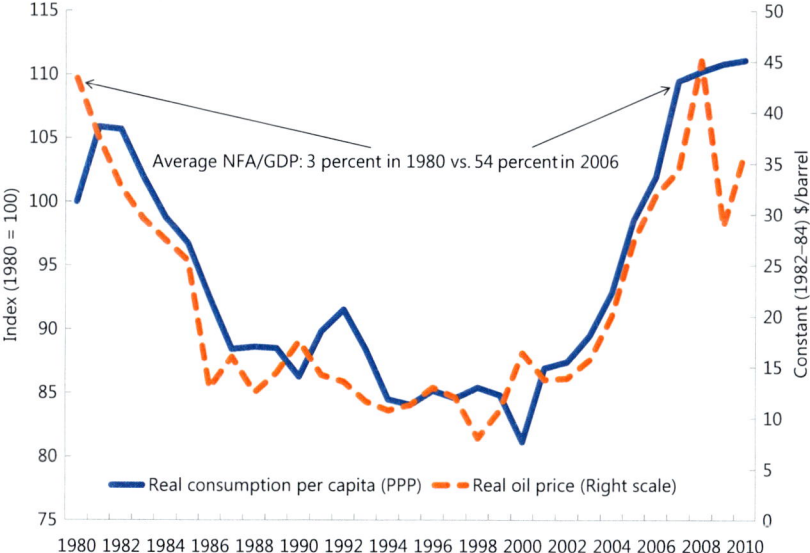

Figure 1.10 Real Consumption per Capita and Real Oil Price, 1980–2010

Sources: IMF, World Economic Outlook database; and Penn World Tables 7.1.

Note: Data come from a sample of oil exporters. PPP = purchasing power parity, NFA = net foreign assets.

Proposition Five

The standard policy advice—implementing structural reforms, improving institutions and business environment, investing in infrastructure, and reducing regulations—is very important, but may not be sufficient to spur tradable production, because of market failures.

Macroeconomic stability, minimum state intervention, and an enabling environment conducive to investment in both physical and human capital are the main ingredients of the standard growth policy prescription for sustainable economic growth. It consists of tackling what is described as "government failures" by Stern (2001) and Rodrik (2005). These failures could stem from the associated high inflation, monopolies, investment impediments, uncertainty regarding property rights, and other types of government-driven distortions. Reforms are ongoing in the GCC to address these issues, yet there has been little progress in export diversification in most countries (see proposition three). Although there is still room for improvement along those dimensions, especially in the legal and bankruptcy framework and cumbersome business regulations in some countries, can the lack of progress in increasing non-oil exports and manufacturing output be attributed to government failures alone? We contend that the binding constraint to developing the non-oil tradable sector lies also in market failures and that tackling both government and market failures is necessary for true development to take place in oil-exporting economies.

A growing body of literature points to the need to rethink industrial policy. It invites economists not to rule out industrial policy as a tool because badly designed industrial policies failed in the past (typically import substitution strategies in the 1970s). Pioneers in the revival of industrial policy include Alice Amsden, Ha-Joon Chang, Ricardo Hausmann, Jomo, Sanjaya Lall, Jose Antonio Ocampo, and Dani Rodrik. The gist of their arguments is that economies face multiple market failures that impede their industrialization.[13] Economies could be trapped in a suboptimal state, not only as a result of distortions imposed by the government or government failures, but as a result of market failures due to learning externalities or coordination failures (Rodrik 2005).

Market failure based on a learning externality[14] implies that firms do not internalize productivity gains, leading to lower allocation of resources into high-productivity sectors. As Matsuyama (1992) argues, some activities, typically manufacturing, entail higher productivity gains for an economy than other traditional activities such as nontradable services or agriculture. Firms may not be fully aware that these productivity gains lead to lower output in high-productivity sectors and lower relative incomes over time. The learning externality could also involve spillover effects in which productivity in other sectors

---

[13] The other main argument is that manufacturing expansion and technological upgrading of export sophistication are key to sustained productivity gains and development in general, as proposition two discusses.

[14] "Learning externality" refers to the positive effects the production activity has on other firms that are not taken into account by a firm performing this activity or paid for it.

increases, while firms are unable to extract the pecuniary benefit from the spillover effect (such as manufacturing's spillover effect on agriculture). In this case, the resource allocation into the traditional sector would also be higher than would otherwise be socially optimal (Rodrik 2005).

The coordination failure is based on the idea that a modern sector (such as manufacturing) needs to reach critical size for a firm to enter it. It would be profitable for a firm to invest in a modern sector only if enough firms were investing simultaneously in other modern sectors. The mechanisms proposed in the literature to explain the spillovers differ (such as demand spillovers). However, they could be summed up as related to reaching a critical market size to justify investment in complex technologies (for example, automotive and aircraft). If many firms invest together in modern sectors, described as the "big push," the economy reaches a higher level of productivity and development. But the existence of market failures requires state intervention to reach a socially superior outcome, with the type depending on the market failure. One could reinterpret the failure of import-substitution strategies as one of misidentifying market failures.

We argue that the GCC countries, and probably other oil exporters, are not plagued so much by "government failures" as by "market failures," though the two are often closely linked. Three arguments indicate that the binding constraint on firms in the GCC, impeding diversification, is not related to government failure:

- The GCC countries have achieved very high infrastructure quality scores and other business quality indicators. Their successes are striking in comparison with other oil exporters that have done poorly in indicators of the ease of doing business, but much better in promoting export sophistication, such as Indonesia and Mexico (Figure 1.11).

- Norway and more recently Canada (Stanford 2012) could not escape Dutch disease, although government failures are basically nonexistent there, in particular in comparison with developing nations. If such advanced economies with a strong record of institutions, governance, skills, infrastructure, and other ingredients of an enabling environment are not immune to Dutch disease, it is highly likely that developing oil-exporting countries are not, either. Moreover, trying to reach their level of institutional quality and openness would certainly not be enough to develop the tradable sector. As Henry and Miller (2009) show, Barbados and Jamaica's real GDP per capita diverged after independence as they pursued different economic policies despite a similar institutional environment, geography, and colonial and legal heritage.

- Diversification in successful oil exporters was taking place as oil revenues were slowly declining. The institutional reforms would have taken a relatively long time to materialize as the diversification process was ongoing. The International Country Risk Guide's bureaucratic quality indices for Malaysia and Saudi Arabia were similar and did not change through the 1980s–1990s as Malaysia was developing its tradable sector, while the quality index was lower for Indonesia.

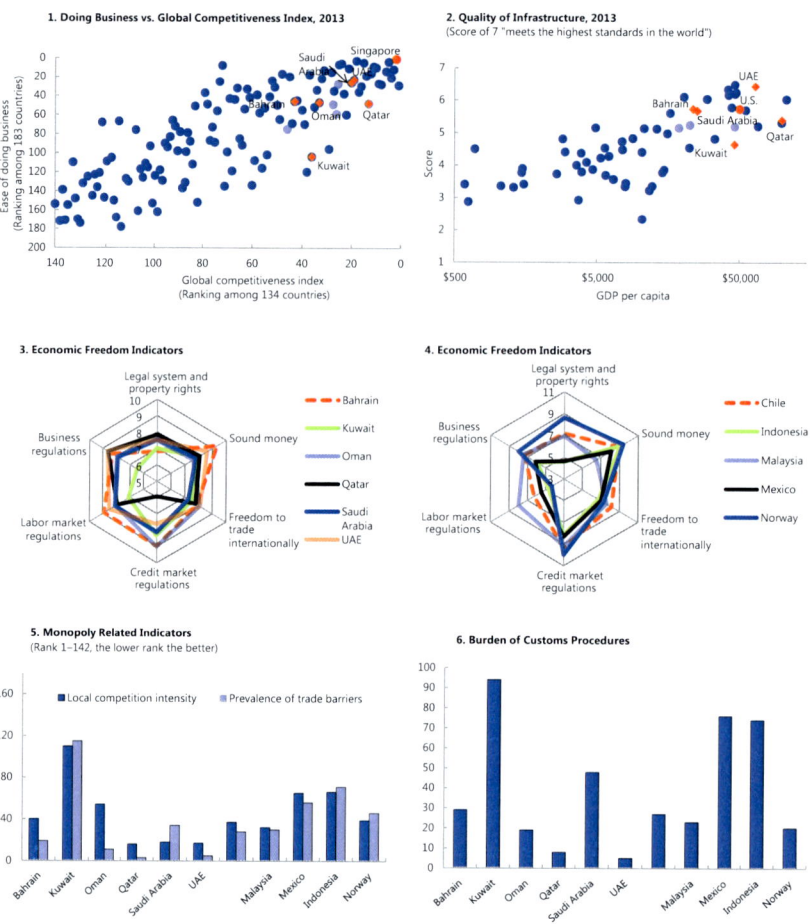

Figure 1.11 Governance and Institutions Indicators

Sources: Fraser Institute; World Economic Forum, Global Competitiveness Indicators (2013–14); and World Bank, Doing Business Indicators.

Note: UAE = United Arab Emirates.

We identify the market failures preventing these economies from developing their tradable sectors. As discussed in proposition three, Dutch disease would lead to a learning failure if firms did not fully recognize the tradable sector's higher potential productivity gains. This is a variant of failure caused by a learning externality, according to the taxonomy of Rodrik (2005). As discussed in proposition three, oil exporters are trapped in a vicious circle in which their relative productivity, or technological gap, in the tradable sector keeps deteriorating. This market failure seems to be the most significant of the theories advanced in the literature.

However, one needs to identify the exact channel relevant for the GCC.[15] We suggest a novel channel of transmission of the Dutch disease in the GCC, and the

---

[15] Standard Dutch disease theory would not fit the GCC picture, with its important assumption that labor is not internationally mobile. If it were, the increase in the revenues from oil exports would not

key to understanding it is the attitude of firms, especially conglomerates. For small and medium-sized enterprises (SMEs), many potential hurdles complicate development of exportable goods—among them access to financing, lack of skills, and poor business services support. In contrast, conglomerates in the region are large, decades-old corporations with access to land, financing, government connections, and the ability to import both skilled and unskilled labor. Moreover, they have access to world-class infrastructure and operate within trade agreements that give access to most advanced markets. In other words, they would be shielded from most forms of government failure or even known market failure, in particular coordination failure. So why do they not diversify into tradable goods as the Korean conglomerates did a few decades ago?

For the GCC, we argue that oil revenues skew the risk-return trade-off between the tradable and nontradable sectors (Cherif and Hasanov forthcoming). Suppose an entrepreneur has to decide whether to enter either the tradable or nontradable sector. The tradable sector is exposed to international competition and requires many years of investment with highly uncertain returns, though the potential for productivity gains is higher. Given high enough oil revenues, the "insurance" mechanism would be at work, and the nontradable sector would be far more attractive to enter than the tradable sector. Access to imported labor would not change this mechanism and would only affect the scale of the output of nontradable goods and profit margins. It could in fact fuel a vicious circle of a further increase in demand for nontradable goods because of the inflow of expatriate workers.

Paradoxically, the government could exacerbate market failure in this environment by engaging in big investment projects in infrastructure, which are by nature nontradable, over multiple years. Commitment to build infrastructure is laudable and most developing economies consider it a priority for development. But if the current binding constraint on producing tradable goods is not infrastructure, the resources may be put to better use developing tradables. In fact, large infrastructure projects may exacerbate the crowding-out of the tradable sector by further increasing risk-adjusted returns in the nontradable sector for monopolistically competitive or oligopolistic firms. The mechanism we described would also apply to SMEs, few of which enter tradable sectors, even when some of the standard hurdles facing them are eased. Government funding programs to encourage SMEs are mostly concentrated in services sectors such as transportation, retail, and restaurants.

Proposition Six

Governments need to change prevailing incentive structures.

The fiscal policies GCC countries follow have helped create very generous social systems, but with limited incentives for risk taking. As noted in proposition

---

lead to real exchange rate appreciation and crowding-out of the tradable sector. This assumption is fairly plausible for most oil exporters, especially those with large populations such as Nigeria or Venezuela. But the GCC economies have had open labor markets with huge inflows of expatriate workers in the past decades, especially from low-income countries.

one, many nationals in the GCC countries are employed by the public sector, where average compensation is relatively high. In the United Arab Emirates, for instance, it is about $4,500 a month compared with less than $2,000 a month in the private sector (IMF 2013a). Energy subsidies represent about 10–20 percent of GDP in the GCC countries, reaching about 30 percent in Bahrain (IMF 2013b). In addition, the legal retirement age is relatively low in the GCC. For instance, Saudi Arabia has a defined benefit system with retirement age of 60 for men and 55 for women, at the low end of the range (IMF 2012). It is even lower, at around 50–55, in Bahrain, Oman, and Qatar. Pension benefits are also high, with a replacement rate of 80 percent in Bahrain, for instance (World Social Security Forum 2013).

The risk-return trade-off channel described in proposition five also applies to the labor market. A risk-free strategy in which nationals can join the public sector for a relatively high salary and generous compensation and benefits does not encourage the uncertain path of entrepreneurship or employment in the tradable sector.[16] Working in the private sector entails higher probability of job loss, longer hours, and maybe even lower pay. The structure of the labor market does not encourage investment in human capital either. If the possibility exists of getting a risk-free job with lifetime employment, generous pension, and relatively high compensation, then the risk-adjusted returns on education need to be very high to justify this investment. In turn, the lack of skills would prevent the private sector from creating enough high-productivity/high-wage jobs to attract workers. The outcome becomes self-reinforcing: the private sector will not create high-productivity jobs given the lack of skills, and the workforce skill set will not improve given a lack of "learning by doing" in high-productivity jobs. So, how can the state change the incentive structure to encourage private sector employment?

The public sector should not be the employer of first resort, offering relatively high compensation and benefits compared with most of the private sector. Government should place firm limits on public sector jobs and wages and clearly communicate to workforce entrants that they should not expect one.

This needs to be matched by programs to ensure that the training and support needed to work in the private sector are available. As in Belgium and Germany, vouchers could be used for training programs on starting a business, accounting and finance, legal issues, information technology and other applied professions, apprenticeship training systems, and vocational education. Safety nets also need to be in place to provide the unemployed a minimum income (as well as the incentive to search for employment).

These approaches would reduce the need to absorb new workers into the public sector, reducing the wage bill, and by reducing the bloated public sector, increase efficiency without disrupting public services. An assured minimum income would also encourage risk taking and, coupled with training programs, provide the necessary support for entrepreneurs.

To attract nationals into the private sector, salaries need to be more competitive, calling for high-value-added jobs and reforms in public employment policy.

---

[16] For evidence on the crowding-out effect of public sector employment, see Behar and Mok (2013).

And to generate such jobs, the private sector has to move from its current business model of reliance on unskilled cheap labor in low-value-added sectors (such as retail, restaurants, transportation, and so on) to more advanced sectors. But this transformation could initially require attracting high-skilled labor and entrepreneurs from other countries, and active policies to create a high-skilled and dynamic national labor force.

Improving skills and changing attitudes should be tackled early; changing incentives as more workers enter the private sector and improving their skills is not enough. Growing evidence suggests that the quality of early childhood education has long-lasting outcomes (Heckman 2008), while Heckman, Pinto, and Savelyev (2013) show that a good-quality early education also has long-term positive effects on test scores. More importantly, Heckman (2008) shows that a program works through its positive effect on noncognitive skills: that is, children with a good early education scored higher on tests later because of more positive social behavior and more academic motivation rather than through higher intelligence. And the positive effects, not limited to labor market outcomes, also included healthier behavior.

In the GCC, even though governments have spent substantially on education and increased years of schooling, education outcomes are still low. GCC countries spend more than 4 percent of GDP on average on education (Saudi Arabia and the United Arab Emirates spend 5.0–5.5 percent of GDP, above the average of high- and middle-income countries; IMF 2013a). Spending per capita is even higher than in most developing economies. However, educational achievements are not in line with this investment, while the average years of schooling is still significantly below that of developing economies (Figure 1.12).

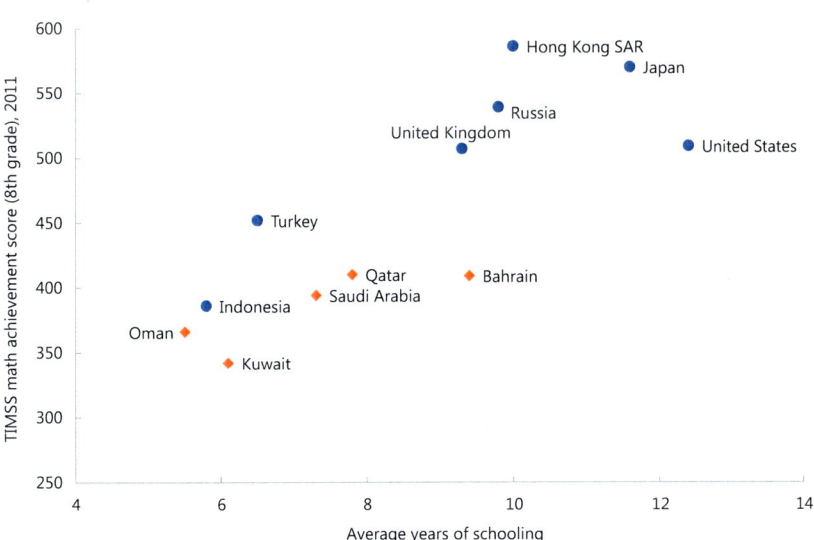

Figure 1.12   Education: Years vs. Quality of Schooling

Sources: Trends in International Mathematics and Science Study (TIMMS); United Nations Development Programme.

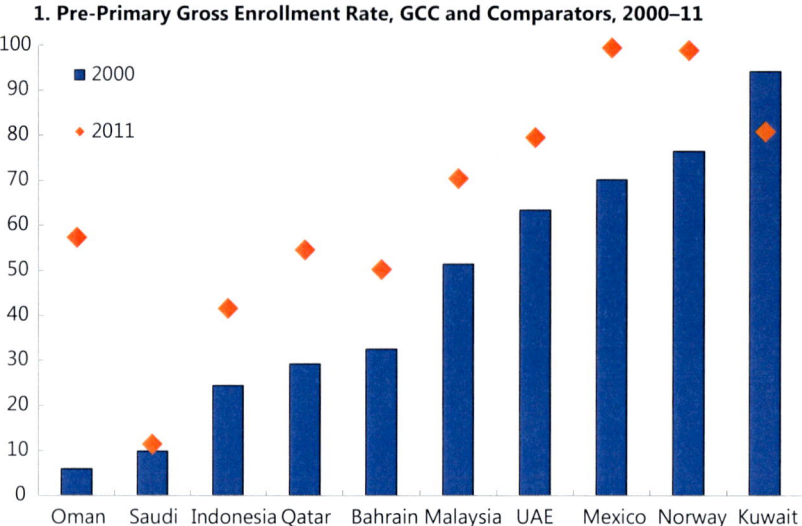

1. Pre-Primary Gross Enrollment Rate, GCC and Comparators, 2000–11

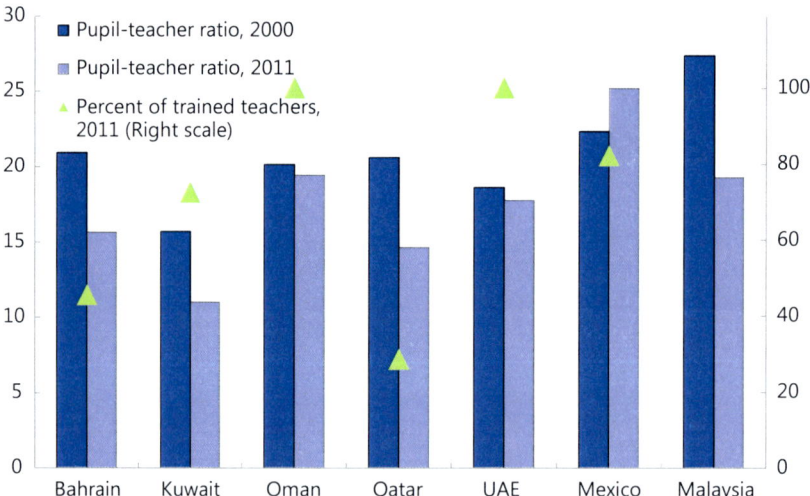

2. Pre-Primary School Statistics, 2000–11

Figure 1.13   Pre-Primary School Statistics, 2000–11

Source: United Nations database.
Note: GCC = Gulf Cooperation Council, UAE = United Arab Emirates.

The amount and quality of early childhood education could be another factor explaining poor results later in life. Several GCC countries have low enrollment rates in early childhood education (Figure 1.13), and countries with the highest enrollment rates in this group also tend to have the highest test scores in secondary school, as shown in Figure 1.12. Student achievement is also highly correlated with teacher quality. This, suggest Dolton and Marcenaro-Gutierrez (2011), depends on how high teachers are in the income distribution of their country. Wages paid have a direct causal effect on teacher motivation, in line with efficiency-wage theory, but they could also act as a proxy for the quality, length of training, and the selectivity of the hiring process. Higher teacher quality also provides a channel for tackling low test scores and the quality of education in general.

Changing societal attitudes toward private sector employment is important, and Korea's experience shows how current attitudes can change. Korea's Saemaul Undong is one social program that changed attitudes and created a link between social and economic development (Kwon 2010; see Chapter 10). It was initially meant as a rural development tool in the early 1970s, but, owing to its success, was rapidly expanded to incorporate urban communities and the public administration.

The program first encouraged communities to undertake small-scale projects to improve their surrounding environment, then to invest in income-generating projects and infrastructure. Government funded and provided the organizational framework, such as type of projects, leadership, accountability, and regional/national coordination, and provided technical assistance. Although the concrete achievements of the program were impressive, the long-term objective was to change social attitudes by encouraging communities to work together, develop self-help, and eventually build the will to contribute to the development of the country.[17] Saemaul Undong "was in a sense, a movement for spiritual reform of Korean people, and has achieved a lot in this respect. It changed people's attitude from laziness to diligence, from dependence to self-reliance, and from individual selfishness to cooperation with others" (Choe 2005).

The social development literature considers Saemaul Undong a role model and an important ingredient of Korea's success (Choe 2005; Kwon 2010). However, the specific conditions of each society should be taken into account when applying programs like the Korean one (Kwon 2010). Even so, Korea's experience shows that through concrete community projects, taking socioeconomic context into account, governments can spur a spirit of self-reliance, innovation, and entrepreneurship. But for this to happen, governments themselves need to change the way they approach development.

Proposition Seven

The state could act as a venture capitalist and foster public-private collaboration to design and implement strategies that go beyond comparative-advantage sectors and target high-value-added sectors with large potential spillovers and productivity gains.

So far we have argued that for GCC countries to achieve sustainable growth a dynamic non-oil tradable sector needs to emerge. We also inferred from the experience of oil exporters in general and the GCC in particular that the main impediment to the emergence of the non-oil tradable sector is not a government failure, but rather a market failure, requiring a redeployment of state intervention. We

---

[17] In the 1970s, for example, 43,000 kilometers of village roads, 61,700 kilometers of agricultural roads, and 79,000 small bridges were built, while 2.7 million households were supplied with electricity (Choe 2005, Table 1).

also argued that it was urgent to start implementing policies to tackle this challenge. This leaves us with the question of how the state should help the process of diversification, in addition to changing the incentive structure in the economy. It is imperative to note that implementing the policies formulated in this proposition without simultaneously tackling the change in the incentive structure of the society, as discussed in proposition six, will work. Without the right change in incentives, the policies proposed would be unlikely to produce the much-needed tradable sector and could lead to destructive misallocation of resources.[18]

The seemingly commonsense answer would be to focus on sectors where the GCC countries have "comparative advantage."[19] But the comparative-advantage theory ignores the fact that to develop new industries a country needs to accumulate industry-specific capital and knowledge. A central assumption of modern comparative-advantage theory is that the same technology is freely available to every country. The only barrier that prevents the poorest developing economy from producing aircraft, robots, or satellites, say, is the capital-to-labor ratio. It ignores the importance of experience in technology acquisition, or learning by doing, and that capital accumulation does not necessarily imply developing new industries. For instance, the GCC countries accumulated impressive general-purpose infrastructure such as roads, ports, and airports. A large buildup of residential and commercial real estate in the GCC would also amount to capital accumulation. Even in a standard Ricardian comparative-advantage framework, Krugman (1987) shows that in the presence of learning externalities (learning by doing), there is a justification for infant industry protection policies. Young (1991) further shows that in a growth model with learning by doing, a country starting with a lower initial level of knowledge would grow less in free trade equilibrium than in equilibrium without trade. Essentially, producing goods in the sector in which learning by doing has been exhausted without attempting to produce goods with learning externalities, would lower growth.

There are also GCC-specific arguments against a pure comparative-advantage strategy. Studies based on "revealed comparative advantage" usually indicate that GCC countries should invest in relatively low-value-added industries such as agro-industry, basic metal manufacturing, and animal skin and leather products. It could be argued that a relatively poor economy could focus on such sectors and approach the upgrading of the industrial sector gradually. However, given that the GCC countries are already high-income countries, it seems unlikely that focusing on these sectors would prevent them from sliding further down the income ladder as they did in the past decades. These low-value-added sectors would not attract enough national workers to tackle the pressing employment issue. In the description of Chang and Lin (2009), the question is not whether comparative advantage should be defied or not, but how far from comparative advantage a state should push.

---

[18] As argued in Cherif and Hasanov (2013), with low productivity in the tradable sector, optimal investment should be relatively low.

[19] Note that if the same logic were applied to Korea in the 1960s, the conclusion would have been to focus on rice or wigs, the main export at the time.

In vertical diversification, the GCC countries have already made significant investment in refining, aluminum smelting, fertilizers, and petrochemicals. As the example of Malaysia showed, the important element is to build domestic capabilities and enter into downstream and upstream activities such as medical materials based on rubber, research in biotechnology engineering to improve palm production, and the international diversification of Petronas, the state oil company (Jomo and others 1997). The emphasis for the future should be on building linkages with the rest of the economy and technological transfer and upgrade.

This could involve creating networks of suppliers around the existing exporting industries. The oil extraction and refining industries, for example, require a large number of manufacturing inputs (machinery, metals, pipes, platforms) as well as high-value-added services (software, geological surveys, engineering studies) with high employment potential. These industries would have the advantage of geographic proximity and knowledge of the specific needs and expected demand.

In this respect, Norway's state policies to develop an oil and gas suppliers' cluster in the 1970s represent an interesting case study. First, the government intervened directly in the procurements of oil operators. The Norwegian Petroleum Code required that operators communicate their lists of bidders to the government, which in turn had the authority to impose the inclusion of Norwegian firms in the list and even to change who was awarded the bid (Leskinen and others 2012). Second, the licensing process required foreign operators to come up with plans to develop the competencies of local suppliers (Heum 2008). Third, starting in the late 1970s, the government ruled that a minimum of 50 percent of the research and development needed to develop a field take place in Norwegian entities (Leskinen and others 2012). Although the restrictions were lifted in 1994 when Norway signed trade agreements with the European Union, the government continued after 1997 to support the suppliers though the INTSOK foundation to encourage them to internationalize their activity. Eventually the suppliers' cluster became highly successful, including on international markets, spanning a large array of high-value-added industries related to the subsea, geology, and seismic fields; developed the required skills; and directly employed about 114,000 workers in 2009, or more than five times the employment of operators in the oil and gas sector (Sasson and Blomgren 2011a, 2011b).

In Singapore, to create "system integrators"—large firms to spearhead sector development—clusters, and "global brands" in the tradable sector, as well as to direct state-owned enterprises (SOEs) to produce tradables, the state itself became what Mazzucato (2013) calls "the entrepreneurial state."[20] Pure coordination failures as discussed in the literature require a "system integrator" or industrial beachheads to provide a "big push" (Murphy, Shleifer, and Vishny 1989) for firms to enter this market. The bigger the technological leap (or the further from the comparative advantage), the bigger the risk and the time it would take to discover the true outcome (Rodrik 2005; Chang and Lin 2009). Horizontal

---

[20] Government-linked companies in Singapore played a significant role in the economy since independence and are run efficiently on a competitive and commercial basis (Ramirez and Tan 2004).

diversification has usually focused on tradable manufacturing and high-tech innovation sectors, including high-skill services. High-tech sectors, or innovation sectors, have large spillover effects on job creation, as shown by Moretti (2012). The growth of global value and supply chains could further support entry of firms and countries to produce specific goods (such as the Asian supply chain). In the current globalized world of trade in tasks and intermediate goods, global value chains are opening up a new avenue for countries to join high-value-added goods production chains.

Entry into the tradable sector provides potentially high returns over the long term, but at high risk in contrast to nontradables that provide high returns in the short term at lower risk. Relevant examples of the risk-return trade-off are Nokia's mobile unit (part of a logging company at the time), which incurred losses for about 20 years, and Toyota, with losses for 30 years, before becoming profitable (Chang and Lin 2009). In contrast, Malaysia's tire industry, for example, did not manage to take off (Jomo and others 1997), showing the importance of competing in international markets and enforcing accountability.

To address the risk-return trade-off in favor of the tradables, governments have used subsidies to support exporters and taxes on firms in the nontradables. The key element in providing support, however, whether to private firms or SOEs, is to make sure that the top management is responsible for the funds they receive, and, if needed, could be fired for nonperformance (Chang 2007). Substantial subsidies and tax breaks are given to large corporations even in advanced economies with the best business environment possible, like the United States and the European Union. As reported by the nonprofit organization Good Jobs First, Boeing had 137 subsidies and tax breaks worth about $13 billion. Alcoa, an aluminum company, received $5.6 billion; Intel, about $4 billion; and Dow Chemical, $1.4 billion over the past decades. According to the World Trade Organization, Airbus received about $18 billion from European governments in the 1990s to the mid-2000s.

Insurance for the tradable sector and access to financing are a second set of policies that countries have used. These are provided through development banks, venture capital funds, and export promotion agencies. Given the long horizon of potential returns and the high risk involved, cheap credit, grants, and access to equity funding would facilitate risk-return trade-off choices conglomerates and SMEs would have to make. There are programs to support innovation through early-stage financing to SMEs in most advanced economies. Lerner (1996) shows empirically that firms that benefited from the U.S. Small Business Innovation Program, which provided more than $6 billion in funding between 1983 and 1995, grew significantly faster than comparable firms. After the failure to attract multinationals to a newly created Science Park in 1980, a Taiwanese venture capital initiative provided financial incentives and tax credits to encourage the setup of firms (Kuznetsov and Sabel 2011). A seed fund provided matching capital contributions to private venture capital funds. Two funds were established and run by U.S.-educated Chinese invited to relocate there. The venture proved successful, and large banks and firms started creating their own venture capital funds.

Even conservative family conglomerates followed suit and started investing in information technology businesses. By the late 1980s, the growth in the venture capital industry was well under way.

The creation of special economic zones, industry clusters, incubators with university links, and the promotion of entrepreneurship constitute a third set of policies that countries have used to promote the development of tradables. Special economic zones have helped tackle countries' specific binding constraints such as land rights and legal/bankruptcy frameworks. Similar to Singapore's Jurong Town Corporation, which specialized in urban planning and made Singapore a location choice for foreign investors, special economic zones would provide business services and support in a short period of time; for instance, to acquire land, facilities, lease agreements, and approval of plans (Minli 2008). Incubators with university links, coupled with research and development funds, would support the promotion of technology transfer and commercialization. Kuwait and Saudi Arabia, for example, have very low research and development spending compared with other oil exporters (Figure 1.14). Another important factor is the link between universities and industry. A relevant example is the Massachusetts Institute of Technology's Technology Licensing Office, which facilitates investment in the development of discoveries and inventions at the university. In 2012, about 200 patents were issued and 16 funded companies established.

Experience suggests that specific-purpose investment is needed to develop a skilled workforce. This is a fourth set of policies. The development of general

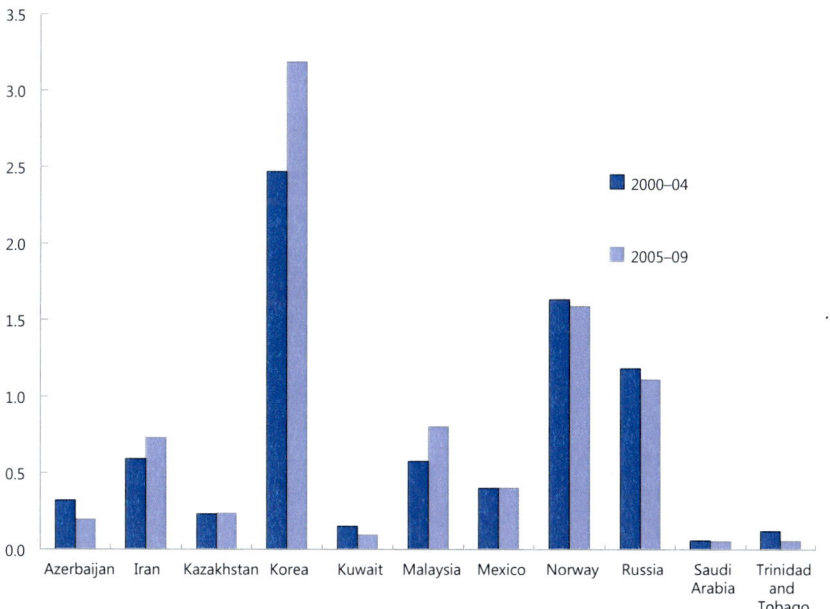

Figure 1.14 Research and Development Expenditures *(Percent of GDP; Averages)*
Source: World Bank, World Development Indicators.

infrastructure and education is important but not sufficient, and a focus on specific-purpose investment is key (Chang 2007). For instance, creating industry clusters necessitates human capital skills relevant to the sector, such as engineering and computer science, along with the required infrastructure and industrial facilities. The polytechnic institute in Guanajuato, Mexico, for example, was created to provide skilled labor geared toward the industrial park outside the campus gates. Internships at auto companies and continued applied education equipped students with skills needed in the industry. As the 2013 survey of 150 executives of fast-growing companies in the United States has shown, a skilled workforce and quality of life were major reasons they located their companies where they did, while taxes and business-friendly regulations were not significant factors (Mazerov 2014). These are the two key elements needed to create industry clusters.

One could argue that the lack of human capital skills is a reason not to pursue many high-value-added and complex activities and to wait until they eventually emerge. However, it is learning by doing or learning on the job that builds up the needed skills. The comparison of Malaysia and Chile since the 1970s provides a good example. While Malaysia has clearly outperformed Chile on export growth and sophistication over the past decades, Malaysia had a significantly less educated workforce. It only caught up in the 2000s.

Universities can also provide relevant skill sets relatively quickly, as Ireland did in the late 1970s. The Irish Development Agency negotiated agreements with electronics firms that substantially increased the demand for electrical engineers. The short-term solution to fill in the gap was to train science graduates through one-year courses, with the expansion of technical programs, courses, and degrees in the longer term. Apprenticeship programs and vocational training need to be formally set up to further increase human capital and skills needed for the targeted industries and clusters. For instance, more than two-thirds of 15- to 16-year-olds enter apprenticeship programs in Switzerland, while more than half of students are apprentices in Germany, with only 25 percent going to college (Nash 2012). In Germany, the retail trade and manufacturing are the largest employers. Government could provide incentives such as directly subsidizing the cost to firms for "hard-to-place" apprentices, as in Germany (Aivazova 2013). The requirement to develop local talent and local suppliers, as is done in Norway, would further produce the needed skill set.

More generally, government can foster linkages between SOEs, multinational companies, and SMEs to promote the development of tradables and exports. A potential way to achieve this is to create a program similar to Ireland's National Linkage Promotion Program (1987–92). Started by the Industrial Development Authority, the program brought together multinationals and potential suppliers to facilitate local sourcing. The government instructed various agencies to help SMEs to navigate through the bureaucracy, to collaborate, and provide an effective service for SMEs that could be fine-tuned depending upon the needs of customers and suppliers. The multinational companies targeted were in the electronics industry and were lobbied extensively to support the development of local firms. They contributed costs for the first two years of the program and provided technical assistance for SMEs, together with state technical agencies. The SMEs were thoroughly assessed before they could participate in the program and were selected together with multinational companies. In the five years of the program's operation, multinational companies increased locally sourced materials from 9 percent to 19 percent of their purchases.

The GCC countries have pursued some of the policies mentioned in this chapter—such as the creation of special economic zones, links between universities and businesses, skills development, SME funds, development banks, export promotion agencies, and, more recently, clusters. However, these policies have yet to deliver the desired results.

CONCLUSION

In this chapter, we have described the main features of the prevailing economic model in the GCC, which relies on oil as the main export and a concentration of economic activity in the low-skilled nontradable sector. We observed that over the past decades this economic model yielded important achievements in human development and infrastructure development. However, in relative economic performance, the model led to stagnation and GCC countries are being outperformed by other countries.

A growing body of literature shows that the lack of a dynamic non-oil tradable sector is the main issue hindering the GCC economic model. We studied a set of oil exporters and inferred from this that Dutch disease is a powerful force at play, which was only mitigated by an initial high level of technology. The few successes at diversification took place only amid dwindling oil revenues combined with decades of adequate policies to prepare the ground.

We contend that a strategy to diversify the non-oil tradable sector must be implemented now, even for the richest GCC countries. We argue that the main hurdles facing diversification in the GCC stem from market failures, rather than government failures, with the incentive structure in society needing to be changed. Although there is room for improving the business environment, infrastructure, skill sets, and institutions, these are unlikely to be enough to spur non-oil exports on their own. To do so, the governments need to change the incentive structure of the economies to encourage individuals to work in the private sector, and to encourage firms to look beyond the confines of domestic markets and seek new export opportunities. Improving the quality of education, especially in early childhood, and implementing a social development program are important elements of changing incentives.

Beyond this, experiences in other countries show that a diversification policy has often followed a mix of vertical diversification in existing export industries and horizontal diversification in suppliers' clusters for those industries, and industrial beachheads into high-value-added and innovation sectors. Crucially, this policy should be implemented in tandem with changing the incentives for workers and firms to achieve the desired results. These countries have used a combination of policies to achieve these results, including the use of venture capital funds, development banks, and export promotion agencies, combined with skills development and the emphasis on technological upgrading and competition in international markets. In the GCC, some degree of coordination on diversification strategies would be helpful to ensure that countries do not all develop in the same area and thereby risk crowding each other out.

ANNEX 1.1. MAIN ECONOMIC CHARACTERISTICS OF OIL EXPORTERS

ANNEX TABLE 1.1.1

Oil Exporters: Selected Economic Indicators

	Population (million)		GDP per Capita (PPP, $)		Percent of Commodity/ Oil Revenues in Total Fiscal Revenues[1]	Percent of Oil Exports in Total Exports of Goods and Services
	1970	Latest[2]	1970	2010	Latest[2]	Latest[2]
Bahrain	0.2	1.2	21,654	23,101	72.3	69.0
Kuwait	0.7	3.9	102,997	41,240	81.7	86.2
Oman	0.7	3.2	6,118	22,390	86.1	65.6
Qatar	0.1	1.9	79,555	136,248	64.7	74.8
Saudi Arabia	6.4	29.6	16,829	20,189	81.8	83.1
UAE	0.2	9.0	24,062	60,175	80.6	30.5
Algeria	13.6	38.1	4,066	6,263	63.2	93.0
Angola	6.0	20.8	2,313	5,108	80.2	96.5
Azerbaijan		9.3		9,474		83.3
Brunei Darussalam		0.4	51,532	44,555	91.9	88.3
Canada	21.3	35.2	17,726	37,104		19.5
Chad	3.6	11.0	879	1,331	61.2	79.0
Congo, Republic of	1.2	4.2	1,348	2,254	74.4	83.7
Ecuador	5.9	14.9	2,916	6,227	33.2	49.4
Equatorial Guinea	.	0.8	737	13,958	158.4	97.9
Gabon	0.7	1.6	8,281	9,896	60.4	80.4
Indonesia	120.3	248.0	816	3,966	17.7	8.6
Iran	28.7	77.1	8,480	9,432	37.9	60.7
Iraq		34.8	2,779	4,537	91.2	97.2
Kazakhstan		17.2		12,303	52.3	58.3
Libya	2.0	6.5	26,814	19,491	96.0	96.8
Malaysia	10.5	30.0	2,046	11,956		10.3
Mexico	50.9	118.2	6,821	11,939		12.2
Nigeria	55.2	169.3	1,572	1,695	80.1	91.6
Norway	3.9	5.1	17,980	50,488		23.0
Russian Federation		141.4		15,068	29.8	47.8
Syria	6.6	21.4	1,753	3,793	18.5	26.4
Timor-Leste		1.2		1,119		
Trinidad and Tobago		1.3	11,110	30,749	49.3	28.4
Turkmenistan		5.7		15,635	49.7	91.4
Venezuela	10.2	30.0	9,366	9,071	30.4	94.3
Yemen		26.7		2,393	46.2	51.4

Sources: IMF, World Economic Outlook (WEO) database and *Regional Economic Outlook: Middle East and Central Asia* (REO); and Penn World Tables 7.1.

Note: MENA = Middle East and North Africa, UAE = United Arab Emirates, PPP = purchasing power parity.

[1] Oil revenue data for MENA and Central Asian countries are from the REO; commodity revenue data for other countries are from the WEO.

[2] Latest = 2013, except Syria = 2010.

ANNEX TABLE 1.1.2

Oil Exporters: Reserves, Horizon, and Production

	Year Oil was First Discovered or Produced[1]	Current Production (million barrels per day)	Reserves as of end-2012 (billion barrels)	Oil Horizon at Current Production Rate (years)
Bahrain[2]		0.1	0.1	6.2
Kuwait	1938	3.1	101.5	88.9
Oman		0.9	5.5	16.3
Qatar	1935	2.0	23.9	33.3
Saudi Arabia	1938	11.5	265.9	63.2
UAE	1958	3.4	97.8	79.3
Algeria	1956	1.7	12.2	20.1
Angola	1955	1.8	12.7	19.5
Azerbaijan		0.9	7.0	22.0
Brunei		0.2	1.1	19.0
Canada		3.7	173.9	127.3
Chad		0.1	1.5	40.8
Congo, Republic of		0.3	1.6	14.8
Ecuador	1921	0.5	8.2	44.7
Equatorial Guinea		0.3	1.7	16.5
Gabon		0.2	2.0	22.4
Indonesia		0.9	3.7	11.2
Iran	1908	3.7	157.0	116.9
Iraq		3.1	150.0	131.9
Kazakhstan		1.7	30.0	47.6
Libya	1959	1.5	48.0	87.2
Malaysia		0.7	3.7	15.6
Mexico		2.9	11.4	10.7
Nigeria	1956	2.4	37.2	42.2
Norway		1.9	7.5	10.7
Russian Federation		10.6	87.2	22.5
Syria		0.2	2.5	41.8
Timor-Leste[2]		0.1	0.0	0.0
Trinidad and Tobago		0.1	0.8	18.8
Turkmenistan		0.2	0.6	7.4
Venezuela	1914	2.7	297.6	299.1
Yemen		0.2	3.0	45.6

Sources: BP *Statistical Review* 2013 data workbook; Energy Information Administration.

Note: UAE = United Arab Emirates.

[1] Data are from the Organization of the Petroleum Exporting Countries. Algeria: first commercial discovery year; Angola: year oil first produced; Ecuador: first productive oil well year; Iran: year first oil well drilled; Kuwait: year first commercial oil well drilled; Libya: year first productive oil well struck; Nigeria: year oil first discovered; Qatar: year oil exploration began; Saudi Arabia: year oil first struck; UAE: year first commercial oil discovered; Venezuela: year first commercial oil well drilled.

[2] Current production and reserves data for Bahrain and Timor-Leste from Energy Information Administration, International Energy Statistics platform.

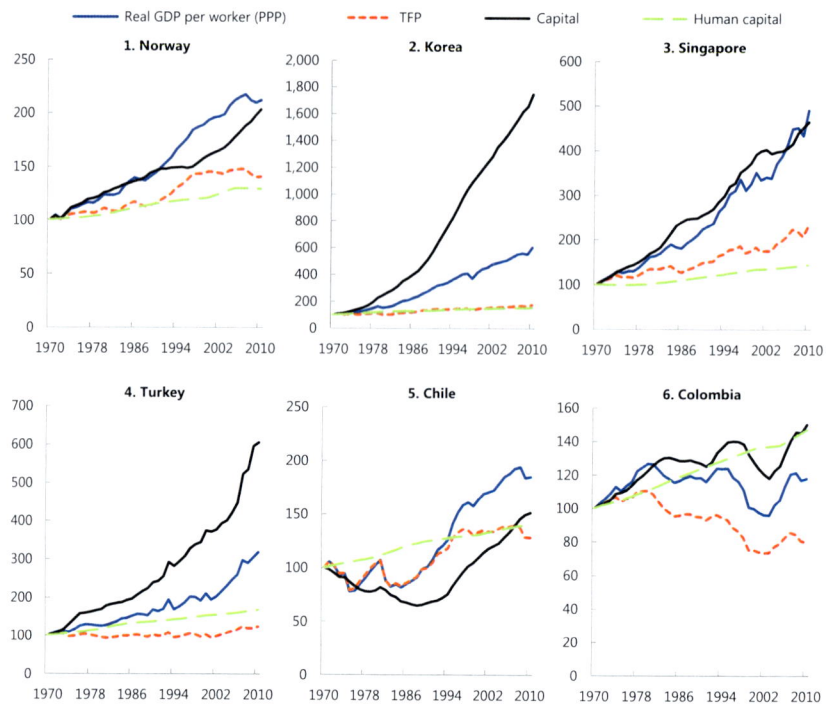

Annex Figure 1.1.1   Selected Countries: Growth Decomposition, 1970–2010 (1970 = 100)

Source: Penn World Tables 7.1.

Note: PPP = purchasing power parity; TFP = total factor productivity.

ANNEX 1.2. DIVERSIFICATION EXPERIENCE OF OIL EXPORTERS

Diversification Trials and Failures

Low-tech/high-oil-revenue countries, particularly Algeria, the GCC, and Venezuela, tried to diversify and industrialize early on and went through three major phases in their approach to export diversification. However, they mostly failed to truly diversify their exports away from oil.

The first phase of the diversification process, taking place in the 1960s–1970s, could be characterized by an oil boom, import substitution policies, and the "heavy-handed" state. Nationalization policies of the late 1950s to the early 1960s expanded the state and the use of central planning. Price controls and production subsidies became widespread. Production was concentrated in state-owned enterprises (SOEs). High tariffs and other protection measures (such as licenses) insulated SOEs from international competition as the state pursued import substitution policy. SOEs were not expected to export, unlike their counterparts in Southeast Asia. The spike in oil prices in the 1970s provided a large flow of oil revenues that could be transformed into an industrial base. In fact, high investment rates followed, in the range of 40 percent of GDP and above, higher than in Korea at the time. The oil revenue transformation into fixed investment spending relied heavily on SOEs as well.

With the strong influence of the state in economic affairs, vertical policies and heavy industrialization were the hallmark of the diversification strategies of this period. Algeria invested in iron and steel, chemicals, and construction materials (Gelb and others 1988). Venezuela built SOEs in steel, aluminum, petrochemicals, oil refining, and hydroelectric power (Di John 2009). Energy- and capital-intensive heavy industries in the Gulf States concentrated in petrochemicals, chemical fertilizers, steel, and aluminum. In joint ventures with foreign companies, Qatar spearheaded the creation of petrochemical, fertilizer, and steel industries in the early 1970s (UN 2001). Saudi Basic Industries Corporation, established in 1976, pursued import substitution projects such as chemicals, plastics, and building materials, followed by large-scale petrochemical projects in the late 1970s and early 1980s (Hertog 2011). Dubai (DUBAL) and Bahrain (ALBA) ventured into aluminum smelting and aluminum rolling industries. Cheap energy and feedstock made these SOEs profitable. For instance, Saudi Basic Industries Corporation was profitable once its large petrochemical plants became operational by the mid-1980s. In contrast, SOEs in Algeria, Venezuela, and Libya mostly ran deficits. Without the pressures of international competition and the need to improve productivity, these deficit-running industries could survive as long as oil prices were high.

During the second phase of the diversification process, as oil prices collapsed in the 1980s–1990s, oil exporters had to adjust their spending and shifted course to pursue liberalization policies. The heavy industries' reliance on imported intermediate goods and inputs did not survive the collapse of oil prices, especially since the goods produced could not be exported to fill the income gap created by falling oil prices. By the mid-1980s, most oil exporters abandoned the import substitution approach in favor of a more flexible economy. Tariffs and price regulations were dismantled or reduced and public enterprises were closed down or privatized to a large extent. This period also saw a drop in the average investment as a share of GDP as the large current account deficits accumulated during the oil slump had to be absorbed. Despite large real exchange depreciation, non-oil exports did not increase much, as there was no industrial base to take advantage of improved competitiveness. Hausmann, Rodriguez, and Wagner (2006) show that out of ten oil exporters that experienced export collapses in 1981–2002 (Algeria, Bahrain, Ecuador, Indonesia, Mexico, Nigeria, Oman, Saudi Arabia, Trinidad and Tobago, and Venezuela), only Indonesia and Mexico managed to develop non-oil exports and grow their economies. Both of these economies had a sufficient non-oil tradables base to increase their non-oil exports.

Henry (2009) argues that it was the reversal of industrialization policies during the bust years that resulted in the failure of the industrialization projects in Algeria. After the death of Algeria's president, Houari Boumediene, in 1978, industrializing technocrats lost their protection and industrialization projects from tires and trucks and automobiles to cement and gas liquefaction plants were stopped. The argument went that the previous policies resulted in a series of disconnected projects that did not produce intra-industry linkages and exchanges of goods and services. However, policies of deregulation, restructuring, and selling of SOEs have not improved the outlook. The deregulation of state monopolies produced a handful of well-connected importers that further discouraged local producers. The manifestation of Dutch disease was the result of policies rather than oil rents per se (Henry 2009).

In contrast, political fragmentation contributed to the failure of heavy industrialization policy in Venezuela. Di John (2009) argues that the populist, clientelist, and factionalized political system of the post-1960s did not bode well for the heavy industrialization projects that required a centralized power capable of mobilizing resources and effectively monitoring these projects. In the 1960s, manufacturing output was growing in chemicals, metals such as steel and aluminum, and metal-transforming industries. The government recognized that import-substitution industries needed to export to continue to grow. In 1973, the Fondo de Exportaciones (FINEXPO, the state export credit fund) provided numerous export credits to help firms enter foreign markets. Most of the support went to manufacturing firms, especially the chemical, aluminum, and steel sectors, but was erratic. Non-oil exports were dominated by these sectors and to a lesser extent, by transport equipment. Despite the non-oil export growth, heavy industries ran into problems. SOEs borrowed heavily in dollars, and external debt skyrocketed. The country went through capital flight, devaluation, and large debt repayment in the early 1980s. The number of SOEs increased to about 400 in 1985, and state employment increased significantly. At the same time, public investment plummeted as personnel expenditures and interest payments on external debt in SOEs went up substantially. The subsidies proliferated, and the number of large manufacturing firms under protection more than doubled in the 1970s–1980s, receiving the most state credits. With the liberalization of the late 1980s, many firms could not survive. Heavy-industry firms witnessed the lowest number of exits because the political costs of closing them down were high, but existing firms were running much below capacity. Policies were misguided, but in large part they were driven by the fragmented political system, which was unable to exclude firms and business interests from state support or discipline them, or coordinate investments and subsidies across the economy (Di John 2009).

By the early 2000s, the third phase of the diversification, as oil prices started rising, oil exporters pursued another investment strategy. Increasing oil revenues led oil exporters to increase spending on investment in infrastructure to compensate for underinvestment during the bust years. After the liberalization policies implemented earlier, international markets were open to them and countries pursued further improvements in business environment to attract foreign capital. Oil exporters invested in general-purpose investment, in particular infrastructure and real estate, and focused further on comparative-advantage sectors to promote export diversification: oil-related and energy-intensive industries such as aluminum and petrochemicals. Algeria, the GCC, and Venezuela's non-oil exports were still mostly chemicals and metals. In addition, the GCC countries focused on developing services, especially in tourism, logistics, and finance.

Diversification Successes

Indonesia, Malaysia, and Mexico have succeeded in diversifying their exports, but more needs to be done.

Malaysia

Malaysia successfully expanded its exports base as well as the sophistication of its manufacturing. The country has promoted specific strategic industries to achieve the maximum technological transfer possible. It relied on both horizontal and vertical development of industries as well as natural-resource-related industries (Yusof 2012; Jomo and others 1997; and Jomo 2001). Above all, Malaysia used active state intervention to spur growth in sectors it deemed important.

Malaysia is richly endowed with diverse natural resources such as palm oil and oil, considered its comparative-advantage sectors. The country pursued vertical policies toward higher-value-added activities related to natural resource industries. Active state intervention produced mixed results. The petroleum industry got going around the time of the spike in oil prices in the early 1970s, when oil was discovered. Petronas, the state oil company, became a very efficient and globalized firm operating in more than 30 countries, involved in exploration, exploitation, refining, and numerous oil-related complex activities. It is ranked among the most profitable firms in the world. Countering oil depletion and exploiting offshore oil fields must have contributed to its active technological upgrade. Palm oil refining could also be considered a success: Malaysia has retained a dominant position in the sector and succeeded in diversifying away from relying exclusively on raw palm oil exports. Investment in refining capabilities followed the imposition of export duties on raw palm oil. However, a similar approach in moving up the value-added chain in the rubber industry to produce tires and in the logging industry to build furniture did not yield the same results. A common thread in all the resource-related manufacturing in Malaysia, in contrast to most other oil exporters, is its emphasis on technology transfers and upgrading and the drive to compete internationally.

In the 1960s, Malaysia followed an import substitution strategy, in heavy industries in particular: steel, cement, and automotive (the Proton car). To protect new industries, state intervention with tariff barriers and subsidies started with public enterprises, although most of them were privatized at least partially at a later stage. This strategy was similar to Korea's a decade earlier, but with much less emphasis on exports and much less performance assessment (Jomo and others 1997; Jomo 2001). So far, these companies have not been as successful as their Korean counterparts in international markets and have relied mostly on domestic markets. Yet it should be pointed out that in other countries successes in these industries was preceded by several decades of losses (such as Toyota and Nokia—Chang 2007).

Malaysia was one of the earliest oil exporters to scale down its import substitution strategy in the 1970s and started relying on an export promotion policy (Jomo and others 1997). As a result, Malaysian manufacturing grew tremendously over the past three decades as it was forced to compete internationally and grow beyond its small domestic market. Today, manufacturing represents more than a third of all exports (and three-quarters if refining and other natural-resource-related manufacturing are included). It is one of the major exporters of electric and electronic manufacturing goods in the world. To achieve this goal, Malaysia used a multifaceted approach: (1) it selectively encouraged foreign direct investment in exports, especially in electronics; (2) it relied on free trade zones; (3) it offered lower taxes; and (4) it provided a stable business environment as well as an educated workforce with competitive wages. However, Jomo and others (1997) note the low number of linkages of these industries with the rest of the economy and the absence of export "champions" in high-value-added goods, as in the other successful East Asian economies, partly explaining why Malaysia did not join Korea's rank as an exporter.

A standard explanation of the success of Asian economies, including Malaysia, is the high rate of saving and investment, which led to a rapid accumulation of physical capital. Jomo (2001) shows that for most of these economies, saving was mainly comprised of corporate saving, while household saving was low. The only countries in this group where households' saving rates were high were Singapore and Malaysia. In Malaysia, high household savings were due to a mandatory, publicly managed retirement fund for employees in the private sector. All employees were required to contribute 10 percent of their income, to which the employer added 12 percent of the employee's salary (on average since 1980). Most of the savings were invested in government securities by law. This forced savings scheme amounted to financial repression and helped the government to finance its investment plans.

In parallel with rapid physical accumulation, one cannot ignore human capital accumulation as another important factor in Malaysia's success. The Malaysian state used public agencies to enforce a continuous retraining and skills upgrading of employees. The Human Resources Development Fund was set up in 1993 and has been financed by a levy on employers (about 1 percent of each employee's salary).[21] Its main target is the manufacturing sector, although many service sectors are included. The firms in the program are eligible to use their contribution for retraining and skills upgrading within the fund's guidelines. At the peak of their scholarship program in 1995, 20 percent of all students were studying abroad, costing the government an estimated $800 million annually, or 12 percent of the current account deficit in 1995.[22] Finally, several agencies were tasked with helping firms, especially SMEs, to upgrade technology and boost quality control to reach international standards. These agencies contributed to helping firms export on international markets by providing consulting services at different levels.

---

[21] The Human Resources Development Fund website. Available: http://www.hrdf.com.my/wps/portal/PSMB/MainEN/Corporate-Profile/About-HRDF.

[22] Patrick Blessinger and Enakshi Sengupta, "Is Malaysia the Regional Leader in International Higher Education?" *The Guardian*, July 2, 2012. Available: http://www.theguardian.com/higher-education-network/blog/2012/jul/02/higher-education-in-malaysia.

Indonesia

Like other oil exporters, Indonesia experimented with an import substitution strategy in the 1970s during the spike in oil prices. It created SOEs involved in heavy industries such as cement and steel to support investment in infrastructure, and fertilizers and agricultural machinery to support agriculture. The growth of manufacturing during the 1970s reached about 15 percent a year (Poot and others 1990). However, the SOEs that operated in isolation from international markets and with little performance control were characterized by inefficiencies and relied on public support (Hill 1988).

With the collapse of oil prices in the 1980s, and contrary to most other oil exporters and, in particular, to other members of the Organization of the Petroleum Exporting Countries (OPEC), Indonesia managed a spectacular turnaround. It adopted a set of new policies meant to attract foreign capital into export-oriented manufacturing. The main instruments of this policy were the creation of free trade zones, tax incentives, the easing of tariff restrictions and nontariff barriers as well as the largest exchange rate devaluation among developing nations in the 1980s (Jomo and others 1997). The result was a substantial growth in labor-intensive manufacturing (textile, footwear, electronics, and others) due to attractive wage levels. Gelb and others (1988) argued that Indonesia was the only OPEC member that used a significant share of its oil revenues to develop its productive capacity, especially in agriculture. However, the low wages may have played a more prominent role, along with Japanese yen appreciation in the mid-1980s and the subsequent offshoring by Japanese firms in Southeast Asia.

More important, oil revenues were already declining rapidly in the 1990s to the extent that Indonesia became a net importer of oil by 2003 (Energy Information Administration 2014). In other words, the intensity of Dutch disease was fading in this period. Between 1985 and 1997, the growth of the manufacturing sector was about 10 percent a year (Dhanani 2000). However, growth in the manufacturing sector has stalled since the Asian financial crisis in 1997–98 to the extent that observers started fearing early deindustrialization (Aswicahyono and Manning 2011). Indonesia remained a good performer in overall growth during the 2000s, but manufacturing was not the engine of growth that it was in the 1990s (Aswicahyono and Narjok 2011).

During liberalization in the 1980s, the government performed a "strategic retreat," but retained several of its strategic projects, in particular in steel and the aircraft industry. The national steel company is considered to be lagging behind other Association of Southeast Asian Nations producers (OECD 2013). The attempt to set up an aircraft industry was viewed negatively and taken as an example of why Indonesia failed to catch up (McKendrick 1992). While agreeing with the inefficiencies and other political economy problems, Jomo and others (1997) note that the experience of Indonesia also shows that, with government commitment, a complex technology industry can be started from scratch in a poor nation (as Indonesia was at the time). Indonesia today is part of a select group of developing economies with clusters of aircraft maintenance and aircraft parts manufacturing. The creation of the national champion, albeit at a large cost, did facilitate the establishment of this cluster.

Mexico

Indonesia and Mexico share several similarities. Both have large populations and followed broadly the same export-led strategy. Both relied heavily on free trade zones focused mainly on labor-intensive industries that were mostly foreign owned. This policy, coupled with attractive wages and business environment, built the export successes of both countries. However, the firms operating in these zones did not climb very far up the value-added ladder and linkages between them and the rest of the economy remained weak (Jomo and others 1997; Verhoogen 2012).

Mexico's experience in the automobile industry in the last 15 years is notable. Most of the industry is located in the center of the country, far from its borders, the traditional land of the *maquiladoras*. Today employment in the sector in Mexico surpasses that of the U.S. Midwest (40 percent of North American employment in Mexico versus 30 percent in the U.S. Midwest in 2012) and is expected to continue its fast growth. Obviously, the North American Free Trade Agreement and exchange rate depreciation in the 2000s helped make the country an attractive place for FDI by automotive companies planning to export to the United States. However, the policies adopted by different states in Mexico in pursuit of building manufacturing clusters, and their performance in terms of productivity and quality upgrading, are of interest. In particular, the State of Guanajuato followed what can be described as a purpose-specific investment strategy in parallel with strong incentives to attract firms. In infrastructure, the state built a 2,600-acre interior port, customs facilities, a railroad depot, and a link to the local airport (Cave 2013). Nearby, there is also a polytechnic university to supply engineers, and the state gives incentives to firms to send workers for training abroad. The state has attracted foreign firms by providing tax incentives, but, more interestingly, by acting "as an overall consultant in terms of support."[23]

More recently, Mexico saw the rapid growth of aerospace clusters reaching total exports of $12.2 billion in 2012 (Araujo 2012). The aerospace industry requires an even higher level of technical skills and is subjected to very high levels of international standards on quality control. So the establishment of more than 300 firms in the aerospace industry is a sign of an improvement in productivity. However, Romero (2010) observes that research and development activity in the sector is almost nonexistent. In his study based on surveys of aerospace firms in several clusters, he shows that the major factors in the location decision of these firms are industrial infrastructure, skilled labor force, and low operational costs. He concludes that as long as the government does not follow a more active policy to encourage research and development and innovation—in particular the creation of domestic "system integrators," that is, a firm constructing and commercializing whole aircraft

---

[23] Norbert Buechelmaier, Getrag's executive vice president of manufacturing, in McCurry, John, "Center of Attention," *Site Selection* magazine, January 2009. Available: http://www.siteselection.com/features/2009/jan/Mexico/

instead of components—the productivity gains and innovation in the sector will remain limited.

REFERENCES

Aghion, Philippe, and Peter Howitt. 1992. "A Model of Growth through Creative Destruction." *Econometrica* 60: 323–51.

Aivazova, Natalia. 2013. "Role of Apprenticeships in Combating Youth Unemployment in Europe and the United States." Peterson Institute for International Economics Policy Brief (August). Peterson Institute for International Economics, Washington.

Araujo, Federico Metzger. 2012. "The Aerospace Industry in Mexico: Baja California, Chihuahua, Sonora and Queretaro." MINERVA Papers. The Center for Latin American Issues, George Washington University, Washington.

Arezki, Rabah, Reda Cherif, and John Piotrowski. 2009. "Tourism Specialization and Economic Development: Evidence from the UNESCO World Heritage List." IMF Working Paper 09/176, International Monetary Fund, Washington.

Aswicahyono, Haryo, and Chris Manning. 2011. "Exports and Job Creation in Indonesia Before and After the Asian Financial Crisis." Departmental Working Papers 2011–11, The Australian National University, Arndt-Corden Department of Economics, Canberra.

Aswicahyono, Haryo, and Dionisius Narjok. 2011. "Indonesian Industrialization." Working Paper Series UNU-WIDER Research Paper, World Institute for Development Economic Research (UNU-WIDER), Helsinki, Finland.

Behar, Alberto, and Junghwan Mok. 2013. "Does Public-Sector Employment Fully Crowd Out Private-Sector Employment?" IMF Working Paper 13/146, International Monetary Fund, Washington.

Cave, Damien. 2013. "In the Middle of Mexico, a Middle Class Rises." *New York Times*, November 18.

Chang, Ha-Joon. 2007. "State-Owned Enterprise Reform." Policy Notes, United Nations, Department of Economics and Social Affairs. http://EconPapers.repec.org/RePEc:une:pnotes:4.

Chang, Ha-Joon, and Justin Lin. 2009. "Should Industrial Policy in Developing Countries Conform to Comparative Advantage or Defy it? A Debate between Justin Lin and Ha-Joon Chang." *Development Policy Review* 27 (5): 483–502.

Cherif, Reda. 2013. "The Dutch Disease and the Technological Gap." *Journal of Development Economics* 101 (C): 248–55.

Cherif, Reda, and Fuad Hasanov. 2013. "Oil Exporters' Dilemma: How Much to Save and How Much to Invest." *World Development* 52 (C): 120–31.

———. forthcoming. "Exports Sophistication, Investment and Growth."

———. forthcoming. "Dutch Disease with Labor Mobility."

Choe, Chang Soo. 2005. "Key Factors to Successful Community Development: The Korean Experience." Discussion Paper 39, Institute of Developing Economies, Japan.

Dhanani, S. 2000. "Indonesia: Strategy for Manufacturing Competitiveness." Vol. II. Jakarta: United Nations Industrial Development Organization.

Di John, Jonathan. 2009. *From Windfall to Curse? Oil and Industrialization in Venezuela, 1920 to the Present*. University Park, Pennsylvania: Penn State University Press.

Dolton, Peter, and Oscar D. Marcenaro-Gutierrez. 2011. "If You Pay Peanuts Do You Get Monkeys? A Cross-Country Analysis of Teacher Pay and Pupil Performance." *Economic Policy* (January): 5–55.

Elbadawi, Ibrahim A. 2009. "Oil, Economic Diversification and Development in the Arab World." Working Paper, Economic Research Forum, Egypt.

El Beblawi, H. 2011. "Gulf industrialization in Perspective." In *Industrialization in the Gulf: A Socioeconomic Revolution*, edited by J. F. Seznec and M. Kirk. London: Center for Contemporary Arab Studies, Georgetown University/Routledge.

Energy Information Administration. 2014. "Indonesia." Country report, March. http://www.eia.gov/countries/cab.cfm?fips=ID.

Espinosa, R., G. Fayad, and A. Prasad. 2013. *The Macroeconomics of the Arab States of the Gulf.* Oxford: Oxford University Press.

Feenstra, Robert C., Robert E. Lipsey, Haiyan Deng, Alyson C. Ma, and Hengyong Mo. 2005. "World Trade Flows: 1962–2000." National Bureau of Economic Research Working Papers 11040, National Bureau of Economic Research, Cambridge, Massachusetts.

Gelb, Alan and Associates. 1988. *Oil Windfalls: Blessing or Curse?* Oxford: Oxford University Press.

Hausmann, Ricardo, Jason Hwang, and Dani Rodrik. 2007. "What You Export Matters." *Journal of Economic Growth* 12 (1): 1–25.

Hausmann, Ricardo, Francisco Rodriguez, and Rodrigo Wagner. 2006. "Growth Collapses." Working Paper Series rwp06–046, John F. Kennedy School of Government, Harvard University, Cambridge, Massachusetts.

Heckman, James J. 2008. "Schools, Skills and Synapses." *Economic Inquiry*, 46 (3): 289–324.

Heckman, James, Rodrigo Pinto, and Peter Savelyev. 2013. "Understanding the Mechanisms through Which an Influential Early Childhood Program Boosted Adult Outcomes." *American Economic Review* 103 (6): 2052–86.

Henry, Clement M. 2009. "Between the Shocks: 'White Elephant' Industrialization in Algeria." In *Viewpoints: The 1979 "Oil Shock:" Legacy, Lessons, and Lasting Reverberations. Viewpoints Special Edition* (summer): 49–52. The Middle East Institute, Washington.

Henry, Peter Blair, and Conrad Miller. 2009. "Institutions versus Policies: A Tale of Two Islands." *American Economic Review* 99 (2): 261–67.

Hertog, S. 2011. "Lean and Mean: The New Breed of State-Owned Enterprises in the Gulf Monarchies." In *Industrialization in the Gulf: A Socioeconomic Revolution*, edited by J. F. Seznec and M. Kirk. London: Center for Contemporary Arab Studies, Georgetown University/Routledge.

Heum, P. 2008. "Local Content Development—Experiences from Oil and Gas Activities in Norway." SNF Working Paper 02/08. SNF, Bergen, Norway.

Hill, H. 1988. *Foreign Investment and Industrialization in Indonesia.* Oxford: Oxford University Press.

Husain, Aasim M., Kamilya Tazhibayeva, and Anna Ter-Martirosyan. 2008. "Fiscal Policy and Economic Cycles in Oil-Exporting Countries." IMF Working Paper 08/253, International Monetary Fund, Washington.

Hvidt, Martin. 2013. "Economic Diversification in GCC Countries: Past Record and Future Trends." LSE Research Online Documents on Economics 55252, London School of Economics and Political Science, LSE Library.

International Monetary Fund (IMF). 2012. *The Challenge of Public Pension Reform in Advanced and Emerging Market Economies.* Occasional Paper 275. Washington: International Monetary Fund.

———. 2013a. "Labor Market Reforms to Boost Employment and Productivity in the GCC." Policy Paper, International Monetary Fund, Washington.

———. 2013b. "Energy Subsidy Reform: Lessons and Implications." Policy Paper, International Monetary Fund, Washington.

Ismail, Kareem. 2010. "The Structural Manifestation of the Dutch Disease: The Case of Oil Exporting Countries." IMF Working Paper 10/103, International Monetary Fund, Washington.

Jarreau, Joachim, and Sandra Poncet. 2012. "Export Sophistication and Economic Growth: Evidence from China." *Journal of Development Economics* 97 (2): 281–92.

Jomo, K. S. 2001. "Growth and Structural Change in the Second-tier Southeast Asian NICs." In *Southeast Asia's Industrialization: Industrial Policy, Capabilities and Sustainability*, edited by K.S. Jomo. Houndmills, UK: Palgrave.

Jomo K. S., Chen Yun Chung, Brian Folk, Irfan ul-Haque, Pasuk Phongpaichit, Batara Simatupang, and Mayuri Tateishi. 1997. *Southeast Asia's Misunderstood Miracle: Industrial Policy and Economic Development in Thailand, Malaysia, and Indonesia.* Oxford: Westview Press.

Krugman, Paul. 1987. "The Narrow Moving Band, the Dutch Disease, and the Competitive Consequences of Mrs. Thatcher: Notes on Trade in the Presence of Dynamic Scale Economies." *Journal of Development Economics* 27 (1–2): 41–55.

Kuznetsov, Yevgeny, and Charles Sabel. 2011. "New Open Economy Industrial Policy: Making Choices without Picking Winners." World Bank PREM notes 161 (September).

Kwon, Huck-Ju. 2010. "Implications of Korea's Saemaul Undong for International Development Policy: A Structural Perspective." *Korean Journal of Policy Studies* 25 (3): 87–100.

Lerner, Josh. 1996. "The Government as Venture Capitalist: The Long-Run Effects of the SBIR Program." NBER Working Paper 5753, National Bureau of Economic Research, Cambridge, Massachusetts.

Leskinen, Olivia, Paul Klouman Bekken, Haja Razafinjatovo, and Manuel García. 2012. "Norway Oil and Gas Cluster: A Story of Achieving Success through Supplier Development." Harvard Business School, Cambridge, Massachusetts.

Looney, R. E. 1994. *Industrial Development and Diversification of the Arabian Gulf Economies*. Greenwich, Connecticut: JAI Press.

Lucas, Robert E. 1993. "Making a Miracle." *Econometrica* 61 (2): 251–72.

Matsuyama, Kiminori. 1992. "Agricultural Productivity, Comparative Advantage, and Economic Growth." *Journal of Economic Theory* 58 (2): 317–34.

Mazerov, Michael. 2014. "More Evidence That You Can't Lure Entrepreneurs with Tax Cuts." Center on Budget and Policy Priorities, February 14. http://www.offthechartsblog.org/more-evidence-that-you-cant-lure-entrepreneurs-with-tax-cuts/.

Mazzucato, Mariana. 2013. *The Entrepreneurial State: Debunking Public vs. Private Sector Myths*. London: Anthem Press.

McKendrick, D. 1992. "Obstacles to 'Catch-up': The Case of the Indonesian Aircraft Industry." *Bulletin of Indonesian Economic Studies* 28 (1): 39–66.

Minli, Han. 2008. "The China-Singapore Suzhou Industrial Park: Can the Singapore Model of Development be Exported?" MSc thesis, National University of Singapore.

Moretti, Enrico. 2012. *The New Geography of Jobs*. New York: Houghton Mifflin Harcourt.

Murphy, Kevin, Andrei Shleifer, and Robert W. Vishny. 1989. "Industrialization and the Big Push." *Journal of Political Economy* 97 (5): 1003–26.

Nabli, Mustapha, Jennifer Keller, Claudia Nassif, and Carlos Silva-Jauregui. 2008. "The Political Economy of Industrial Policy in the Middle East and North Africa." In *Industrial Policy in the Middle East and North Africa: Rethinking the Role of the State*, edited by Ahmed Galal, 109–136. Cairo: Egyptian Center for Economic Studies.

Nash, Betty J. 2012. "Journey to Work: European Model Combines Education with Vocation." *Region Focus*, Fourth Quarter, Federal Reserve Bank of Richmond: 17–19.

Organisation for Economic Co-operation and Development (OECD). 2013. "The Structure and Prospects of the Indonesian Steel Industry." http://www.oecd.org/sti/ind/Item%205%203%20OECD%20Naoki%20-%20Copy.pdf.

Papageorgiou, Chris, and Nicola Spatafora. 2012. "Economic Diversification in LICs: Stylized Facts and Macroeconomic Implications." IMF Staff Discussion Note 12/13, International Monetary Fund, Washington.

Poot, Huib, Arie Kuyvenhoven, and Jaap Jansen. 1990. *Industrialisation and Trade in Indonesia*. Yogyakarta: Gadjah Mada University Press.

Ramírez, Carlos, and Ling Hui Tan. 2004. "Singapore Inc. versus the Private Sector: Are Government-Linked Companies Different?" *IMF Staff Papers* 51 (3): 510–28.

Rodrik, Dani. 2005. "Growth Strategies." In *Handbook of Economic Growth*, edited by Philippe Aghion and Steven Durlauf. Amsterdam: Elsevier.

———. 2011. "Unconditional Convergence." NBER Working Papers 17546, National Bureau of Economic Research, Cambridge, Massachusetts.

Romero, Javier Martínez. 2010. "The Development of Aerospace Clusters in Mexico." Working Paper, 2010–03, The Global Network for Economics of Learning, Innovation, and Competence Building System.

Sasson, Amir, and Atle Blomgren. 2011a. "Knowledge Based Oil and Gas Industry." Knowledge-Based Norway, March, Report No. 4.

———. 2011b. "Developing NODE: Mediating Strategy for Sustainable Growth." Working Paper, Norwegian Business School, Oslo.

Stanford, Jim. 2012. "A Cure for Dutch Disease: Active Sector Strategies for Canada's Economy." Technical Paper, Canadian Center for Policy Alternatives.

Stern, N. 2001. "A Strategy for Development." ABCDE Keynote Address. World Bank, Washington.

Verhoogen, Eric. 2012. "Industrial Structure and Innovation: Notes toward a New Strategy for Industrial Development in Mexico." Working Paper, Columbia University, New York.

United Nations. 2001. "Economic Diversification in the Oil Producing Countries." Economic and Social Commission for Western Asia, United Nations, New York.

United Nations Department of Economic and Social Affairs. 2009. *World Population Prospects: The 2008 Revision.*

World Social Security Forum. 2013. "Civil Retirement and Social Insurance Systems in GCC-Reality and Challenges." International Social Security Association, Geneva.

Young, Alwyn. 1991. "Learning by Doing and Dynamic Effects of International Trade." *Quarterly Journal of Economics* (May): 369–405.

Yusof, Zainal. 2012. "Economic Diversification: The Case of Malaysia." Revenue Watch Institute, New York.

CHAPTER 2

The Riddle of Diversification

Clement M. Henry

As Reda Cherif and Fuad Hasanov conclude in Chapter 1, petro-states face daunting challenges—really a riddle for policymakers—to assure sustainable and diversified economies. Late-late developers[1] must climb ever steeper quality ladders to generate sophisticated and competitive exports. Mere import substitution will not do if diversification is to be sustained. Within the Middle East and North Africa (MENA) region, the Gulf Cooperation Council (GCC) could lead the way, possibly inspired by the successes of Korea, Malaysia, and Singapore—as subsequent chapters discuss. This chapter examines the successes and failures to date of some of the oil-rich states of the region, but it is necessary first to examine the possible criteria of success. Why bother at all to diversify?

If the principal yardstick is income per capita, diversified economies usually do better than undiversified ones in the long term. On the shorter horizons of policymakers, however, the priority is political survival rather than potentially destabilizing economic reform. Within the MENA region, moreover, there are significant differences in oil and gas revenues and their contributions to national budgets. Looming budgetary squeezes are more likely to concentrate policy minds on diversification than long-term prospects. In 2013, IMF and GCC policymakers could share concerns about future fiscal balances as state expenditures rose and oil prices were not keeping up with the fiscal breakeven prices of a number of other petro-states (IMF 2013). Fiscal concerns may drive some efforts to diversify hydrocarbon-based economies, even in GCC countries where (with the exception of Bahrain and Oman) ratios of natural gas and oil reserves to production promise many decades of healthy revenue. The volatility of oil prices may concern policymakers in Kuwait, Qatar, and the United Arab Emirates, countries enjoying extraordinarily high rents per capita (Table 2.1).[2] However, an abundance of capital may tempt some of them to diversify their sources of revenue through sovereign wealth funds rather than by generating dynamic export-driven private sectors.

---

[1] Late-late developers are usually economies that started developing in the second half of the twentieth century, such as Korea.
[2] Oil rents in general are defined as the value of oil production at world prices less costs of production, which are mostly fixed costs incurred in the past.

TABLE 2.1

Oil and Gas Revenues					
Country	Rents per Capita, 2009 (Dollars)	Rents per Capita, 2012 (Dollars)	Rents per Citizen, 2012 (Dollars)	Rents, Percent of GDP, 2012	Rents, Percent of Government Revenue, 2012
Qatar	24,940	22,447	153,398	24	62
Kuwait	19,500	31,077	103,517	55	83
United Arab Emirates	14,100	9,938	86,620	24	89
Oman	7,950	9,904	14,033	42	88
Saudi Arabia	7,800	12,896	18,857	50	90
Libya	6,420	–	–	–	–
Bahrain	3,720	5,469	11,549	24	87
Algeria	1,930	1,211		23	65
Iraq	1,780	3,044		46	92
Iran	1,600	1,614		25	44
Syria	450	503		18	–
Egypt	260	365		11	56
Yemen	270	217		16	56
Sudan	260	88		5	16[1]
Tunisia	250	222		5	17
Indonesia	140	110		3	22
Malaysia	860	905		9	41
Russian Federation	2,080	2,469		19	30%
United States	730	421		1	5%

Sources: Ross (2012); World Bank, World Development Indicators; IMF (2013, 12); and IMF Article IV consultation reports.
[1] 58 percent in 2011 before loss of Southern Sudan.

Even when the very wealthy smaller states diversify their economies, their initiatives resemble overseas portfolio investment in that the new economic activities are largely in the hands of expatriate management and labor. In Qatar, for instance, nationals comprise only 5 percent of the labor force, and almost all of them are government employees (Chapter 1). In Kuwait, national participation in the labor force is greater, at 18 percent, but more than three-quarters of it is in government, and a mere 5 percent of employees in the private sector, despite official carrots and sticks. The government offers private firms subsidies to hire more Kuwaitis and requires that they meet quotas to be eligible for government contracts (for instance, that at least 10 percent of the engineers in a consultant firm be nationals). Nevertheless, most Kuwaitis, including engineers and architects, prefer less demanding jobs at higher salaries in government service. Data are not available for the United Arab Emirates, but Dubai's spectacular diversification into a variety of international service industries also obviously depends heavily on expatriates.

Portfolio diversification, whether accomplished through sovereign wealth funds or on the ground, can hardly be rated a success—at least not in the larger oil-exporting states—unless it achieves gainful employment for the local citizenry. Sustainable employment, expanding to accommodate the surge in youth numbers, is surely the most politically significant yardstick by which to evaluate experiences of diversification in most of the MENA region. Oil wealth carries additional burdens. Being capital intensive, the industry directly employs few people, even if, as in the national oil company, Saudi Aramco, it has replaced most foreign staff with locals.

Moreover, the oil and gas industries lie on the periphery of densely interrelated product spaces (Abdon and Felipe 2006; Hausmann and others 2008; Hausmann and Hidalgo 2010). Hydrocarbons have few direct spillovers into other industrial or manufacturing sectors. Unlike textiles, say, they do not develop capacities that are readily transferrable to the production of other tradable exports. Oil-exporting countries may have less promising prospects for sustainable development than ones with fewer resources, given that "a sustainable growth model requires a diversified tradable sector" (Chapter 1). The further requirement not only of export sophistication, but also of full participation of the national workforce poses almost insurmountable problems. Any serious response to the riddle of diversification for oil-exporting economies must meet the requirements for human capital.

In examining partial successes and failures to date, this chapter seeks to define the mix of policies that might foster sustainable diversification of the MENA region's hydrocarbon-based economies. No state in the region has developed the human capital and skills needed to generate "sophisticated" exports. Some of the smaller GCC countries have begun to invest in human capital to engage more citizens in their development strategies. The two most populous Arab oil states, Algeria and Saudi Arabia, for example, each took human and financial capital into account to break dependence on hydrocarbon revenues. Both highlight the issue of human capital formation in the context of late-late development, as the quality ladder to be globally competitive becomes an ever steeper climb.

ALGERIA'S INDUSTRIALIZATION AND LOST OPPORTUNITIES

Algeria's experience in the 1960s and 1970s deserves attention as the first Arab country to fully nationalize its oil industry, in 1971, ahead of Iraq and other Gulf states. It tried to translate its revolutionary legacy—as the only country in the region to wage a successful full-scale war of liberation against the colonial power—into an industrial revolution. Algeria had a total vision of rapid development and diversification: the newly discovered oil would provide the capital to develop its gas fields and then liquefy the gas, using technologies that were relatively new in the 1970s for transport to Europe and beyond. Hydrocarbon income would be reinvested in petrochemicals, iron and steel, and cement factories. These were what French development economist Gérard Destanne de Bernis (1963, 1966) called "industrializing industry," giving rise to other industries, or planned industrialization from above. But in the words of its chief architect, Belaid Abdesselam:

> The Algerian strategy of industrialization was exclusively conceived and elaborated by the authorities of the Algerian Revolution. In no way did its

choices and ultimate goals derive from external sources . . . contrary to ideas deliberately propagated by the foreign media, particularly in France . . . Destanne de Bernis had no role in the definition of this conception. The goal of industrialization policy was to enable Algeria to insure by itself the largest possible assortment of inputs into its economy and the needs of its population . . . Our industries were to result to the greatest possible degree in inputs in basic and semi-finished products through inter-industrial exchanges operating in our national territory. (Abdesselam 2007, 1–2)

This 1960s' "Development Decade" vision of revolutionary self-sufficiency or autarchy is easy to criticize in retrospect, after half a century of growing interdependence connoted by globalization. Algeria's vision offered no room for tradable exports, because the revolutionaries had little interest or experience in international marketing. Moreover, heavy industrialization was capital, not labor, intensive. Other countries, such as Egypt and Tunisia, had embarked on similar schemes of import substitution by industrialization from above but could not afford to sustain their plans. They terminated their experiences in 1966 and 1969, respectively, once they had nationalized many privately held assets, for the most part foreign, and were running out of foreign exchange. Algeria's greater oil and gas rents enabled the country to pursue its revolutionary dreams for an additional decade.

Possibly, had President Houari Boumediene not died in late 1978, Belaid Abdesselam could have pursued his strategy even longer. In 1977 he was demoted at his request from being minister of industry and energy to minister of the weakest part of his old portfolio, light industry, so as to cultivate those "inter-industrial exchanges." He claims to have enjoyed Boumediene's continued support and to have been one of the few ministers expected to remain in top decision-making circles after the president reconsolidated his power in a *Front de Libération Nationale* Congress planned for 1979 (Bennoune and El-Kenz 1990).

Boumediene's death of a rare disease put an end to these plans and enabled Abdesselam's many political opponents to reverse his industrial policies—in fact to "assassinate industry," as Mohammed Liassine, his close colleague and successor as minister of heavy industry, asserted at an academic conference in 1990 (Moore 1994, 25).

Ironically, the about-turn in economic policy occurred just as oil and gas revenues were rising. And when they fell, Abdesselam's liquefied natural gas contract with the United States' El Paso Company would have offset them with annual revenues of $2–$3 billion had Abdesselam's opponents not abrogated the contract (Abdesselam 1990, 293). Algeria under President Chadli Bendjedid instead went on a consumer spending spree, helped by an overvalued foreign exchange rate that resulted in a major debt crisis and, by 1987, shortages of basic products, inadequate maintenance of new industrial fixed assets, and steady declines in manufacturing value added. By 2007, Algeria was producing no more manufactured goods than Tunisia, a country with less than one-third of its population (Figure 2.1).

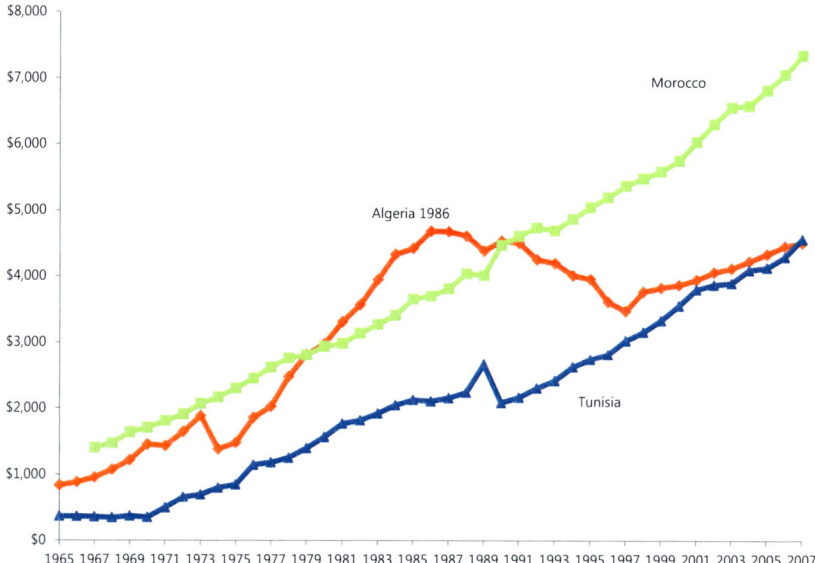

Figure 2.1   Manufacturing Value Added in Algeria, Morocco, and Tunisia 1965–2007
(Constant 2000 U.S. dollars)
Source: World Bank, World Development Indicators.

Although it is easy to criticize Algeria's vision of autarchic development, its shortcomings may sharpen our understanding of the challenges ahead there and elsewhere in the MENA region. Algeria was an outlier in human capital. For purposes of industrialization or even agriculture (dominated by French proprietors and foremen) education and skill levels were virtually nil in 1960, compared, say, to Korea in the same year (Chapters 5 and 10). At the outbreak of its 1954 revolution, Algeria had only 165 physicians, 354 lawyers, 350 civil servants, 100 French army officers, and fewer than 30 engineers (Malek 2010, 206). By independence in 1962 student leaders could boast that the revolution had already produced more university graduates than during the previous 124 years of colonial rule (Pervillé 2004, 30, 136).

Nevertheless, Algeria still had far fewer educated cadres than its much smaller neighbor, Tunisia, and direct French rule had offered them little administrative experience. Consequently the new industry came in ready-made turnkey projects, supplemented by "product-in-hand" contracts, reflecting an excessive dependence on foreign experts. With such limited supervisory capacities of so few university graduates, it was perhaps easier for Algeria to engage in a small number of major projects, such as the Hadjar (ex-Duzerville) iron and steel complex, expanding on a French plan to export pig iron, than to invest in a large number of light manufacturing projects. The complex became Algeria's principal showcase in the 1970s, although the costs of the foreign expertise required to run it steadily increased rather than diminished as a percentage of total labor costs (El-Kenz 1985).

Acutely aware of Algeria's shortages of managerial and technological capabilities, including skilled labor, the new public enterprises such as Sonatrach (Société Nationale pour la Recherche, la Production, le Transport, la Transformation, et la Commercialisation des Hydrocarbures) established a wide variety of technical higher institutes that were tied to their respective industries and were independent of the national education system inherited from colonial times. By the academic year 1984–85, the technical sector, originally funded by the ministry of industry rather than the ministry of higher education, had 58 percent of the resources earmarked for its teaching and research staff. The remaining 42 percent funded teaching and research staff in the traditional universities, who outnumbered the technical staff by a ratio of almost 2 to 1 (El-Kenz 1992, 232). As industrial production foundered, with most factories working well under capacity, a new problem emerged—the underutilized human capital of unemployed engineers and technicians. Research and development capabilities were neglected, and experienced Algerian cadres found employment in GCC countries and elsewhere.

Sadly, Algerian exports today are even less diversified than those of other oil exporters in the MENA region, and its tiny non-oil basket of exports is not only unsophisticated, but also as peripheral as hydrocarbons to other product spaces. In other words, the fixed assets, skilled labor, infrastructure, regulations, and the like that produce the very limited number of Algerian exports—only 184 products, compared to Saudi Arabia's 336 (Hausmann and others 2008, 65)—are not readily transferrable to other product spaces. The revolution lost much of Algeria's productive capability accumulated over 132 years of colonial rule with the departure of most of the settlers in the summer of 1962. Workers repossessed their farms, but then an agrarian revolution accelerated a rural exodus and decline of agricultural production under state management. Trade disputes with France resulted in the destruction of most Algerian vineyards, and only recently have efforts been made to restore them so as to exploit one of Algeria's comparative advantages. Finally, many people trained for Algerian industry had to look for jobs elsewhere. Sharp discontinuities in the country's economic policies still have unfortunate and unintended consequences, and skills and practices that were built up in one generation have not transferred into the next.

Yet, Algeria's relatively small inventory of capabilities associated with peripheral product spaces may still guide new beginnings. An analysis of these capabilities in 2008, evaluating the potential for developing clusters of product spaces given existing capabilities, pointed to a variety of new products worth developing (Hausmann and others 2008). In order of priority, it identified "the most attractive nearby export opportunities for Algeria" as:

- Meat, milk, and fishing products
- Other agro-industrial products and chemicals
- Steel and aluminum, metal products, and shipbuilding

Interestingly, the study disagreed with the government's planning for petrochemical industries downstream from its core oil and gas capabilities, arguing that they were still too far removed from the upstream product spaces.

As an extreme case of colonial domination and emancipation, Algeria may be an outlier. It also puts into sharper focus some of the mistakes that were committed in its Promethean effort to diversify the economy. The state had less administrative capacity than neighboring Morocco or Tunisia, yet had substantially greater funds at its disposal. Its leadership also conflated Algerian and French entrepreneurs as enemies of the people, and faced the horror of nationalizing much private Algerian property. All the banks were nationalized (as in Nasser's Egypt) and grouped into three large banks corresponding to foreign trade (mainly hydrocarbons), other industry and agriculture, and the service sectors (Naas 2003, 44–55).

Although private enterprise enjoyed greater respect after 1980, the statist banking legacy has stonewalled all reform efforts since 1986. Whether out of popular distrust for public institutions in general or because of Muslim objections to interest, Algerians tend to avoid banks. More than 25 percent of the broad money supply is kept at home, compared to roughly 15 percent in Egypt and Tunisia. Banks, in turn, offer little to the private sector. Traditionally serving as cash cows for state enterprises, they still tend to leave businesses to finance themselves unless they are public enterprises or have government connections. Table 2.2 compares Algeria's distribution of credit to the private sector with other countries and comparators in the region and shows only Iraq, Sudan, Syria, and Yemen with similar profiles.

Algeria illustrates that without a dynamic private sector, any sustained effort to diversify an economy seems doomed. Yet servicing a booming private sector is

TABLE 2.2

Bank Credit to the Private Sector, 2011

Country	Money (M2) in Banks (Percent)	Private Sector Credit to GDP (Percent)	Credit (Billions of dollars)	Credit per Capita (Dollars)
Qatar	97.1	36.5	66.7	32,526
Kuwait	95.5	55.8	99.3	30,549
United Arab Emirates	–	59.1	226.7	24,627
Bahrain	95.0	70.0	20.0	15,188
Oman	89.2	41.1	28.0	8,443
Saudi Arabia	89.0	36.4	228.9	8,092
Algeria	72.8	14.5	27.9	725
Iran	–	12.5	62.9	823
Iraq	52.6	6.0	10.1	309
Sudan	69.5	12.0	7.3	196
Egypt	81.5	29.1	73.5	911
Morocco	76.2	73.3	71.4	2,196
Malaysia	95.0	117.8	323.3	11,057
Turkey	91.9	57.9	411.5	5,561
Indonesia	86.7	35.0	268.6	1,088
Kazakhstan	79.7	36.7	67.7	4,032
Russian Federation	72.0	48.1	853.1	5,958

Sources: IMF, World Economic Outlook database; World Bank, World Development Indicators; and Saudi Arabian Monetary Agency, Yearly Statistics.

clearly not sufficient, unless it is also hiring nationals. Algerian efforts to educate its labor force deserve attention. Only 1.9 percent of the population was in school in 1890 (Guerid 2007, 62), and by 1954 only 13.7 percent were literate. Formal education was almost exclusively in French, so that of the three-quarters of the tiny minority that read French, only one-third were bilingual in Arabic, while the remaining quarter, products of traditional schools, could only read Arabic (Lardjane 2007, 325).

Overly ambitious plans to Arabize the education system after independence came into conflict with Algeria's massive undertaking to train cadres for modern industry. In the 1970s, observers pointed to a two-track system reminiscent of *janissaries* and *ulama*: French training for the captains of industry, Arabic for cultural and political figures (Gellner 1981). But Algeria's cultural revolution conflicted with the needs of its industrial one (El-Kenz 1992): Arabization of the humanities and social sciences, including management, undermined industrial training efforts. Arabized cadres had to learn French to function on the factory floors (Madi 1994). The great cultural divide was also one of the background factors leading to civil war in the 1990s.

Although other oil producers never experienced Algeria's cultural polarization, the Algerian experience may bear some relevance to the current clash of paradigms in the region. Algeria alerts us to the political implications of modern labor training and to the need to tailor it to meet the changing needs of economic diversification. Also worth noting is that despite the abundance of trained Algerian technicians and engineers, as well as unskilled labor, they have not developed effective linkages, either with businesses or trade unions. The government engages in massive infrastructure projects by importing labor forces, much like the GCC countries. And the research potential accumulated in the defunct industrial sector is largely ignored for lack of demand. Research and development is underfunded even by regional standards,[3] and what remains of Algeria's skilled manpower remains underemployed.

SAUDI ARABIA'S INCOMPLETE PATH TO DIVERSIFICATION

In the 1970s, Saudi Arabia, enjoying record oil revenues, was as active as Algeria in promoting heavy industry to diversify its economy. Like Algeria, it engaged in ambitious economic planning and is currently implementing its ninth four-year plan. Yet unlike Algeria, the Saudis not only stayed the course, but also did so by welcoming joint ventures with traditional American corporate partners and other multinationals. Instead of investing in turnkey projects advised by American consultants, they benefited from international alliances for tapping new export markets in downstream petrochemical and other heavy industrial projects.

The Saudi Basic Industries Corporation (SABIC) is the government's industrial arm. SABIC is a publicly traded company that is 70 percent government-owned and was founded in 1976. Though hardly dependent on support from private

---

[3] World Bank, World Development Indicators.

investors, SABIC issues annual reports, just as most of its multinational partners do, and conveys a sophisticated and friendly image to international business, quite unlike its Algerian government counterpart.

The corporation's objectives, fueled by much greater oil revenues than Algeria, were equally radical. SABIC built the factories for Saudi Arabia's two industrial cities, Jubail and Yanbu, from the late 1970s, and went on to build even more that required heavy investment, principally in petrochemical industries designed to take advantage of cheap petroleum feedstock. More recently, SABIC's plan is for 27 more industrial cities (Kingdom of Saudi Arabia 2013, 119). As stated on its web page:

> SABIC has pioneered a system of partnerships in our manufacturing activities that is often cited as a model for industrial progress in developing countries. This strategy is central to our business growth. To create our advanced manufacturing plants, SABIC enters into joint ventures with industry leaders from around the world. We offer a share in our resources in exchange for technology and expertise in human resources and global marketing.[4]

Like Algeria, SABIC also built an iron and steel complex, managed by its subsidiary, the Saudi Iron and Steel Company (Hadeed). Hadeed was founded in 1979, opened operations in 1983, and gradually expanded its initial output of 800,000 metric tons of long products to 3.3 million while adding an additional 2.2 million tons of flat products and another million tons of miscellaneous products.[5] By contrast, Algeria's El Hajdar complex, with a theoretical capacity of 2 million tons, achieved only 1 million in 2001. After El Hajdar was subsequently privatized and placed under foreign management, its production diminished to 500,000 tons in 2012. In 2013, the Algerian government regained majority control of the joint venture with ArcelorMittal by buying back 21 percent of the company for a symbolic Algerian dinar ($0.01).

The Saudi strategy ensured quality standards and international markets for its petrochemical exports. It avoided Algeria's mistakes and succeeded in developing a slightly less concentrated basket of exports with twice as many products, albeit heavily weighed down by its gigantic petroleum sector.

In newly founded industrial cities, Saudi Arabia also implemented further downstream integration, not only exporting the petrochemicals, but also fostering light industries to use some of the inputs from SABIC's factory complexes. Private enterprises moved in to take advantage of the excellent infrastructure provided by Bechtel and Parsons, hired respectively by the Royal Commission for Jubail and Yanbu. Figure 2.2 documents Saudi Arabia's rapid progress in generating value added in the manufacturing sector. In constant U.S. dollars per urban inhabitant, it has reached Malaysian levels, at about $2,500, whereas the equivalent measure for Algeria has plummeted.

Unlike Algeria, the Saudis offered a world-class, business-friendly environment. The kingdom joined the World Trade Organization in 2005, whereas

---

[4] SABIC. http://www.sabic.com/corporate/en/ourcompany/manufacturing-affiliates/.
[5] SABIC. http://www.sabic.com/corporate/en/productsandservices/metals/.

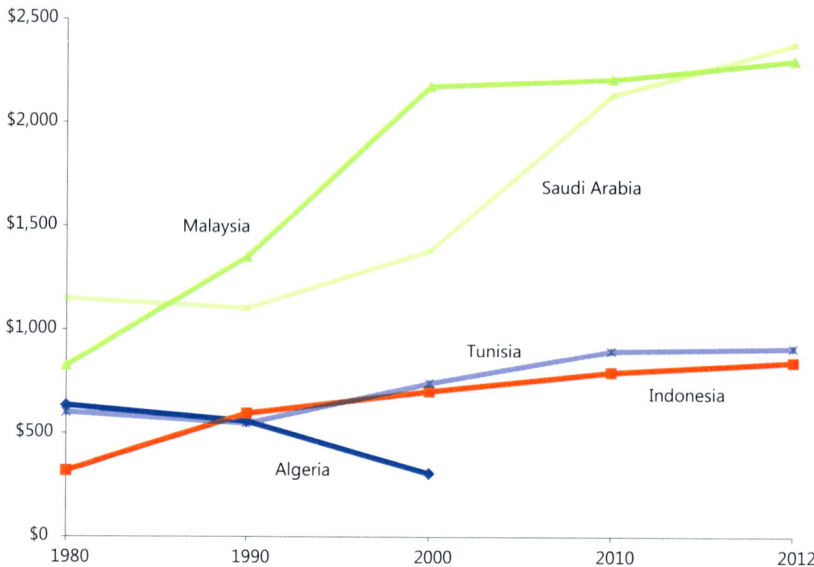

Figure 2.2   Manufacturing Value Added per Urban Inhabitant, 1980–2011
(Constant 2005 U.S. dollars)
Source: World Bank, World Development Indicators.

Algerian negotiations began in 1989 and are still pending. The World Economic Forum placed Saudi Arabia 22 out of 148 countries in 2013, whereas Algeria lagged at 100 (World Economic Forum 2013). Table 2.3 presents the overall rankings of the MENA region's oil-exporting countries and selected comparators, together with their respective ranks on education, business sophistication, technological readiness, and innovation potential.

Rather than relying, like the Algerians, on state investment in light industry to flesh out linkages with its heavy industrial base, the Saudis relied on incentives to the private sector, including foreign investors. In other words, SABIC, Saudi Arabia's functional equivalent of Algeria's Ministry of Industry and Energy in the 1970s, wholly owned its iron and steel complex and engaged in joint ventures in the petrochemical sector, but did not become directly involved in most of the nearly 6,000 factories built since the 1970s. Moreover, the Saudi commercial banking system—originally a product of joint ventures with multinational banks—generated much more credit to the private sector as a percentage of GDP and per capita (see Table 2.2). The Saudi government provided additional cheap consumer credit to its citizens through specialized funds.

SABIC has also helped propagate a Saudi image of innovation that suggests an ability to climb that steep ladder of export prowess into the global economy. Its 2013 annual report highlights the creation of industrial research centers at home and overseas, in China, India, and Singapore as well as Europe and the United States. Much space is devoted to high-tech products, including quality Saudi steel and other inputs. King Saud University is another important initiative: the

TABLE 2.3

World Economic Forum Rankings 2013–14 (out of 146 countries)					
Country	Overall	Higher Education and Training	Technological Readiness	Business Sophistication	Innovation
UAE	19	35	28	16	28
Bahrain	43	53	32	53	73
Kuwait	36	84	69	77	118
Oman	33	57	56	32	45
Qatar	13	29	31	10	16
Saudi Arabia	20	48	41	28	30
Algeria	100	101	136	144	141
Iran	82	88	116	104	71
Iraq	–	–	–	–	–
Sudan	–	–	–	–	–
Egypt	118	118	100	84	120
Morocco	77	102	80	92	106
Turkey	44	65	58	43	50
Malaysia	24	46	51	20	25
Indonesia	38	64	75	37	33
Kazakhstan	50	54	57	94	84
Russian Federation	64	47	59	107	78

Source: World Economic Forum, *Global Competitiveness Report.*
Note: UAE = United Arab Emirates.

cutting-edge research of its world-class scientists can be applied directly to Saudi industry through the SABIC centers. Yet, as Zahlan (2012, 195) observes, "No Arab country has yet developed a national science and technology system in order to build a knowledge-based economy."

The impressive Saudi initiatives still run into the same problem as smaller GCC states in their efforts to promote service sectors. Like those of Dubai or Qatar, they may be largely viewed as exercises in portfolio diversification, rather than sustainable development, because expatriates occupy so many of the critical positions, especially in research and development.

Like the Algerians, however, the Saudis have made determined efforts to train indigenous labor and build up human and industrial capital. Like the Algerians a decade earlier, the Saudis started with a very weak base. Like Algeria, too, SABIC developed parallel systems to train industrial cadres and engage in applied research. As well as investing heavily in a national university system, the government has resumed sending tens of thousands of Saudis abroad. Efforts have been made since 2001 to reform education so as to better match schooling with the skills demanded by the private sector, but in 2011 only 11.1 percent of private sector employees were Saudi. In the very top 0.8 percent, to be sure, more than 80 percent of the 65,000 administrative and business directors were Saudi in 2011, and included 5,934, an increase from 2,328 in the previous year (Saudi Arabian Monetary Agency 2013, 187) and offsetting the retirement or demotion of some 7,000 Saudi men. Saudis, however, comprised only 15 percent in the next rung of the hierarchy, the technical specialists who constituted about 5 percent of private sector workers.

It is still not clear whether Saudi education is producing more employable graduates, or whether those many thousands studying abroad will fit into the Saudi economy on their return, assuming that they return. Despite the many potential openings in rapidly expanding non-oil sectors, close to 30 percent of young Saudis were unemployed in 2006–10 (Looney 2014, 475), reflecting either inadequate training, poor motivation, or, like the Kuwaitis, a preference for government jobs, already largely in Saudi hands.

Despite excellent monetary policy and astutely planned allocation of tasks between the public and private sectors, the Saudis cannot be said to have resolved the riddle of sustainable diversification. While prudently mixing strategic capital investment with carefully crafted incentives to private business, the Saudis have not been able to engage many of their citizens in their model of development. Consequently Saudi Arabia faces risks similar to those that beset Algeria—potential polarization between a technocratic elite and the masses.

Necessary political reforms are beyond the scope of this chapter, but one possible response to public concern about economic management is to increase the transparency of government operations. No major Arab oil producer has yet voluntarily joined the Extractive Industries Transparency Initiative launched in 2002. One could argue that joining the initiative, an international nongovernment organization, is considered unnecessary for countries that do not need foreign direct investment. But joining might reinforce Saudi Arabia's high standing, not only with the international business community, but also with its public at home.

Economic visions and sustainable strategies of diversification clearly cannot rely on trickle-down effects. They need private business involvement and support and understanding from broader segments of the workforce. The Korean experience discussed in Chapter 10 offers one illustration of how rural folk were prepared to move into the modern economy.

THINKING OUTSIDE THE BOX

The Saudi experience in industrial diversification may be instructive, but new initiatives will be needed to engage the citizenries of the GCC for any of their respective projects to be sustainable. The region clearly enjoys capital abundance but needs to develop the human capital to cultivate it. To date, much of the recent investment in human capital has been top-down, bringing in the foreign experts to transfer cutting-edge science and technology. Qatar and Abu Dhabi host branches of top American universities servicing their international business plans, while King Saud University picks up academic stars. Highly qualified expatriates tend to be mobile, however, and their science and technology will not acquire roots to survive their departure. Inspiration and innovation need local roots.

To be sure, the development state is needed, to build schools and universities and to send students abroad, possibly emulating the meticulous interventions of

Singapore (Chapter 3). The state may also be viewed as a venture capitalist needed to nurture export sophistication and climb up the quality ladder, but the ventures are perhaps better accomplished in association with more experienced multinationals, as the Saudi model illustrates.

The state's primary challenge is to set appropriate incentives for capital and labor. The Saudis and others compete to offer appropriate incentives for capital and "business friendliness," but what about the workers? How, if at all, can the state make people want to work and to acquire the skills needed to be gainfully employed? What sort of environment can favor the construction, so to speak, of human capital from below?

States may, like Saudi Arabia and Algeria, generate human capital from above, but movement from below is also needed and presumably starts at a very early age. Women's education in much of the MENA region lagged a generation behind that of Southeast Asia. Now that the mothers are literate (Figure 2.3), they may read their children story books. The content matters. As David McClelland (1961) pointed out half a century ago in *The Achieving Society*, stories about hard work and upward mobility may make small children higher achievers later in life. The state or some charity might sponsor contests for writers, perhaps young mothers among them, to write good stories. Poetry contests may blend Bedouin tradition with Arab legacies. Smart toys can introduce children to the robots of industrial and post-industrial society. Informal as well as formal education should inculcate values of hard work and respect for nontraditional avenues of achievement, by technicians and plumbers as well as worldly managers.

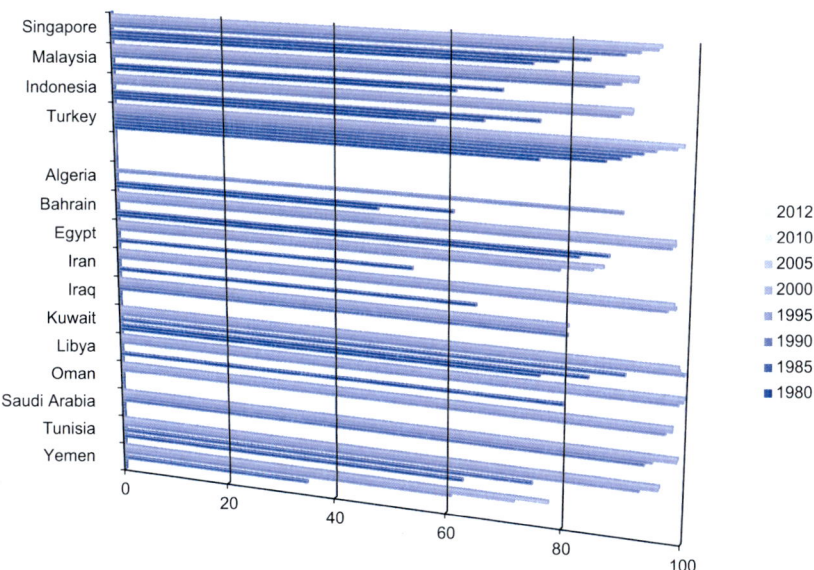

Figure 2.3 Female Literacy *(Percent, aged 15–24)*
Sources: UNESCO Institute for Statistics; and World Bank, World Development Indicators.

If their citizens are to participate fully in diversified economies, states must develop a work ethic in their citizens from an early age and help them to become competitive with their peers in other advanced countries. Rather than obsessive attention to portfolio diversification and imports of high-tech expertise and brand-name universities, the highest priority must be given to ground-up primary education to rectify the poor showings in mathematical proficiency and other basic skills demonstrated in Trends in International Mathematics and Science Study testing. Finland may have lessons for many countries' primary and secondary schools, including those of the United States. Finnish schoolteachers are well respected and properly paid members of their communities—not unlike the *ulama* and village teachers of precolonial times in the MENA region.

Cutting-edge services need not be focused exclusively on global competition. The GCC is part of the Arab region, sharing the lofty vision of Arab cultural, educational, and economic integration articulated by the Economic and Social Commission for Western Asia of the United Nations. The GCC may enjoy a certain locational advantage from proximity to Arab Bedouin traditions with minimal disruption compared to Western intrusions into Algeria or even Egypt. That oil production enclaves were so peripheral to these Gulf societies gave them a certain historical advantage. In the much wider Dar al-Islam they lie at the center of a vibrant global civilization (Bianchi 2013). Value-added hajj tourism, staffed by faculty and students specialized in religious studies, could develop into a high-tech global service space.

Islamic finance is another key service area of great potential. Wealthy Saudis are already its driving force, cultivated today primarily by big London- and New York-based banking monoliths. The growing set of Islamic financial practices seems bound to grow, given the beliefs of millions of Muslims who avoid conventional interest-based banking. Why not encourage labor-intensive microfinance that most conventional banks shun? Experiments in Egypt show greater receptivity among villagers to a sharia-compliant procedure (interest free) than to the Grameen Bank's method based on interest (El-Komi and Croson 2013; Ali 2012; El-Gamal and others 2014). Egypt is potentially a huge market, and public opinion in other Arab countries shows even greater distrust of conventional banking and, hence, potentially a fertile field for Islamic finance. More finance for small and medium-sized enterprises might encourage enterprises to emerge from the shadows of the informal economy and alleviate the credit shortages underlined in Table 2.2.

Table 2.4 records the responses of representative national samples in the MENA region to Arab Barometer surveys conducted in 2006–08 and in 2011 to the question of whether bank interest accords to the teachings of Islam. Large majorities in most of the countries surveyed considered interest forbidden, despite findings by some religious authorities that it was acceptable under certain conditions.

A second question in the 2011 surveys was whether conventional banks should be allowed to charge interest, given the needs of the modern economy. Here opinion was more divided. Still, over half of the respondents opposed conventional banks charging interest, except among the Lebanese and Egyptians, some of whom were Christian, and the Tunisians. Sophisticated Islamic financial services might offer another tradable niche in the global economy.

TABLE 2.4

Arab Attitudes toward Bank Interest			
	Charging interest by banks contradicts teachings of Islam (Percent agreed)		Banks should not be allowed to charge interest (Percent agreed)
Country	2006-2008	2011	2011
Algeria	89	86	56
Egypt	–	72	45
Iraq	–	80	69
Jordan	86	87	54
Kuwait	76	–	–
Lebanon	65	69	38
Morocco	86	–	–
West Bank and Gaza	85	86	69
Saudi Arabia	–	77	74
Sudan	–	64	59
Tunisia	–	85	48
Yemen	81	77	67
Average	82	78	58

Source: Arab Barometer I and II, www.arabbarometer.org.

There are no easy solutions to the riddle of sustainable diversification. Starting with relatively modest reserves of human capital, combining labor-intensive activities with export sophistication is a daunting challenge. Cultural services deserve greater attention as one of several approaches, and these, too, may constitute "sophisticated" exports to the 1.5 billion Muslims scattered across the globe. There is no substitute, however, for an expanding set of sophisticated, high-tech exports of goods and services. Cultural services and even import substitution possibly can be added to the mix, and planners might envision stages of human capital formation that combine strategies from above and below to escape the oil ghetto of product spaces.

REFERENCES

Abdesselam, Belaid. 2007. "La Politique de Developpement Appliquee par L'Algerie au Lendemain de Son Independance." October 2007. http://www.belaidabdesselam.com/?page_id=81.

———. 1990. *Le Gaz Algérien: Strategies et Enjeux*. Algiers: Editions Bouchene.

Abdon, Arnelyn, and Jesus Felipe. 2011. "The Product Space: What Does It Say About the Opportunities for Growth and Structural Transformation of Sub-Saharan Africa?" Working Paper 670, Levy Economics Institute of Bard College, Annandale-on-Hudson, New York. http://www.levyinstitute.org/pubs/wp_670.pdf.

Ali, S. Nazim, ed. 2012. *Sharia-Compliant Microfinance*. London and New York: Routledge.

Bennoune, Mahfoudh, and Ali El-Kenz. 1990. *Entretiens avec Belaid Abdesselam*. Algiers: ENAG.

Bianchi, Robert. 2013. *Islamic Globalization: Pilgrimage, Capitalism, Democracy and Diplomacy*. Singapore: World Scientific.

Destanne de Bernis, Gérard. 1963. "L'industrialisation en Algérie." In *Problèmes de l'Algérie indépendante*, edited by François Perroux, 125–37. Paris: Presses Universitaires de France.

———. 1966. "Industries Industrialisantes et Contenu d'une Politique d'Intégration Régionale." *Economie Appliquée* 19 (3/4): 415–73.

El-Gamal, M. A., M. El-Komi, D. Karlan, and A. Osman. 2014. "Bank-Insured RoSCA for Microfinance: Experimental Evidence in Poor Egyptian Villages." *Journal of Economic Behavior and Organization* 103: 56–73.

El-Kenz, Ali. 1985. *Le Complexe Siderurgique d'el Hadjar*. Paris: Editions du CNRS.

———. 1992. "Les Deux Paradigmes (Algérie)." In *L'industrie et la Recherché*, edited by Roland Waast and A. El Kenz, 230–38. Marseilles: Institut de Recherche pour le Développement.

El-Komi, Mohammed, and Rachel Croson. 2013. "Experiments in Islamic Microfinance." *Journal of Economic Behavior and Organization* 95 (2013): 252–269.

Gellner, Ernest. 1981. "The Unknown Apollo of Biskra: The Social Base of Algerian Puritanism." In *Muslim Society*, 149–173. Cambridge: Cambridge University Press.

Guerid, Djamel. 2007. "Algerie: Dualite de la Societe et Dualite de L'elite: Les Origines Historiques." In *Elites et Sociétés: Algérie et Egypt*, edited by Omar Lardjane, 55–67. Algiers: Editions Casbah.

Hausmann, Ricardo, and César Hidalgo. 2010. "Country Diversification, Product Ubiquity, and Economic Divergence." CID Working Paper No 201, Kennedy School of Government, Harvard University, Cambridge, Massachusetts.

Hausmann, Ricardo, Bailey Klinger, and José R. López-Cálix. 2008. "Export Diversification in Algeria." In *Trade Competitiveness of the Middle East and North Africa: Policies for Export Diversification*, edited by José R. López-Cálix, Peter Walkenhorst, and Ndiamé Diop. Washington: World Bank.

Henry, Clement M. 2009. "Between the Shocks: 'White Elephant' Industrialization in Algeria." In *Viewpoints: The 1979 "Oil Shock:" Legacy, Lessons, and Lasting Reverberations. Viewpoints Special Edition*: 49–52. Washington: The Middle East Institute.

International Monetary Fund (IMF). 2013. *Economic Prospects and Policy Challenges for the GCC Countries*. Prepared for the Annual Meeting of Ministers of Finance and Central Bank Governors, October 5, 2013.

Kingdom of Saudi Arabia. 2013. "Achievements of the Development Plan: Facts and Figures (version 30)." http://www.mep.gov.sa/themes/BlueArc/index.jsp.

Lardjane, Omar. 2007. „Les Médersiens: Destinées d'une Elite." In *Elites et Sociétés: Algérie et Egypte*, edited by Omar Lardjane. Algiers: Editions Casbah.

Looney, Robert E. 2014. "The Saudi Arabian Model." In *Handbook of Emerging Economies*, edited by Robert E. Looney, chapter 25. London and New York: Routledge.

Madi, Mustapha. 1994. "Arabization and Industrial Organization in Algeria (Arabic)." In *Maghreb et Maîtrise Technologique: Enjeux et perspectives*, edited by Henry Clément Moore, 495–526, Actes de colloque. Tunis: Centre d'Etudes, de Recherches et de Publications and Centre d'Etudes Maghrébines à Tunis.

Malek, Redha. 2010. *Guerre de Liberation et Revolution Democratique*. Algiers: Casbah Editions.

McClelland, David, C. 1961. *The Achieving Society*. Princeton, New Jersey: Princeton University Press.

Moore, Henry Clément, ed. 1994. *Maghreb et Maîtrise Technologique: Enjeux et Perspectives*. Actes de colloque. Tunis: Centre d'Etudes, de Recherches et de Publications and Centre d'Etudes Maghrébines à Tunis.

Naas, Abdelkrim. 2003. *Le Système Bancaire Algérien; de la Décolonisation a L'économie de Marché*. Paris: Maisonneuve et Larose.

Pervillé, Guy. 1997. *Les Etudiants Algériens de l'Université Française 1880–1962*. Algiers: Editions Casbah. Reprinted, Centre National de la Recherche Scientifique, 2004.

Ross, Michael L. 2012. *The Oil Curse: How Petroleum Wealth Shapes the Development of Nations*. Princeton, New Jersey: Princeton University Press.

Saudi Arabian Monetary Agency. 2013. "48th Annual Report." Riyadh.

World Economic Forum. 2013. *Global Competitiveness Report 2013–2014*. Geneva: World Economic Forum. http://reports.weforum.org/the-global-competitiveness-report-2013–2014/.

Zahlan, A. B. 2012. *Science, Development, and Sovereignty in the Arab World*. New York: Palgrave Macmillan.

PART II

Experiences of Diversification in Asia and Latin America

CHAPTER 3

Going Beyond Comparative Advantage: How Singapore Did It

PHILIP YEO

Singapore has been transformed economically, socially, and politically since independence in August 1965. The country's industrial development strategy evolved from labor intensive in the 1960s, skill intensive in the 1970s, capital intensive in the 1980s, and technology intensive in the 1990s to knowledge and innovation intensive from the 2000s onward (Figure 3.1). Four industries—electronics, precision engineering, chemicals, and biomedical sciences—have anchored the city's approach to industrial development.

1960S: LABOR INTENSIVE

GDP was S$2.2 billion (US$0.7 billion) in the 1960s, and by 2013 had expanded to S$372.8 billion (US$298.0 billion). Income per capita had reached US$54,662 from US$428 in the span of about 50 years (Singapore Department of Statistics 2014a). This phenomenal growth can be attributed to an economic transition through different industrial phases (as shown in Figure 3.1).

Marked by high unemployment, Singapore focused on labor-intensive industrialization in the 1960s. The Jurong Industrial Estate, transformed from a mangrove swamp in the west of the island, initiated the country's industrialization program with factories producing garments, textiles, toys, mosquito coils, wood products, and hair wigs (EDB 2014a). The overriding strategy at that time was to spearhead rapid industrialization that would urgently create new jobs and promote economic development.

Industrialization was a new experience for independent Singapore, as the economy had been wholly dependent on the *entrepôt* trade since the British founded it in 1819. Hence, active leadership and timely execution by the fledgling Singapore government was needed to promote industrialization. The Economic Development Board (EDB) carried out industrial planning, development, and investment promotion, while Jurong Town Corporation, spun off

Research and assistance in the preparation of this chapter were provided by Dr. Yew Kwan Choong, Economic Development Innovations, Singapore.

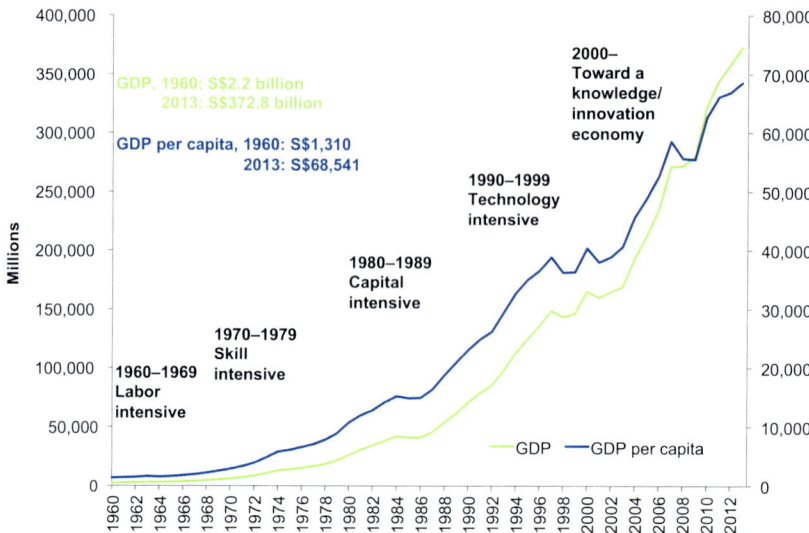

Figure 3.1 Five Phases of Singapore's Economic Development, 1960–2013 (Singapore dollars)
Source: Singapore Department of Statistics.

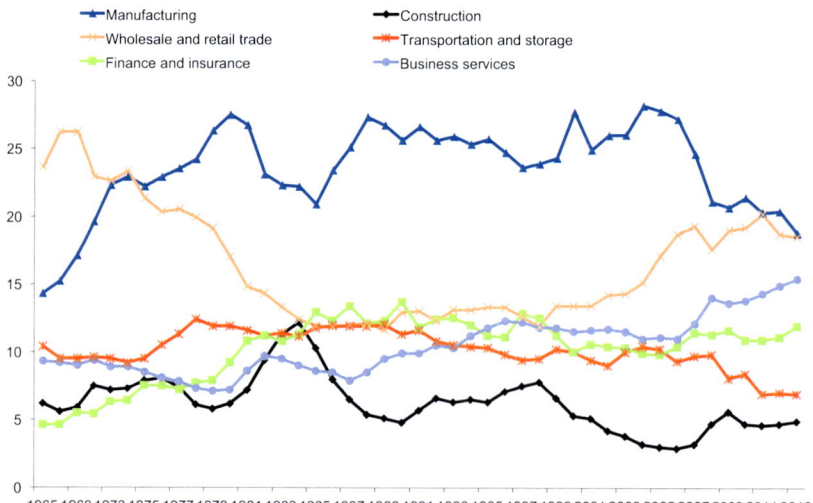

Figure 3.2 Share of GDP by Industry at 2013 Market Prices *(Percent)*
Source: Singapore Department of Statistics (2014b).

from the EDB's Land Department, focused on the development and management of industrial estates.

By the mid-1970s the manufacturing sector contributed a significant share of GDP, solidifying the successful transition from an entrepôt into an industrialized economy (Figure 3.2). Realizing the limitations of the domestic market to support local industries and the lack of raw resources, the government proactively went to the global marketplace to engage and attract foreign investors.

Singapore accompanied industrialization in its economic development with early social investments. The evidence of 50 years of growth is clearly reflected in the transformation of the Singapore River itself, a cornerstone of the city state's modern history. Located within the central region and acting as an economic lifeline, it was originally a busy—and polluted—port, earning it the nickname "Dead Chicken River" in the 1970s for the proliferation of poultry farms along its banks.

Various government departments embarked on a 10-year program to clean it up. Riverside squatters were resettled in public housing and hawkers in hawker centers. And with completion of the cleanup in the 1980s, the Urban Redevelopment Authority embarked on a comprehensive long-term plan to transform the river precinct. The plan covered the length of the river all the way to its mouth at Marina Bay, where the downtown area now sits, anchoring the city's competitive edge as a premier financial and business hub. Planned as early as the late 1960s, land was reclaimed as part of the new downtown area for a seamless extension of the central business district. Today, the Singapore River is an aesthetically pleasing, functional reservoir supporting tourism and commercial activity.

The social needs of the population included infrastructural investment and housing development. To address these priorities, the country established the Housing and Development Board in 1960 to build low-cost housing. At its inception, only 9 percent of residents lived in public housing; today more than 80 percent do (Housing & Development Board 2014).

The Urban Redevelopment Authority[1] was set up to redevelop the city area into a vibrant modern commercial center. Among its key tasks in the early 1960s was to resettle residents living in slums and move industries to new locations. Once land was amalgamated and parceled, the government started the sale of sites for modern commercial development.

Authorities drew up the first Concept Plan in 1971 and laid the foundation for the physical landscape, such as housing developments outside of the city and developing key transport infrastructure, with the first mass rapid transit lines and expressways, as well as Changi International Airport.

The Urban Redevelopment Authority also started conserving historical buildings as physical anchors to Singapore's past and social memories. Close to 7,200 buildings have been conserved so far. As Singapore's national land use planning authority, the Urban Redevelopment Authority works with other government agencies such as the National Parks Board to "green" Singapore's urban environment through parks, park connectors, and "vertical greenery," incorporating plants within buildings' vertical surfaces.

---

[1] Initially known as the Urban Renewal Unit of the Housing Development Board.

1970S: SKILL INTENSIVE

As industrial development gathered momentum, the government saw an opportunity to upgrade the economy from low-cost, labor-intensive industries to higher-value-added skilled jobs and businesses by developing technical and business skills and expertise.

Significant effort was made to attract foreign investment from Europe, north Asia, and the United States into Singapore by positioning the country as a global business hub for a company's entire value chain of activities. Investments poured into an emerging electronics industry, in particular high-tech products, including computer parts, peripherals, software packages, and silicon wafers. Multinational companies were encouraged to relocate to Singapore or develop research and development activities locally as an extension of their manufacturing operations. Many showed their willingness to make such long-term investments. Texas Instruments set up manufacturing operations in Singapore to produce semiconductors and integrated circuits, a major investment highlight in the coordinated push to develop a local electronics industry. Other firms followed, including Hewlett Packard of the United States, SGS (now ST Microelectronics, Europe), and NEC (Japan). The continued success of the manufacturing industry was proven when, in the late 1970s, it surpassed the trading sector for the first time.

Recognizing the need to upgrade the local workforce to support this economic growth, efforts were made to train skilled technicians, engineers, and managers from the local population. This started with the EDB's establishment of the Singapore Institute of Management and of various industrial training institutes, including the French-Singapore Institute, German-Singapore Institute, and the Japan-Singapore Institute, which were combined into the country's third polytechnic institute, Nanyang Polytechnic, in 1993.

To cope with the immediate shortfall in skilled professionals resulting from accelerating economic growth, Singapore took the radical step of liberalizing its immigration and work permit systems for foreign professionals to be employed by foreign firms, solving a potential squeeze in human capital in the operations of multinational corporations (Mathews and Cho 2007).

1980S: CAPITAL INTENSIVE

In response to rapid globalization in the 1980s, Singapore introduced a new national economic strategy, the Second Industrial Revolution: The Economic Development Plan for the Eighties (Parliament of Singapore 1981). The manufacturing sector's focus under the plan was on transitioning toward capital-intensive operations, as emphasized in the 1980 budget (Parliament of Singapore 1981, paragraph 24):

> Our industries will require more land as they become more capital intensive. On the other hand, the large claims for land for social and recreational purposes will continue unabated. The Ministry of National Development

must accord higher priority to industrial land and set aside more land in or near housing estates for the clean and higher value-added industries.

In 1985, Singapore's growth was interrupted by its first recession. The government realized the need to diversify economic activities, and a second engine of growth in exportable services was initiated by positioning the city state as a "total business center"—a methodology combining industry and technical know-how with the strategic formation of business relationships. It did this to attract international service corporations in the financial, educational, lifestyle, medical, information technology, and software sectors (EDB 2014a). Greater emphasis was put on higher value-added industries at all levels. Among the large-scale initiatives launched was the establishment of Science Park next to the National University of Singapore to spur research and development by the private sector. In addition, local enterprises were encouraged to grow through loans and incentives.

1990S AND 2000S: A TECHNOLOGY-INTENSIVE AND KNOWLEDGE- AND INNOVATION-BASED ECONOMY

The government's Strategic Economic Plan (Singapore Ministry of Trade and Industry 1991) in the 1990s focused Singapore's efforts to "attain the status and characteristics of a first league developed country within the next 30 to 40 years."

A key initiative was the building of a research and development environment to create a knowledge-based and innovation-driven Singapore. The National Science and Technology Board was established in 1991 to focus on applied research, and transformed into the Agency of Science, Technology and Research (A*STAR) in 2002 to focus on research and development and human capital training through local and overseas PhD scholarships. Two research-oriented councils were created: the Biomedical Research Council, which supports, oversees, and coordinates public sector biomedical sciences research and development activities in Singapore; and the Science and Engineering Research Council, which fulfills similar functions in physical sciences and engineering.

SINGAPORE TODAY

In 2013, as Singapore's GDP reached S$373 billion, 70 percent of nominal value added was generated by the service industries, and close to 25 percent by goods-producing industries (Singapore Department of Statistics 2014b). Manufacturing, which includes major industry sectors such as chemicals, electronics, precision engineering, transport engineering, and biomedical science, accounts for 19 percent of total GDP (Figure 3.3 and see Annex Table 3.1.1).

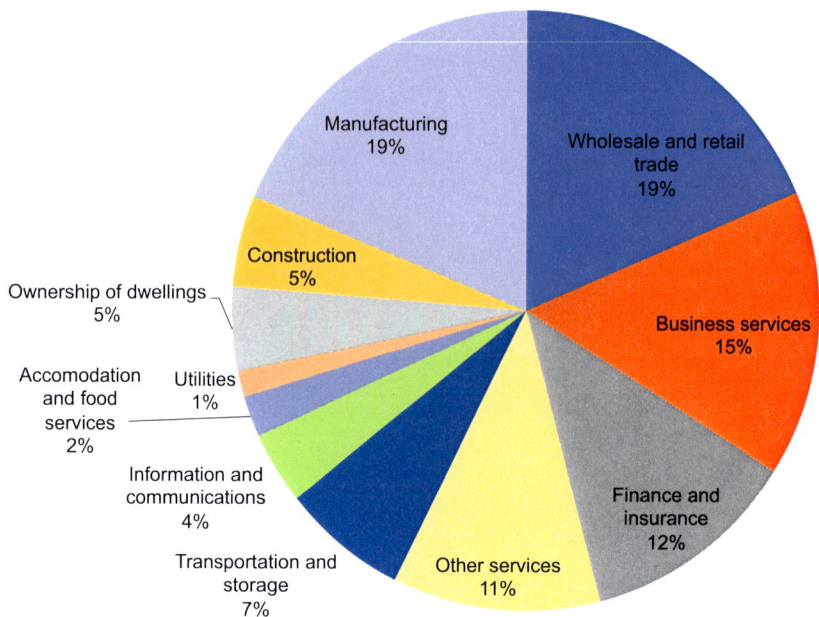

Figure 3.3 Share of Singapore GDP by Industry, 2013
Source: Singapore Department of Statistics.

A key item to note is the value added achieved in each sector.[2] As a country with no natural raw materials, Singapore has to import raw supplies needed for the chemical industry; hence the value added achieved was only 6.9 percent, in contrast with the biomedical sciences industry, where a significant 20.5 percent value added was achieved through the high-value proprietary products manufactured. This was made possible by heavy investment in research and infrastructure, and foreign investment in the development of the biomedical sciences industry.

The path taken to achieve high, long-term growth rates despite the lack of natural resources and a large domestic market enabled Singapore to become one of the four Asian Tiger economies, along with Hong Kong Special Administrative Region, Korea, and Taiwan Province of China. In 1992 the Economic Development Institute of the World Bank attributed Singapore's remarkable success largely to sensible and effective policies and early attention to infrastructure and manpower resources.

Accompanying this economic growth was a tangible transformation in the infrastructure and social make-up of its people. Urban redevelopment proceeded

[2] The value added equation used is as follows: value added = labor cost to employees + interest to lenders of money + depreciation for reinvestment in machinery and equipment + profits retained by the organization + other distributed costs (for example, tax) (Spring Singapore 2011).

at a very rapid pace to cope with the expansion of the population from 1.6 million in 1960 to 5.4 million in 2013.[3]

THE DEVELOPMENT THEMES OF THE SINGAPORE APPROACH—EXAMPLES OF FOUR INDUSTRIES

Singapore was forced to focus its efforts on specific industries for development, precisely because it had no domestic market and no natural resources. It started with the electronics industry in the 1970s, precision engineering in the 1980s, and chemical and biomedical industries in the 1990s.

It took an *investment promotion* approach to build and solidify its position as a "total business center." Through each decade of change, the country took a prioritized approach when selecting an industry to develop. Following research on that industry, international companies were identified as foreign investors and partners, and relationships formed with key executives of those companies. This proactive approach to building an international network of business relationships allowed it to search out foreign direct investment opportunities across all continents.

Singapore today has garnered investments from 37,400 international companies, including 3,200 from China, 4,400 from India, and 7,900 from the Association of Southeast Asian Nations (excluding domestic companies). In addition, some 7,000 multinational corporations (60 percent of which have regional responsibilities) have made Singapore their home base.

The Electronics Industry—Creating Value Added

Electronics manufacturing is the backbone of the Singapore economy, contributing 30 percent of total manufacturing value added (see Figure 3.3 and Annex Table 3.1.2). According to the EDB (2014b), Singapore's electronics industry, in 2013, attracted numerous investment projects, totaling S$3.3 billion of fixed assets investments, and S$0.6 billion of total business expenditure. These projects are expected to contribute S$1.8 billion in value added per year to GDP and create 1,310 skilled jobs when they are fully implemented.

Electronics was the first industrialized manufacturing industry developed in the 1960s that benefited from the availability of low-cost labor. This industry is still relevant today because further investment was made during the capital-intensive phase of the 1970s to enable electronics manufacturing to progress up the value chain. Process-intensive semiconductor fabrication complemented by assembly and testing activities, which require high-cost skilled labor, still comprises a significant share of Singapore's electronics industry. Through this phase, a development theme of *creating value added* can be identified.

---

[3] The number of citizens increased from 1.9 million in 1970 to 3.3 million in 2013, while permanent residents rose from 0.14 million to 0.53 million in the same period (Singapore Department of Statistics 2014c).

The Precision Engineering Industry—Building around the Value Chain

The precision engineering industry emerged in response to the need to grow the support infrastructure for the electronics industry. Its development was capital intensive, and considerable investments were made in the development of infrastructure and skills.

Alongside the electronics industry, the precision engineering industry today is a core enabler of associated industries, including marine, aerospace, oil and gas, and medical devices. Precision engineering skills and products also support the manufacturing of semiconductor chips and the large drill bits for oil exploration. In 2013, the industry contributed 11.4 percent, S$33 billion, to manufacturing GDP, or 2.2 percent to Singapore's GDP (see Figure 3.3 and Annex Table 3.1.2).

The precision engineering industry can be divided into two categories that, combined, create a self-sustaining cycle in the sector: precision modules and components, and machinery and systems (equipment). Companies in the first category produce specialized components, some of which then supply companies in the second category to build equipment. Companies can then use this equipment in the precision modules and components category. The developments within this industry bring a second developmental theme of *building around the value chain*.

The Chemicals Industry—Developing Clusters

In 2013 the chemical industry contributed 33 percent, S$97 billion, to Singapore's manufacturing output, and it has been the largest contributor to the country's manufacturing output since 2006 (Annex Table 3.1.2; Singapore Department of Statistics 2014d).

The chemical industry started with oil, an integral part of the country's economic history. Oil trading began in 1891, and the three main activities were refining, trading, and logistics (EDB 2011). Today, Singapore is recognized as one of the world's top three export oil refining centers, even though it has no oil reserves of its own. Investment, moving to higher-value-added production in developing the chemical industry, follows the two economic development themes of *creating value added* and *building around the value chain*.

A game changer for Singapore's chemical industry was the development of 3,000-hectare Jurong Island, through a S$7 billion land reclamation of seven smaller islands, which became the heart of the chemical industry. Besides clustering chemical suppliers, producers, and service providers, Jurong Island segregates the more polluting manufacturing processes from the main island. Jurong Island has attracted more than S$40 billion of investments with over 100 companies across the entire chemical production value chain, and some 40,000 people commute to it daily.

Jurong Island provides a "plug-and-play" capability to its clustered stakeholders, such as oil refineries, crackers, gas synthesis, petrochemicals, and specialty chemicals. It does this by developing infrastructure that allows access to feedstock and simplified logistics through co-location, reducing the cost of production for companies operating there. Singapore had effectively taken a proactive step to undertake the cost of infrastructure development in Jurong Island. Emphasis on *cluster development* can be seen as the third economic development theme.

Following the successful development of Jurong Island, Singapore turned to the next phase of growing its chemical industry, through the so-called Jurong Island Version 2.0 initiative and development of research activities. This was launched in 2010 to seek out investments to increase optimization, robustness, and options for resources. One of these was the Jurong Rock Caverns liquid hydrocarbon storage facility, located 130 meters under the Banyan Basin on Jurong Island. It is Southeast Asia's first underground liquid hydrocarbon storage facility, and was developed for liquid hydrocarbons such as crude oil, condensate, naphtha, and gas oil. Phase One has a storage capacity of approximately 1.47 million cubic meters (Energy Market Authority 2011). Other key infrastructure developments include a gasification plant, a liquefied petroleum gas terminal, and a multiuser product grid.

Research activities under Jurong Island Version 2.0 were executed through joint industry scholarship programs and the creation in 2002 of a public research institute, the Institute of Chemical and Engineering Sciences. From these endeavors, a fourth economic development theme emerges: *research and development.*

The Biomedical Sciences Industry—Focusing on Research and Development

The biomedical sciences initiative was launched in June 2000 to develop this industry cluster as a new, knowledge-based and knowledge-intensive pillar of the economy. In 2013, the biomedical sciences industry contributed 8.2 percent to GDP and, more importantly, contributed a value added of 20.5 percent (second only to the electronics industry, at 30.3 percent).

The two key sectors of Singapore's biomedical science manufacturing industry are pharmaceuticals and medical technology. Pharmaceuticals manufacturing investments were enabled by the establishment of a reclamation project at the western tip of the country to form the Tuas Biomedical Park. As of 2013, the park is home to seven of the top 10 international pharmaceutical companies, including 29 commercial-scale manufacturing plants for active pharmaceutical ingredients, biologics, cell therapy, and nutrition. The medical technology sector, meanwhile, is made up of 30 manufacturing plants, more than 10,000 employees, and six research and development centers in Singapore.

In addition to attracting manufacturing investment in the pharmaceutical and medical technology sectors, the biomedical sciences initiative included a bold plan to attract industry research and seed start-up ventures to cover four biomedical sciences industries (pharmaceuticals, medical technology, health care services and delivery, and biotechnology and biologics) from bench (research) to bedside (service delivery to patient). To support industry research and commercialization, publicly funded research institutes were created to build up capabilities in areas spanning bioprocessing to genomics and cell biology.

This initiative was implemented in three distinct phases. In the first (2000–05), Singapore invested in public research institutes that covered core research capabilities, including bioprocessing, chemical synthesis, genomics and proteomics, molecular and cell biology, bioengineering and nanotechnology, and computational biology. The second phase (2006–10) focused on strengthening translational and clinical research with the aim of translating basic discoveries from the lab into clinical applications to improve health care. The third phase (2011–15) aims to achieve commercialization, research partnerships with industry, and spin-offs. An essential aim of the third phase is the availability of financing and support, and one such approach is through co-investment with strategic partners for capital and value added, or commercialization grants. Some 40 local medical technology start-ups are currently in this program (the Agency for Science, Technology, and Research Biomedical Sciences Initiative).

The development of the biomedical sciences industry follows the four development themes of creating value added, building around the value chain, utilizing a cluster development approach, and making investments in research and development (Figure 3.4).

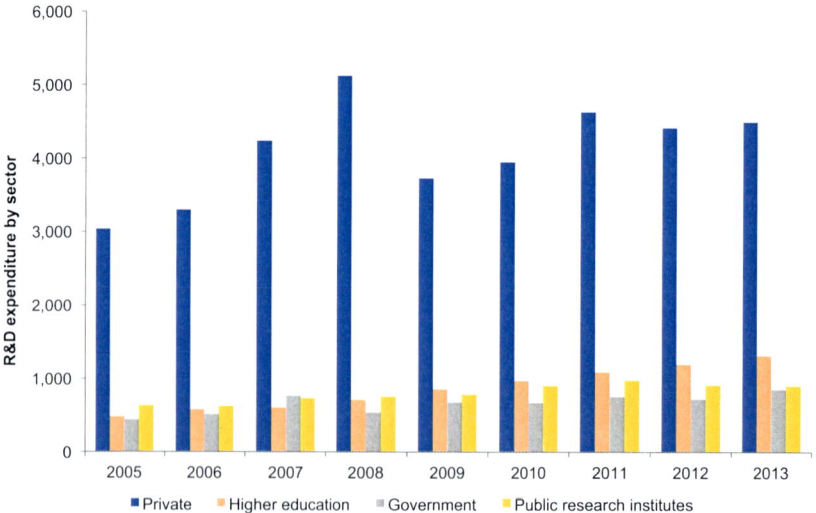

Figure 3.4 Research and Development Expenditure by Sector *(S$, millions)*
Source: Singapore Department of Statistics (2014e).

GOING FORWARD AS A KNOWLEDGE- AND INNOVATION-BASED ECONOMY

Significant investments have successfully transitioned Singapore's economy from a dependence on manufacturing and services to one based on knowledge and innovation, through investments in knowledge, innovation, and human capital. Evidence of its success is in the rise in publications, patents, and licensing revenue arising from research in Singapore during the 2000s (Figure 3.5).

1. Public Sector

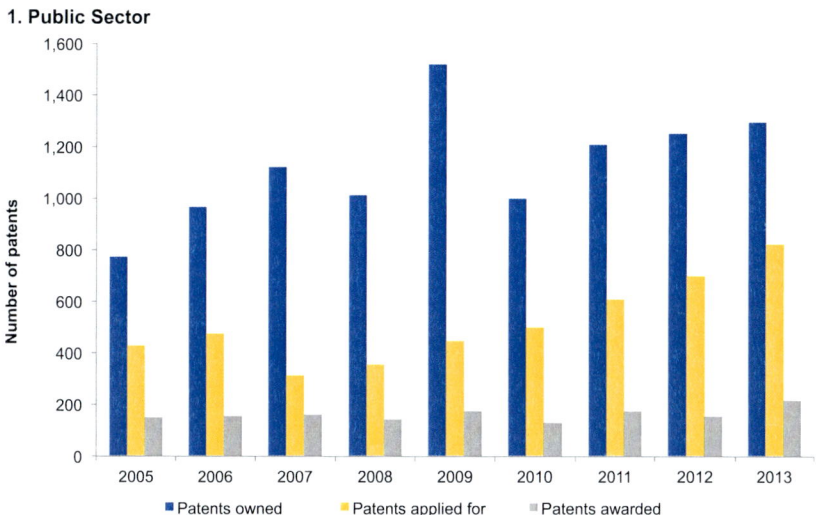

2. Private Sector

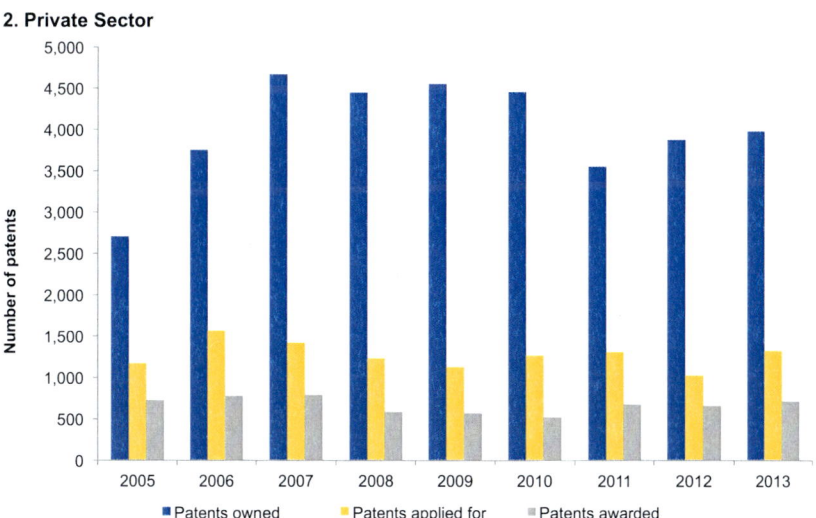

Figure 3.5   Patents Applied for, Awarded, and Owned in the Private and Public Sectors, 2005–13
Source: Singapore Department of Statistics (2014e).

Long-term human capital development remains a priority and senior figures from the international scientific community are invited to Singapore to lead research institutes and teams and to develop local talent (Figure 3.6). New scholarships were introduced to encourage Singaporeans to pursue PhDs, and more than 1,200 PhD scholarships have been awarded to develop research and development talent since 2001. Some 350 scholars have completed their PhD studies and are contributing to the research, innovation, and enterprise development environment (Figure 3.7).

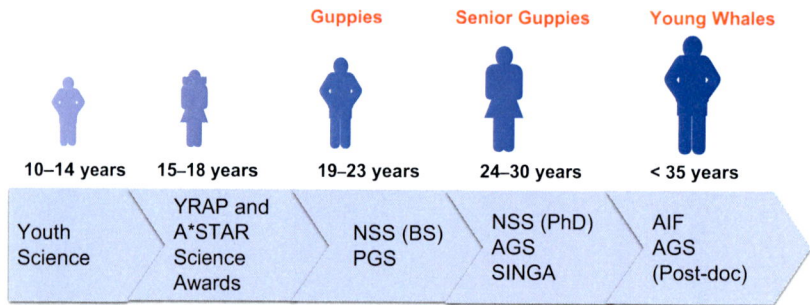

Figure 3.6 Long-Term Human Capital Investment Pipeline

Source: Agency for Science, Technology and Research (A*STAR).

Note: AGS = A*STAR graduate scholarship; AIF = A*STAR international fellowship; NSS = national science scholarship; PGS = pre-graduate scholarship; SINGA = Singapore international graduate award; YRAP = young researchers attachment programme.

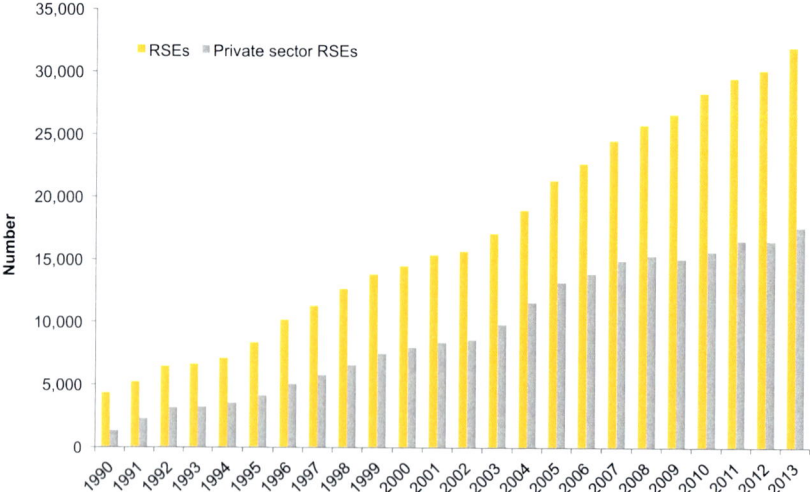

Figure 3.7 Research Scientists and Engineers, 1990–2012

Source: Agency for Science, Technology and Research (2014).

Note: RSE = Research scientists and engineers.

Infrastructure development is a cornerstone in Singapore's move to become a knowledge- and innovation-intensive economy, as shown by the 200-hectare purpose-built, high-tech zone known as the "one-north" development. Here, hubs such as Biopolis and Fusionopolis house public and private institutes and organizations. The one-north differentiation is in its integrated work-live-play-learn concept. The co-located work facilities the hubs provide are close to public amenities and residences to stimulate an exchange of ideas and to create a holistic environment. In essence, one-north has comprehensively captured the four economic themes of *creating value added, building around the value chain, cluster development*, and *research and development*.

Biopolis is the hallmark of Singapore's biomedical research and development. Construction of the seven buildings in Biopolis Phase 1 began in December 2001 and was completed in 18 months. Biopolis colocates public sector research institutes with corporate laboratories to facilitate a collaborative culture while providing access to state-of-the-art facilities, shared infrastructure, and specialized services. It is also strategically located near the National University of Singapore and National University Health System to facilitate translational and clinical research. Fusionopolis is an integrated urban development that is dedicated to research and development in information and communication technology, media, physical sciences, and engineering industries. It serves as a platform to fuse and synergize knowledge from different scientific domains, bringing together the public and private sectors.

Having started its development ascent as a poor island in the 1960s and possessing no comparative advantage in any specific industry, Singapore has transformed itself from a labor-intensive economy to a knowledge- and innovation-based one within a few decades. It has established international partnerships and industrial parks to share knowledge and explore opportunities in China, India, Indonesia, and Vietnam. Yet the city state cannot rest on its achievements—it must continue to learn and adapt to remain relevant in the face of increasingly complex global economic challenges.

ANNEX 3.1. SINGAPORE'S MANUFACTURING INDUSTRY

ANNEX TABLE 3.1.1

Value-Added of Singapore Manufacturing Industry, 2013

	Employment		Remuneration		Total Output		Value Added		Remuneration per Worker	Value Added per Worker
	Number	Percent	Million S$	Percent	Million S$	Percent	Million S$	Percent	Thousand S$	Thousand S$
Electronics	76,402	18.4	4,271.0	21.1	80,860.0	27.8	17,469.0	30.3	55.9	228.6
Semiconductors	40,659	9.8	2,468.0	12.2	46,260.0	15.9	10,861.0	18.8	60.7	267.1
Computer peripherals	10,170	2.4	494.0	2.4	8,195.0	2.8	2,188.0	3.8	48.6	215.2
Data storage	9,645	2.3	394.0	1.9	4,877.0	1.7	1,744.0	3.0	40.8	180.9
Infocomms and consumer electronics	9,129	2.2	602.0	3.0	19,510.0	6.7	2,010.0	3.5	66.0	220.2
Other electronic modules and components	6,799	1.6	312.0	1.5	2,018.0	0.7	665.0	1.2	45.9	97.9
Chemicals	24,909	6.0	2,362.0	11.7	97,114.0	33.4	3,977.0	6.9	94.8	159.7
Petroleum	4,087	1.0	740.0	3.7	51,316.0	17.7	72.0	0.1	181.0	17.6
Petrochemicals	5,577	1.3	539.0	2.7	34,581.0	11.9	1,015.0	1.8	96.6	182.0
Specialty chemicals	10,291	2.5	803.0	4.0	9,369.0	3.2	2,377.0	4.1	78.0	231.0
Others	4,954	1.2	281.0	1.4	1,848.0	0.6	513.0	0.9	56.7	103.6
Biomedical Manufacturing	16,704	4.0	1,098.0	5.4	23,677.0	8.2	11,793.0	20.5	65.7	706.0
Pharmaceuticals	6,272	1.5	608.0	3.0	18,593.0	6.4	9,795.0	17.0	96.9	1,561.7
Medical technology	10,432	2.5	490.0	2.4	5,085.0	1.8	1,998.0	3.5	47.0	191.5
Precision Engineering	89,682	21.6	4,227.0	20.9	33,143.0	11.4	7,508.0	13.0	47.1	83.7
Machinery and systems	42,173	10.1	2,336.0	11.5	22,367.0	7.7	4,192.0	7.3	55.4	99.4
Precision modules and components	47,509	11.4	1,891.0	9.3	10,777.0	3.7	3,316.0	5.8	39.8	69.8
Transport Engineering	111,404	26.8	4,890.0	24.1	32,172.0	11.1	9,772.0	16.9	43.9	87.7
Marine and offshore engineering	85,378	20.5	3,089.0	15.2	21,000.0	7.3	5,939.0	10.3	36.2	69.6
Aerospace	19,856	4.8	1,424.0	7.0	8,749.0	3.0	3,046.0	5.3	71.7	153.4
Land	6,170	1.5	376.0	1.9	2,343.0	0.8	787.0	1.4	61.0	127.5
General Manufacturing Industries	96,740	23.3	3,415.0	16.9	23,509.0	8.1	7,144.0	12.4	35.3	73.8
Food, beverages, and tobacco	28,181	6.8	947.0	4.7	8,492.0	2.9	2,300.0	4.0	33.6	81.6
Printing	14,882	3.6	683.0	3.4	2,279.0	0.8	1,168.0	2.0	45.9	78.5
Miscellaneous industries	53,677	12.9	1,784.0	8.8	12,739.0	4.4	3,677.0	6.4	33.2	68.5
Total manufacturing	415,841	100.0	20,262.0	100.0	290,476.0	100.0	57,661.0	100.0	48.7	138.7

Source: Singapore Department of Statistics (2014f).
Note: Refers to all manufacturing establishments. The industries are classified according to SSIC 2010.

ANNEX TABLE 3.1.2

Manufacturing Sectors, 2013

	Total Output		
	Million S$	**Percent**	**Percent of Manufacturing GDP**
Electronics	80,860.0	100.0	27.8
Semiconductors	46,260.0	57.2	15.9
Infocomms and consumer electronics	19,510.0	24.1	6.7
Computer peripherals	8,195.0	10.1	2.8
Data storage	4,877.0	6.1	1.7
Other electronic modules and components	2,018.0	2.5	0.7
Precision Engineering	33,143.0	100.0	11.4
Machinery and systems	22,367.0	67.5	7.7
Precision modules and components	10,777.0	32.5	3.7
Chemicals	97,114.0	100.0	33.4
Petroleum	51,316.0	52.8	17.7
Petrochemicals	34,581.0	35.6	11.9
Specialty chemicals	9,369.0	9.6	3.2
Others	1,848.0	1.9	0.6
Biomedical Manufacturing	23,677.0	100.0	8.2
Pharmaceuticals	18,593.0	78.5	6.4
Medical technology	5,085.0	21.5	1.8

Source: Singapore Department of Statistics (2014d).

ANNEX 3.2. SINGAPORE OUTPUT BY INDUSTRY

ANNEX TABLE 3.2.1

Share of Gross Domestic Product by Industry at 2013 Market Prices *(Percent)*

Year	Manufacturing	Construction	Wholesale and Retail Trade	Transportation and Storage	Finance and Insurance	Business Services
1965	14.3	6.2	23.6	10.4	4.6	9.3
1967	15.2	5.6	26.2	9.5	4.6	9.2
1969	17.1	5.9	26.2	9.5	5.5	9.0
1971	19.6	7.5	22.9	9.6	5.4	9.4
1973	22.3	7.2	22.6	9.5	6.3	8.9
1974	22.9	7.3	23.3	9.2	6.4	8.9
1975	22.2	7.9	21.3	9.5	7.5	8.5
1976	22.9	8.1	20.3	10.5	7.5	8.1
1977	23.5	7.4	20.5	11.3	7.2	7.8
1978	24.2	6.1	19.9	12.4	7.7	7.3
1979	26.3	5.8	19.1	11.9	7.9	7.1
1980	27.5	6.2	17.0	11.9	9.2	7.2
1981	26.7	7.2	14.8	11.6	10.8	8.6
1982	23.1	9.4	14.3	11.2	11.2	9.7
1983	22.3	11.3	13.3	11.4	10.8	9.5
1984	22.2	12.2	12.4	11.1	11.3	9.0
1985	20.9	10.3	11.9	11.8	12.9	8.6
1986	23.4	8.0	11.8	11.9	12.3	8.5
1987	25.1	6.5	12.0	11.9	13.4	7.9
1988	27.3	5.4	12.1	11.9	12.1	8.5

(Continued)

ANNEX TABLE 3.2.1 (CONTINUED)

Year	Manufacturing	Construction	Wholesale and Retail Trade	Transportation and Storage	Finance and Insurance	Business Services
1989	26.7	5.1	11.6	12.0	12.3	9.5
1990	25.6	4.8	12.9	11.3	13.7	9.9
1991	26.6	5.7	13.0	11.6	11.8	9.9
1992	25.6	6.6	12.3	10.8	12.4	10.5
1993	25.9	6.3	13.1	10.5	12.5	10.3
1994	25.3	6.5	13.1	10.4	12.0	11.2
1995	25.7	6.3	13.3	10.3	11.2	11.8
1996	24.7	7.1	13.3	9.8	11.1	12.3
1997	23.6	7.5	12.6	9.4	12.8	12.2
1998	23.9	7.8	11.9	9.5	12.5	11.8
1999	24.3	6.6	13.4	10.2	11.2	11.8
2000	27.7	5.3	13.4	10.0	10.0	11.5
2001	24.9	5.1	13.4	9.4	10.6	11.6
2002	26.0	4.2	14.2	9.0	10.4	11.7
2003	26.0	3.8	14.3	10.0	10.3	11.5
2004	28.2	3.2	15.1	10.4	9.9	11.0
2005	27.8	3.0	17.1	10.2	9.8	11.1
2006	27.2	2.9	18.7	9.3	10.4	11.0
2007	24.6	3.2	19.3	9.7	11.4	12.1
2008	21.1	4.7	17.6	9.8	11.3	14.0
2009	20.7	5.6	19.0	8.1	11.6	13.6
2010	21.4	4.7	19.2	8.4	10.9	13.8
2011	20.3	4.6	20.2	6.9	10.9	14.3
2012	20.4	4.7	18.7	7.0	11.1	14.9
2013	18.8	4.9	18.5	6.9	11.9	15.4

Source: Singapore Department of Statistics (2014b).

REFERENCES

Economic Development Board (EDB). 2014a. "Our History. Future Ready Singapore." http://www.edb.gov.sg/content/edb/en/about-edb/company-information/our-history.html.

———. 2014b. Electronics Fact Sheet 2014. Future Ready Singapore webpage. https://www.edb.gov.sg/content/edb/en/industries/industries/electronics.htmlhttp://www.edb.gov.sg/content/dam/edb/en/industries/Electronics/downloads/ElectronicsFactsheet-2014.pdf.

———. 2011. "Energy Facts Sheet 2011." Singapore. http://www.edb.gov.sg/content/dam/edb/en/resources/pdfs/factsheets/Energy% percent 20Factsheet.pdf.

Energy Market Authority. 2011. "Statement of Opportunities for the Singapore Energy Industry." Singapore. https://www.nccs.gov.sg/sites/nccs/files/SOO_US_LETTER_Finalversion.pdf.

Housing & Development Board. 2014. "Annual Report 2008–2009 and 2013–2014." Annual Reports. http://www.hdb.gov.sg/cs/infoweb/about-us/news-and-publications/annual-reports.

Matthews, John A., and Dong-Sung Cho. 2007. *Tiger Technology: The Creation of a Semiconductor Industry in East Asia*. Cambridge: Cambridge University Press.

Parliament of Singapore. 1981. "Singapore's Economic Development Plan for the Eighties." Highlights, Annex I. http://sprs.parl.gov.sg/search/resource/NonPDF/1981/19810306/19810306-HA-0400357.htm.

Singapore Department of Statistics. 2014a. Time Series on Annual GDP at Current Market Prices and on Per Capita GDP, 20 May. http://www.singstat.gov.sg/statistics/browse-by-theme/national-accounts.

———. 2014b. GDP by Industry. Accessed February 20, 2014. http://www.singstat.gov.sg/statistics/browse-by-theme/national-accounts.

———. 2014c. Key Demographic Indicators, 1970–2013.
Accessed February 20, 2014. http://www.singstat.gov.sg/statistics/browse-by-theme/population-and-population-structure.

———. 2014d. Manufacturing (Statistical Tables from Yearbooks). Accessed February 20, 2014. Available: http://www.singstat.gov.sg/statistics/browse-by-theme/manufacturing.

———. 2014e. Research and Development (Statistical Tables from Yearbooks). http://www.singstat.gov.sg/statistics/browse-by-theme/research-and-development.

———. 2014f. Principal Statistics of Manufacturing by Industry Cluster, 2013. Accessed February 20, 2014. http://www.singstat.gov.sg/statistics/browse-by-theme/manufacturing.

Singapore Ministry of Trade and Industry. 1991. "The Strategic Development Plan: Towards a Developed Nation." Executive Summary. Singapore. http://www.mti.gov.sg/ResearchRoom/Documents/app.mti.gov.sg/data/pages/885/doc/NWS_plan.pdf.

Spring Singapore. 2011. "A Guide to Productivity Measurement." http://www.spring.gov.sg/resources/documents/guidebook_productivity_measurement.pdf.

CHAPTER 4

Malaysia's Move Toward a High-Income Economy: Five Decades of Nation Building—A View from Within

AHMAD TAJUDDIN ALI

Malaysia is blessed with quite a few advantages that have enabled it to diversify economic activities and achieve a high quality of life. It has a strategically favorable location in Southeast Asia and enjoys a good year-round climate that helps keep it relatively free of natural disasters. Its arable land is fertile for plantations; its rainforest is biodiverse and rich in resources, including timber; and valuable deposits of mineral and metal oxides are found throughout the country. These commodities and products have been exported to other countries and have contributed significantly to the nation's economy.

Since independence in 1957, Malaysia, in many ways a microcosm of Asia, has achieved sustained economic growth marked by low inflation and unemployment. This is reflected in the country's current ranking in global indicators and indices. In 2014, it placed 17th in the World Bank's Ease of Doing Business Index, 33rd in the Global Innovation Index,[1] 20th in the World Economic Forum's Global Competitiveness Index, and 25th for its quality of infrastructure. Malaysia's population reached 30 million in 2014; 54 percent of the population represent the country's middle class, with per capita income of about $10,000. Moving up the ranking in the Global Competitiveness Index from 24th in 2014 to 20th in 2015 (World Economic Forum 2012, 2014). Malaysian competitiveness improved owing to the economy's successful horizontal and vertical diversification, while inflation and wage pressures remained contained.

The education system is an important element in supporting intergenerational equity. As part of an ambitious transformation effort for the education system, the government continues to invest about 16 percent of the federal budget in education (Ministry of Education Malaysia 2013). However, educational outcomes are not yet commensurate with the level of funding.

The author wishes to acknowledge the contribution of Rushdi Abdul Rahim of the Malaysian Industry-Government Group for High Technology in the preparation of this chapter.
[1] The Global Innovation Index is copublished by Cornell University, INSEAD, and the World Intellectual Property Organization (an agency of the United Nations).

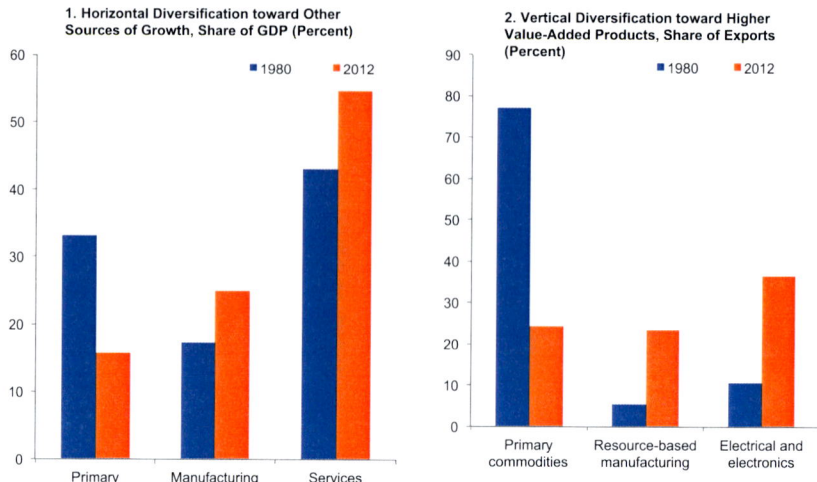

Figure 4.1 Horizontal and Vertical Diversification of the Malaysian Economy away from Commodities

Source: Malaysia, Department of Statistics, Economic Planning Unit.

Malaysia is one of the very few resource-rich countries that invests more than the resource wealth extracted. Figure 4.1 shows a significant reduction in reliance on the primary sector as a result of the rapid pace of the economy's horizontal diversification, with robust growth in the manufacturing and services sectors. Of equal importance, the economy has diversified vertically by moving up the commodities value chain from upstream to downstream activities (Bank Negara Malaysia 2013).

A lid on inflation and wage growth has supported the diversification efforts. Malaysia recorded inflation of 2.3 percent from 2002 to the first quarter of 2013, lower than its peers (at a compounded annual growth rate). Productivity growth of 3.2 percent exceeded wage growth of 2.7 percent in the same period.

Reflecting the growth of the nation, Kuala Lumpur has undergone tremendous development to become one of Asia's most iconic cities. The country has a progressive outlook on development, and offers an attractive business environment with quality infrastructure.

PREREQUISITES FOR DEVELOPMENT

Malaysia's success so far is due to its ability to leverage visionary leadership, political stability, sound planning mechanisms, and abundant natural resources. Visionary leadership and political stability provided a strong base for development and the implementation of national strategies, leading to a sound planning mechanism. This in turn helped sustain growth, expand both foreign and domestic direct investment, and supported the tourism industry—an ever growing contributor to the economy.

Since independence, Malaysia has been led by five prime ministers, who have influenced the nation's growth. Malaysia gained its independence on August 31, 1957, when the country's first prime minister, Tunku Abdul Rahman Putra Al-Haj, known as the Father of the Nation, was handed power by the British. In 1970 he was succeeded by Tun Abdul Razak. After his untimely demise, Tun Hussein Onn became prime minister. During this period, the nation's social and economic foundations were laid down.

In 1981, Tun Dr Mahathir Mohamad became prime minister. He embarked on an energetic drive to increase economic activities and build Malaysia's competitiveness. He is known as the Father of Industrialization, because of the significant advancement made during his administration in the industrial and manufacturing sector. Citing personal reasons, Mahatir retired in 2003 after 23 years at the helm.

Balancing social needs within the economic development, Malaysia's fifth prime minister, Tun Abdullah Ahmad Badawi, promoted human capital development before handing the post to his deputy, current Prime Minister, Dato' Sri Mohammad Najib bin Tun Haji Abdul Razak, who has relentlessly pursued the nation's sustainability agenda by focusing on encouraging more downstream activities and expanding manufacturing.

Political stability complementing good leadership allowed for the effective implementation of policies. These supported a conducive business environment and helped attract high foreign investment.

Malaysia, as noted, is fairly safe from natural calamities such as earthquakes and volcanic eruptions. Its geographic location also protects it from tornadoes (though it experiences occasional floods during the monsoon season). Malaysia benefits from tropical weather throughout the year, encouraging the growth of various plants, some of which have been converted into major sources of income.

The abundance of natural resources has been a prerequisite for Malaysia's success story, with rubber and palm oil being the first commodities produced. During the early postindependence years, tin ore, rubber, and palm oil contributed significantly to the nation's wealth. These commodities, in later years, blossomed into other economic activities, such as manufacturing; that is, instead of exporting raw materials, consumer and industrial products were made and then exported. And this downstreaming is still under way.

Notwithstanding the stability Malaysia has enjoyed through the years, the country has weathered occasional challenges caused by its dependence on commodities and natural resources, including economic fluctuations due to the trend of decreasing resources and volatility in commodity prices, and rising environmental concerns.

Not only does diversification have a profound impact on an economy, but it can also influence a country's environmental landscape and social structure.

When the development of Malaysia's rubber and palm oil industries started in the 1960s and 70s, the government, researchers, and planters made efforts to improve the ecosystem to make these industries more resilient. They have also enjoyed strong support through the development of infrastructure and good governance. Today, as environmental concerns increase, continuous research on sustainability is being undertaken to ensure balanced growth for the nation, both economically and environmentally.

Rubber

In 1877, the first rubber tree seedlings were brought from the Amazon Basin and planted on an experimental basis before attempts were made to produce rubber on a commercial scale. The British, the colonial power at that time, provided capital for forest clearing and planting rubber trees, and also provided a market for rubber. Skilled labor from India was transported to work on the rubber estates. Rubber became one of the major commodities in Malaysia with the help of important national initiatives, such as establishing the Rubber Research Institute in 1926 (Malaysian Rubber Board 2011). In 2013, Malaysia exported 1.31 million metric tons of natural rubber, and was the world's third-largest exporter of natural rubber after Thailand, at 2.8 million tons, and Indonesia, at 2.45 million tonnes (Malaysian Rubber Board 2013).

Palm Oil

In 2014, palm oil cultivation covered about 5.4 million hectares of land in Malaysia, producing 19.7 million tons of palm oil and 2.3 tons of palm kernel oil. Malaysia is one of the largest producers and exporters of palm oil in the world, accounting for 12 percent of global oils and fats production and 27 percent of the export trade in oils and fats. Malaysia's palm oil industry provides employment to more than half a million people and livelihoods to an estimated 1 million (Malaysian Palm Oil Council 2014). It accounts for 5 percent to 6 percent of GDP.

In the early 1960s, palm oil cultivation expanded at a fast pace under the government's agricultural diversification program, which was introduced to reduce the nation's economic dependence on rubber and tin. Later, the government introduced land settlement schemes for planting palm oil to eradicate poverty among landless farmers and smallholders. Malaysia's palm oil plantations are largely based on the estate management system and smallholder scheme. A key driver for this effort was the Federal Land Development Authority, established in 1956 to promote socioeconomic responsibility in the development of plantation land for the rural poor and landless (Malaysian Palm Oil Council 2012).

The palm oil industry has consistently contributed toward poverty eradication and narrowing the income gap between rural and urban residents. It has created rural townships where workers enjoy good quality of life with adequate social infrastructure (for example, housing, health, and religious facilities), contributed to social security and peace, and reduced migration of the labour force from rural to urban areas.

SOCIAL AND POLITICAL CHALLENGES

During the British colonial era, Chinese laborers were brought in to work in tin ore mines, and Indians to help run the civil service and work in the plantations. In doing so, the British colonial system created ethnic communities based on economic activities. But this system created an imbalance in the working structure for the local population, as Chinese and Indians were brought in to work in the economically productive sectors, disadvantaging locals (Yusof 1998). However, since independence, affirmative action has minimized the gap.

Demographically, Malaysia is a young nation. Since the 1970s, the proportion of its working-age population has increased in tandem with the rapid development of the nation (Mahari 2011). However, different age groups, with different roles and needs, require tailored development programs.

On average, a Malaysian spends at least 10 years in school before joining the workforce. Education has supported the development of the country's social fabric. Mutual understanding and respect are key in developing and maintaining the harmony of Malaysians.

Although Malaysia's main political parties are race-based, they usually form coalitions or alliances during elections. Several parties are represented in the current ruling coalition, Barisan Nasional (National Front).

ECONOMIC CHALLENGES

Despite occasional social flux and economic volatility, Malaysia has managed to climb the economic ladder through a series of practical development plans, along with continuous public infrastructure development, and the integration of science, technology, and innovation in the economy.

To recap, economic activities in the early years after independence were highly dependent on primary commodities, namely rubber and tin, which accounted for 70 percent of total export earnings, 28 percent of government revenues, and 36 percent of employment (Economic Planning Unit 2013). However, reassuring as this performance may have been, diversification was crucial to reducing the nation's dependence on commodities.

Malaysia's development is rooted in its series of five-year national plans. These began with the First Malaya Plan, from 1956 to 1960, and the Second Malaya Plan from 1961 to 1965. After the formation of Malaysia in 1963, this five-year plan, known as the Malaysia Plan, ran from 1966 to 1970. The 10th Malaysia Plan is the current one, and preparations for the next one, covering 2015–20, are under way.

Because of the British colonial legacy of keeping economic activities divided among races, by the late 1960s gaps were beginning to show in economic development between the predominant Malays in rural areas and the Chinese in urban areas. This disparity and inequality, fueled by an uncertain political future, contributed to the race riots following the 1969 elections. To avoid a repetition of these events, the government brought the various political parties, organizations, and political personalities together to formulate strategies to deal with the sensitive issues of poverty and inequality among ethnicities and regions. This led to a critical evaluation and a major shift in the formulation of development policies, resulting in affirmative action—the New Economic Policy. The policy is characterized by two main goals: to eradicate poverty irrespective of race and to restructure the society. The New Economic Policy highlights the basic philosophy of national growth and unity.

In the 1980s Malaysia embarked on a diversification strategy, moving from an agriculture-based economy to a resource-based one. The "Malaysia Incorporated" concept launched by former Prime Minister Mohamad in 1983 represented a new approach to national development. Both the public and private sectors adopted the idea that the nation was a corporate or business entity, jointly owned by both sectors and working together in pursuit of a common mission. In the same year, a privatization policy was announced and developed to underscore the increased role of the private sector in the development of the economy. During this period, the manufacturing sector recorded its fastest growth, rising from 10.4 percent of GDP to 22.6 percent in the 1980s, surpassing the contribution of the agricultural sector (Economic Planning Unit 2013). Exports were also diversified; the main exports included electronic equipment, petroleum and liquefied natural gas, wood and wood products, textiles, and chemicals.

The pace of development changed rapidly as the economy underwent structural transformation under the National Industrial Policy and Industrial Master Plan of the mid-1980s. Subsequent plans to enhance development included measures to aggressively promote manufacturing and services in the 1990s.

Nevertheless, a nation's development should not be approached solely in economic terms. Given that social transformation requires "well-being" as a key component, development and growth had to occur along all dimensions: economic, political, social, spiritual, psychological, and cultural. Vision 2020, launched in 1990, set out a road map for Malaysia to become by 2020 a united nation, with a strong democratic society, infused with moral and ethical values.

TRANSFORMING THE NATION AND SUPPORTING GROWTH

In 2010 the National Transformation Programme was launched as the main agenda of national development through the Government Transformation Programme and the Economic Transformation Programme.

The Government Transformation Programme covers structural issues, and aims to enhance the efficiency of the civil service. Under the program, six National Key Results Areas were identified:

- Reducing crime
- Fighting corruption
- Improving student outcomes

- Raising living standards of low-income households
- Improving rural basic infrastructure
- Improving urban public transport

These areas represent important issues that require government involvement.

The Economic Transformation Programme aims to lift the nation's gross national income per capita from $6,700 to $15,000 in 2020, an increase that would raise Malaysia to a high-income country. Under the program, the 12 National Key Economic Areas have the potential to contribute a quantifiable amount of growth (PEMANDU 2013):

- Oil, gas, and energy
- Palm oil
- Financial services
- Tourism
- Health care
- Communications, content, and infrastructure
- Business services
- Electronics and electrical
- Wholesale and retail
- Education
- Agriculture
- Greater Kuala Lumpur

Lead ministries are responsible for the implementation of the National Key Results Areas; the implementation of the National Key Economic Areas is a collaboration between the private sector and the government.

As well as strategic growth plans, major investments were made in infrastructure development to support the economic transformation. Physical infrastructure and well-equipped transportation hubs—world class airports, sea ports, and a network of well-maintained expressways—were built to enable the efficient movement of people and goods. Malaysia has seven international sea ports, five international airports, and 500 industrial estates and free industrial zones, including technology parks such as the Multimedia Super Corridor which specializes in multimedia technology. Malaysia also has a high quality telecommunications network and services (Malaysian Industrial Development Authority 2015).

Various government agencies were established with specific tasks and authority to support and facilitate economic growth. Agencies under the Ministry of Trade and Industry, for instance, play significant roles in supporting business growth; among them, the Malaysian Industrial Development Authority, the Malaysia External Trade Development Corporation, the Malaysia Productivity Corporation, and SME Corporation Malaysia.

In addition, these initiatives were complemented by and harmonized with business policies and tax packages to ensure that doing business in Malaysia is an attractive proposition. The main incentives include pioneer status, investment tax and reinvestment allowances, and support for high technology industries, strategic projects, and for setting up international and regional service-based operations.

The focus on human capital development is also significant. Here, the government has continuously invested in developing talent, after realizing early on that Malaysians needed to be equipped with the necessary knowledge and skills to compete globally. Each of Malaysia's five-year development plans put a high priority on education and skills development, thereby ensuring that the quality of Malaysia's workforce is one of the highest in the region.

2020 AND BEYOND: FOCUS ON SCIENCE, TECHNOLOGY, AND INNOVATION

There is no doubt that Malaysia has been quite successful in reaping the benefits of its endowments. However, if it is to sustain growth and stay ahead of competitors, complacency is not an option. As the saying goes: We do not inherit the world from our ancestors, we borrow it from our children. Thus, any plans made today should put a high consideration on the young, because positive values can be engrained through education that prepares the quality leaders of tomorrow.

In tandem, technology advancement and know-how are essential for industry to grow. A continuous supply of skilled and knowledgeable workers is critical to sustaining economic growth, and, again, education is crucial for developing human capital.

As reflected in the Rukun Negara (National Principles), the Malaysian national pledge, the nation aspires to build a progressive society that will make use of science and modern technology as the foundation for moving forward socially and economically.

To meet global and local science and technology challenges, Malaysia is striving to master science, technology, engineering, and mathematics. Having a supportive education system in which these areas are prioritized is vital for generating quality human capital at various academic levels. In 1967, the Higher Education Planning Committee proposed that a 60:40 ratio of science to arts students would fulfil future demand. To date, however, tertiary enrolment shows a 30:70 ratio.

The emphasis on science, technology, and innovation runs through Malaysia's development programs, including the Malaysia Plans, the Industrial Master Plans, the National Science, Technology, and Innovation Policy, and Public Research Assets.

The general thrust of the National Science, Technology, and Innovation Policy, launched in 2013, is to strengthen basic foundations in these areas; namely, competency in generating and deploying knowledge, strengthening human capital, elevating the innovative potential of local industry, enhancing governance, and developing a society receptive to science, technology, and innovation. The policy and its implementation plans are expected to imbue a new vigor for science that will propel the nation's economic trajectory to a higher plane.

The Ministry of Science, Technology and Innovation is the lead ministry for implementing programs to promote science and technology, including the bulk of national research and development activities in these areas. Moreover, its agency, Academy Science of Malaysia, plays a vital role in pursuing, encouraging, and enhancing excellence in science, engineering, technology, and innovation.

The Global Science and Innovation Advisory Council was set up in 2010 to improve and optimize national capabilities through international networks. Industry leaders and prominent academicians from around the world are on the council, as well as members of the New York Academy of Sciences President's Council. Officials from key Malaysian ministries and local corporate leaders are also on the council.

The Science to Action (S2A) initiative is the latest national agenda to ensure that Malaysia maintains sustainable growth beyond 2020. Its goal is for Malaysia to be not only a consumer of technologies, but also a producer through a "science transformation" initiative to bolster fundamentals in the science, technology, and innovation ecosystem. To achieve this, the initiative was streamlined into three thrusts to facilitate sustainable growth. The three thrusts, according to the Malaysian Foresight Institute (2014) are:[2]

- Science for Industry to strengthen current industries, create new industries and entrepreneurs by identifying new growth areas, as well as increasing private sector participation in science and technology development.

- Science for Well Being to improve the quality of people's lives through the use of science and technology. This includes popularizing science and improving the uptake of the Science, Technology, Engineering and Mathematics exploration center.

- Science for Governance to strengthen public services and governance to ensure a conducive ecosystem for the development and uptake of science and technology.

CONCLUSION

Malaysia, in common with many other nations, has found that not all targets it has aspired to have been met or achieved as planned. This can be attributed to factors that include resource limitations, implementation issues, and different externalities. Moreover, like other nations, Malaysia is not immune to wage pressures, inflation, and global economic uncertainties. Yet by diligently working on overcoming these obstacles, it has become stronger and attained a better position for achieving the national vision of becoming a high-income nation by 2020.

---

[2] Interview with Professor Tan Sri Zakri Abdul Hamid on the Science to Action Programme. Malaysian Foresight Institute. Available: http://www.myforesight.my/index.php/architects/insights-leaders/612-science-to-action-s2a-programme.html

REFERENCES

Bank Negara Malaysia. 2013. "Economic Developments in 2013." Annual Report 2013. http://www.bnm.gov.my/files/publication/ar/en/2013/cp01.pdf.

Economic Planning Unit. 2013. "Economic History." http://www.epu.gov.my/en/economic-history;jsessionid=AB199A4C187395F9CA5EB3F7B8251E18

Mahari, Zarinah. 2011. "Demographic Transition in Malaysia: The Changing Roles of Women." Paper presented at the 15th Conference of Commonwealth Statisticians, New Delhi, India. 7–10 February.

Malaysian Foresight Institute. 2014. "The Science to Action (S2A) Programme." Interview with Professor Tan Sri Zakri Abdul. http://www.myforesight.my/index.php/architects/insights-leaders/612-science-to-action-s2a-programme.html.

Malaysian Industrial Development Authority. 2015. "Why Malaysia." http://www.mida.gov.my/home/why-malaysia/posts/.

Malaysia Palm Oil Council. 2012. "Malaysian Palm Oil Industry." http://www.mpoc.org.my/Malaysian_Palm_Oil_Industry.aspx.

———. 2014. "Annual Report 2014." http://www.mpoc.org.my/More_Publications.aspx.

Malaysian Rubber Board. 2011. "The Origin and Establishment of the Rubber Research Institute Malaysia." http://www.lgm.gov.my/general/rrim70yrs.aspx.

Malaysian Rubber Board. 2013. "Natural Rubber Statistics 2013." http://www.lgm.gov.my/.

Ministry of Education Malaysia. 2013. "Malaysia Education Blueprint 2013–2025." Kementerian Pendidikan Malaysia, Putrajaya, Malaysia.

Performance Management and Delivery Unit (PEMANDU). 2013. "Economic Transformation Programme Annual Report 2013." Prime Minister's Department. http://etp.pemandu.gov.my/annualreport2013/.

World Economic Forum. 2012, 2014. "Global Competitiveness Report 2012–13 and 2014–15." http://www.weforum.org/reports/global-competitiveness-report-2014-2015.

Yusof, Ahmad Mohd. 1998. "Impact of National Policies upon Malaysia's Employment Sector." Essay, Graduate School of Policy Science, Saitama University, Japan.

CHAPTER 5

Industrial Diversification in Korea: History in Search of Lessons

MEREDITH WOO

Koreans define their predicaments in terms of absences. One of the first absences they will lament is that of exportable natural resources, from which stemmed a path of industrialization squarely focused on manufacturing and on continually moving up the industrial ladder in order to survive in an inhospitable world for economic upstarts. What lessons Korea can offer the Gulf Cooperation Council (GCC) nations is an intellectually challenging question, because their starting points are as different as can be, as are the paths they have travelled in the past century. One can describe how the Koreans jump-started their economy, then diversified and upgraded it, but description does not make a prescription for the GCC nations to follow.

A long tradition in Western social sciences says that starting points do not really matter, nor does history, for an eventual economic convergence to occur. "Modernization theory" posits that in spite of unevenly paced development, nations progress along more or less a linear path and eventually resemble each other. Karl Marx thought Western capitalism would knock down the walls of China and drag it, kicking and screaming, into modernity; or that Germany, a country late to unified statehood and modern industrialization, would see, in the mirror the United Kingdom held, a reflection of its future self.

The idea that capitalist development is more or less homogenizing at each of its stages has been debated ad nauseam. If, however, countries already have similar attributes (in factor endowments, history, outlook and institutions, and perhaps geographical proximity), it is indisputably easier to move as a pack through the Rostowian "stages of growth" (Rostow 1962). In the pack, nations learn from each other—through examples, conversations, conferences, and simple travel—and the lessons can be meaningfully implemented because the institutional and cultural contexts are familiar and recognizable.

In that sense, the United Kingdom did hold a mirror for Germany, as did Japan for Korea. Singapore held the mirror for so many cities that dot the coasts of China; and Korea, with its history of industrial policy has lessons for Beijing (if not for Shanghai), as it did for Mahathir Mohamad's Malaysia.

In spite of geographical and cultural distance, it is still possible that nations of the Middle East and East Asia can learn from each other. Some countries have similar trajectories. Dubai has much in common with Singapore and Hong Kong: they have long been committed to being open cities, more oriented toward trade, more *laissez-faire* in their attitude than some of their surrounding countries. They are also hub cities—in education, transportation, and finance—for their regions, and they grapple as best they can with the challenges and opportunities of running multiethnic cities that employ large expatriate populations.

Algeria also had, until the end of the 1970s, a trajectory not dissimilar to Korea's. Both were colonized by countries that were themselves late industrializers, France and Japan, with soft spots in their hearts for industrial policy and economic planning. This planning tendency was carried on into the independent period in both Algeria and Korea. Houari Boumedienne (1965–78) and Park Chung Hee (1961–79) had long tenures as authoritarian rulers, presiding over extremely ambitious projects of social and industrial transformation—and with not inconsiderable success. They were in some ways "industrial sovereigns." Unfortunately, the relative economic success and stability of the Boumedienne years were not sustained in Algeria, as they were in Korea.

This chapter distinguishes among East Asian countries by crude ideal types, based on their historical and institutional trajectories, and attempts to draw a more meaningful comparison and identify greater possibilities for generating "lessons" from experiences between these countries—mostly Korea—and the GCC countries. Using the analytical requirements discussed in Chapter 1 of this volume by Reda Cherif and Fuad Hasanov, the chapter then describes how Korea overcame the obstacles to growth. Some of the Korean experiences may resonate, in context and history, with policymakers in the GCC countries.

There are three very different worlds in East Asia, and these worlds came into being over a long period. The first world was created by Japan, starting in the late nineteenth century. It took shape through the intense mobilization and transformation of itself and its colonies—Taiwan Province of China first, then Korea, then Manchuria, and later pockets of territories occupied in the Pacific War. This world bore the birthmark of its creator—nationalistic, insular, militaristic, and state-oriented in its policies. Like Japan, these colonies eventually became oriented toward manufacturing, using multiyear plans and industrial policies based on intense mobilization of the population. Largely homogeneous in racial makeup and culture (although one could argue this point about Taiwan Province of China), they remained intact as nations for a relatively long time, which made national mobilization for economic growth less problematic.

Another world was created by Western colonialism, particularly in Southeast Asia—Hong Kong Special Administrative Region, Indonesia, Malaysia, the Philippines, Singapore—but also in the old treaty ports along the coasts of China. This is a world that is quite different from that of the former Japanese imperium. Born as maritime trading cities or *entrepôts*, they are open to the world (and the West), more market friendly and *laissez-faire*. These countries are multiethnic and multicultural, and thus the effort at both institution building and economic transformation involved some ethnic give and take, a balance predicated on some reasonable expectation of trickle-down from an ever-growing economic pie.

Third there is the world that China inhabits. Its multiple tendencies have persisted over time: a nationalist orientation in Beijing, with the same preferences as in other Northeast Asian countries toward multiyear planning, industrial policy, and manufacturing. But throughout coastal China a pronounced pattern similar to maritime Southeast Asia exists: trade-oriented, open, munificent, multiethnic, easygoing. The capitalism that developed in coastal China has often been described as "petty capitalism," or "peddler capitalism," which thrived in the interstices of whatever big-picture nationalist policy was brewing in the minds of the rulers in Beijing. Finally, China has a tendency that derives from its socialist past. China's hinterland, especially in its west, still needs to develop a viable consumer base with the help of the government to redistribute resources from the coastal area to inland through various fiscal and financial incentives. Only when this happens will China have a truly unified national market, much as the United States created one through the intervention of the state.

Chapter 1 provides a useful scaffolding to enable comparison across time and place—a kind of elegant *sine qua non* for sustainable development. In Cherif and Hasanov's analysis of the GCC countries, the hurdles to sustainable growth are immediately recognizable to those familiar with recent industrial histories of East Asian nations, as varied as they have been. Their arguments are based on economic theory, one that is validated by successful practices and experiences, particularly in the past few decades, in a constellation of countries in East Asia. What they suggest is that there is a kind of unshakable truth about development economics—all the gyrations of emphasis over the past seven decades notwithstanding—that is borne out by real industrial experiences.

Cherif and Hasanov argue that the standard prescriptions for growth—open economies, avoidance of government failures, macroeconomic stability, investment in infrastructure, and so on—are important; and it is true that the GCC countries have done relatively well in this regard, with impressive results in improvement along the numerical indices on quality of life, from health, life expectancy, and education. But for growth to be sustainable and with improved productivity, the *tradable* industries have to be promoted, deepened, and constantly upgraded. Even Dubai, a city long committed to openness and which has had spectacular success in diversifying away from natural resources, has not been as successful in broadening its exports, which remain predominantly in gold and jewelry.

Cherif and Hasanov also argue that the deepening of the tradable sector has to be meaningfully articulated with the rest of the economy to reap the benefit of externalities. Economic diversification is not a new agenda in GCC countries and dates back to the 1970s, if not earlier; but this diversification, mostly with a focus on the petrochemical and metal industries, has lacked linkage with the rest of the economy.

Industrial deepening in the tradable sector, and its linkage with the rest of the economy, requires an active agent: the market cannot accomplish this on its own. This is where Cherif and Hasanov's third argument comes in: the critical role of the government, if no longer as an all-seeing master planner, then as a "coordinator," an honest broker, venture capitalist, and partner with the civil sector. (Vibrant civil society and civil sectors are required for this to occur.)

Let me take these three prescriptions for growth, and see how they were followed in Korea—over a relatively long period. Historical origins are important—social scientists have an infelicitous phrase to underscore this point, "path dependency"—but locating this origin (the "path") is a bit more complicated than simply saying that origins matter.

In my brief sketch of the three worlds of East Asian capitalism, I suggested that the Korean path to industrialization cannot be understood except through its experience throughout the entire twentieth century. This is another way of saying that, impressive as Korean economic growth has been, it did not exactly bolt out in the 1960s like Athena from the head of Zeus.

Korea was an integral part of the Japanese colonial empire, one that was unlike anything that the Europeans—let alone Americans—created. It was not far-flung. It was based on addition of contiguous territories, so Japan had the core country, which was Japan itself; it had a semi-periphery, which was Taiwan Province of China, Korea, and later, Manchuria; and then it stretched, during the war years, on to coastal China.

Western colonialists in Southeast Asia were primarily interested in resource extraction, and thus their expedient economic model was a dual or enclave economy, and the political model was "divide-and-conquer" along ethnic or tribal lines. In the first half of Japanese colonialism in Korea, Japan too followed this Western model. Korea served as a breadbasket, its economic structure geared toward exporting agricultural commodities to Japan. In some ways, Japanese policy exhibited a pattern parallel to the one that Albert O. Hirschman described for Germany vis-à-vis its trading partners before World War I: namely the attempt to prevent the industrialization of its agricultural partners, thus to create export markets for the colonizer's goods and to destroy the competitive industries already established.[1] In both the German and Japanese cases, there was remarkable coherence in the planning and execution of this policy.

Japanese policy aborted Korean industrialization in two ways: a cadastral survey and agricultural reorganization to transform Korea into an exporter of rice, and later, a Corporation Law that empowered the colonial government to control and dissolve, as necessary, new and established businesses in Korea. The effect of the decade-long cadastral survey was to establish a system of capitalist ownership in the countryside, stripping peasants of the motley benefits that feudal arrangements had guaranteed them, and confiscating or snatching up at fire-sale prices vast tracts of unclaimed land for the benefit of Japanese colonizers, most of them originally from Kyushu. The Corporation Law, on the other hand, limited Korean ownership and was aimed at insuring a monopoly position for Japanese manufactured goods, and severely curtailed investment in the nonagricultural sector; no Korean was permitted to start a factory without permission (which was almost always denied) and direct private Japanese capital inflow was discouraged,

---

[1] See Hirschman (1945).

lest colonial industries compete with those at home. Through 1919, therefore, industries that thrived in colonial Korea were mostly household concerns that did not require company registration; industrial production accounted for only 13 percent of agricultural production in 1920—mainly in cottage industries such as dyeing, papermaking, ceramics, leather processing, rice milling, soy sauce making, brewing, rubber shoemaking, candlestick making, and so forth.[2]

The 1930s changed all that. Ironically, the global depression relieved the Korean landscape of its stagnant monocrop export economy, and thrust it fully into the Japanese industrial complex as an integral part. The precipitating factor was the deterioration of the Japanese rural economy, which, to reverse the trend, required a halt to the expansion of Korean rice production. More important, however, was a complex set of policy changes in Japan as a response to domestic crisis and the rapidly fluctuating international environment: the decision, following the boycott of Japanese products by other nations through tariffs and quotas, to pursue autonomous development, to create a self-sufficient economy within its sphere of influence.

Ugaki Kazushige, the Governor-General of Korea from 1931 to 1936, believed deeply in the need for a Japanese imperium of economic autarky and industrial self-sufficiency. Thus, in the 1930s, the real growth of Korea's manufacturing production and value-added would average over 10 percent a year, and the value added from Korea's mining sector increased at an annual compound rate of 19 percent, more than four times the rate of growth achieved before 1927. In other words, these were the first years of Korean "double-digit growth," although Koreans, who were ruthlessly exploited, found it rather less than "miraculous."

Colonial Korea was, in ways that Japan proper was not, a "capitalist paradise." Taxes on business were minimal in order to attract the *zaibatsu*, or conglomerates, there was nothing equivalent to the "law Controlling Major Industries" that regulated business in Japan proper, legislation for protecting workers was nonexistent, and wages were half of what they were in Japan. The Government-General of Korea granted financial priority and preferential treatment to the *zaibatsu* with respect to capital, materials, and equipment procurement; mining firms received a subsidy for prospecting and for the processing of low-grade iron ores. For producers of synthetic petroleum, mica, aluminum, and tungsten, the subsidy was over 90 percent.

The colonial state also offered big business the two most fundamental preconditions for investment: the guarantees of political stability and of state investment in the infrastructure necessary for industrialization. Relying on a special budget set aside for a five-year industrial plan for Korea, and other subsidy funds and revenues from bond sales in Japan, the colonial government invested heavily in railways, ports, roads, and communications.

The colonial government also took upon itself the leading role in creating this "spurt" of industrialization; its share of capital formation in Korea was consistently high, becoming more than half in the 1930s and declining thereafter as the

---

[2] See Chapter 2 of Woo (1991).

Japanese *zaibatsu* began moving into the peninsula. Most critical in the Japanese private sector's decision to invest in Korea was the financial incentives created by the Japanese government and the latter's willingness to share the risk should investments turn unprofitable.

In a relatively short time, the grip of *zaibatsu* groups on the Korean economy became tight and concentrated, and by the 1930s they substituted for the national policy companies as the spearhead of the industrial expansion drive. Three-quarters of capital investment in Korea was estimated to have been made by leading Japanese *zaibatsu* in 1940, the roster containing names like Mitsubishi, Mitsui, Nichitsu, Nissan, Asano, Mori, Riken, Sumitomo, and Yasuda (Woo 1991).

Politically, economic transformation and reorganization of this magnitude demanded a vast strengthening of the colonial state's functions: repression, legitimation, and intervention with the aim to restructure social relations. This phenomenon was not confined to Korea, and occurred in Japan proper and in Taiwan Province of China. Yet, it was more accentuated in Korea, in part because the populace proved particularly recalcitrant, and in part because of the suddenness and magnitude of change.

This colonial experience, so painful that many Koreans would prefer it expunged from memory, made a feeble reappearance in the 1970s. The Korean state in the 1970s was consanguineous with the earlier state some 40 years back, in much the same way that the corporatist state of Brazil in the 1930s made an atavistic return in 1964 with the inauguration of the Castello Branco regime. What makes such a return visitation possible still remains, on a theoretical level, moot.

Postindependence Korea could not see itself finding a usable past in the wartime industrialization of the 1930s; the very idea was anathema to Koreans. But sometimes history proceeds as a straightforward text, and at other times important forces appear—as it were—in the parentheses. The 1930s bequeathed a set of patterns, a model, that could be a silent companion of Korean development, and the unspoken force of the truth that people make their own history but not in the circumstances of their own choosing.

The lesson of the colonial industrialization pattern was that *it worked*, and that its success was based on close collaboration between the state and the *zaibatsu,* and on building economies of scale. Perhaps nobody knew and appreciated this better than President Park Chung Hee, a military cadet in Manchuria in 1940 and a lieutenant in the Kwangtung Army—the architect of industrialization in Japan's continental territory—when the war came to a halt in 1945.

The kind of industrial deepening—and its overall articulation with the rest of the economy—Cherif and Hasanov describe took place in Korea in the 1970s. Perhaps not so surprisingly, it happened at the time of a global shift in political and economic orientation, as in the 1930s.

The Korean economic boom in the late 1960s, much of it helped by American patronage, was a splurge on borrowed time. As American fortunes turned for the worse in Vietnam at the close of the decade, Korea braced for hard times and a new set of tasks: how to bargain with America so as to prevent the turning-off of the economic and military spigot that the Korean and Vietnam Wars had kept open, and how to handle the predictable eventuality of a U.S. troop reduction in Korea. But what the Korean leadership failed to anticipate—and the same could be said of all American allies—was just how systematic and imperious the devolution of the U.S. global burden was to be.

The new world according to Richard Nixon was an unfriendly and unforgiving one, where God only helped those who helped themselves: the Nixon Doctrine wrote off Indochina, and shoved off, through protectionism, economic parvenus like Korea. No longer could Korea find refuge in the indulgence of the Mutual Security Act and the exuberance of the Development Decade.

In what were perceived as the waning days of Pax Americana, the end of the Bretton Woods system, and the quadrupling of petroleum prices—a veritable disaster for a nation utterly bereft of oil—the first provision for survival was to purge all uncertainties from both the body politic and industry through the elimination of electoral uncertainties and the replacement of a self-regulating market with a regulated one. With the steering mechanism thus made predictable, the nation then veered toward the Big Push: massive investments in steel, automobiles, shipping, machine building, metals, and chemicals. The ambition was to turn Korea in the span of one decade from the final processor of export goods to one of the world's major exporters of steel, ships, and other producer goods. The development of basic industries also held the promise of a vibrant defense industry to end reliance on American largess in weaponry and various attendant political inconveniences.

In 1973, six industries—steel, chemical, metal, machine building, shipbuilding, and electronics—were officially targeted for rapid growth, becoming objects of intense government scrutiny and development. The Heavy and Chemical Industrialization Plan sought to create one large industrial complex with "state of the art" production facilities for each target industry. Once ensconced, the enterprises were the first to receive available foreign capital (and the last to pay it back), with low interest to boot. They were first to receive government funding to purchase raw materials and machinery; first to be directed through administrative guidance; and first to receive discounts on freight rates, harbor-use fees, and on the cost of water, electricity, and gas. Heavy and chemical industries swiftly moved into these complexes. The projected economies of scale for the plan were truly breathtaking.

What was highly *unusual* about Korea's Heavy and Chemical Industrialization Plan was that the production of producer goods had to substitute for imports *and simultaneously* (or with as little lag as possible) to be good for export.

There were three ways to finance the new export industries. One was through the banking system, the Bank of Korea rediscount rate; the second was fiscal, taken out of the state budget; and the third was through the National Investment Fund and other policy loans, which together accounted for over 40 percent of total domestic credit through the second half of the 1970s.

Of all policy loans, export credits and National Investment Fund loans were the most compelling for the Big Push. Export loans at *real* interest anywhere between minus 19 percent and minus 10 percent were the most plentiful loans to get: exporters merely had to produce letters of credit from foreign buyers to turn on the spigot.

The tight sequencing of import substitution industrialization, as found in Latin America, became condensed in Korea, and entailed a huge risk, given the massive economies of scale for heavy and chemical industrialization: if markets for new exports could not be found, then enormous waste, idle capacity, unemployment, and serious financial problems would ensue.

To avoid this problem, the state also became a harsh disciplinarian. Export credits were wonderful gifts but to get them, one had to be deserving, otherwise licenses were immediately revoked. Every year, the state slapped stringent performance criteria on the big exporters with respect to their capital, export volumes, and the minimum number of export items, destinations, and overseas branches required. Companies meeting these requirements were allowed the dollar amount of the letter of credit at favorable exchange and interest rates.

The Heavy and Chemical Industrialization Plan coasted along (even hovered above) the basic 1973 projection, and it was completed before the end of the decade. Just as the World Bank and other detractors of the Korean plan feared, Koreans achieved their goals by claiming a disproportionate share of resources for heavy industry. This was by design, not accident; the guiding principle of the heavy industrialization scheme had always been the achievement of scale economies through exporting and by participation of a few handpicked monopoly conglomerates.

The Korean "industrial deepening" of the 1970s is difficult to comprehend without the security threat, real and perceived, from outside. And the timing makes no sense without paying attention to the decline in American prowess that left Korea—its longtime ward—out in the cold. This was really what set Korea apart from the Latin American version of the "industrial deepening" that was orchestrated in the absence of a massive security threat.

If existential threats were the environmental factors that enabled economic diversification in Korea, one might say that the same enabling factors exist for GCC countries: existential threats to statehood emanate not only from region-wide political instability but also from domestic economic problems. At home, the GCC countries struggle with overgrown state sectors that sustain employment for most of the working population. The pressure this places on the state budget, along with the problem of the large population of young people and the joblessness that afflicts them, should make industrial diversification (and the job creation and skills acquisition it promises) a priority for government.

The Korean path to industrialization is perhaps too draconian for emulation; in any event, the world trade regime today is very different from the 1970s, and export subsidies of the kind the Korean government was able to provide to private enterprises—with all the carrots and sticks—are anathema in the current climate. It is also true that countries do not emulate, even if it were desirable, the entire economic *Gestalt* of another country unless it happens in colonial contexts or through voluntary associations (as in economic unions).

There are other ways to learn from each other, piecemeal. Those lessons abound in this volume: best examples from education and skills acquisition that can be emulated; the roles that development banks have played in another resource-dependent country, Brazil, which has diversified its industrial base over the past eight decades; the roles that governments play to affect technological leapfrogging by nurturing scientific talent—if not at home, then abroad, by recruiting students from inside and outside the country and educating them at the best universities in the world. Singapore is a fine example of this, as is Saudi Arabia. This volume also contains another chapter on Korea, focused on *Saemaul Undong*—one might call this the Great Leap Forward that actually worked—a self-help program to increase rural income, promote cottage industries, and stop the hemorrhage of rural population to cities. This massive mobilization of the countryside had a political purpose to serve, but it also accomplished its goal on its own terms, giving agency and purpose to rural inhabitants who had remained in the shadow of the intense glare of heavy industrialization. *Saemaul Undong* played an essential role in achieving balanced growth in Korea.

Good examples of how disparate countries learn from each other piecemeal can be found in East Asia. The notion of "the Pacific Rim" added some specificity to the promise of globalization, with the "three worlds" of East Asia coming closer together in their economic practices. In spite of varying economic origins and paths travelled, they have become, instead of members of the "three worlds," members of "the Pacific Rim," learning from each other through intense interactions, comparing notes, competition, simple travels, and conversations—as well as through conferences and books, just like this one. There are, in other words, many mirrors of the future that policymakers hold for each other the world over, at different times and places. The point of it all is to have the imagination and willingness to find one's reflection in a few of them.

REFERENCES

Hirschman, Albert. 1945. *National Power and the Structure of Foreign Trade.* Berkeley: University of California Press.

Rostow, Walt Whitman. 1962. *The Stages of Economic Growth.* London: Cambridge University Press.

Woo, Jung-En. 1991. *Race to the Swift.* New York: Columbia University Press.

CHAPTER 6

Economic Diversification in Latin American Countries: A Way to Face Tough Times Ahead

JOSÉ MIGUEL BENAVENTE

During the past decade, Latin American countries enjoyed some of their best economic times in recent memory. Most of the good performance is attributed to unusually favorable international prices, especially for natural-resource-based products and services. Investment was promising, inflation rates were in single digits for most countries in the region, and unemployment reached its structural levels.[1] Other macro indicators looked healthy compared with past figures and, more important, poverty was significantly reduced.

However, it seems that these tailwinds are losing strength. Commodity prices have dropped significantly for the past two years and foreign direct investment, which had flourished, is in a long-term decreasing trend. Today, several countries are facing fiscal problems, especially in the Caribbean, where governments are under pressure to maintain or increase social expenditures to weather the storm. Even though several welfare indicators have improved in most Latin American countries, recent events may jeopardize this performance and the issue has grabbed the attention of local and international policymakers.

One of the main characteristics of the region's countries is their disproportionate dependence on a highly concentrated bundle of products, most of them natural resources. This dependency explains their recent success, but also their fragility. A natural resources bonanza has kept countries from developing more valued-added sectors that could have buffered economies in lean times. Yet what is most striking in the region's long-term growth figures is an evident stagnation of total factor productivity (TFP) in almost every country; indeed, it has been on a decreasing trend, and not only in recent years.

This chapter argues that intimately linked issues such as export and output concentration and stagnant productivity need more attention, especially considering the potentially hard times coming in which, as always, policies seem insufficient to sustain increases in growth of income per capita across the region.

I want to thank Fuad Hasanov and Reda Cherif for comments, and Jocelyn Olivari for assistance during the preparation of this chapter.
[1] Essentially due to skills mismatch between workers and firms.

BACKGROUND: WHAT WE KNOW

Imagine that the position of a country in a cycling race depends on its income per capita. Australia, Hong Kong Special Administrative Region, the United States, and several European economies lead the race (Figure 6.1); some, such as the United States or Canada, have led it for a long time, while others, like Australia, joined the frontline only in recent decades. Another bunch of developed countries (based on income per capita) trails just behind, but is fast catching up—the Asian tigers such as Korea, Taiwan Province of China, and Singapore, alongside New Zealand and Slovenia—all of them growing faster than their predecessors.

In a third group, about half as wealthy as the previous group, are a few Latin American countries. Argentina and Chile are leading this group of less-developed economies—together with East European countries—most of them heavily favored by high natural resource prices in the 10 years through 2011.

In proposing guidelines for reaching the lead position, it is useful to compare a handful of leading economies that have abundant natural resources, small domestic markets, and are far from international markets with similar Latin American countries. Before embracing a new development strategy, we argue that the focus should not be on what these leading and similar countries are doing now, but on the strategies they implemented when they had income levels comparable to those in the third group.

The first lesson this analysis reveals is the type of "fuel" the leading economies used to boost growth rates: *inspiration*, meaning TFP improvements. Latin American economies, by contrast, relied on *perspiration* to enhance growth rates. During the last decade, saving and investment figures have increased, complemented by lower, if not the lowest, unemployment rates. Yet even though this perspiration approach

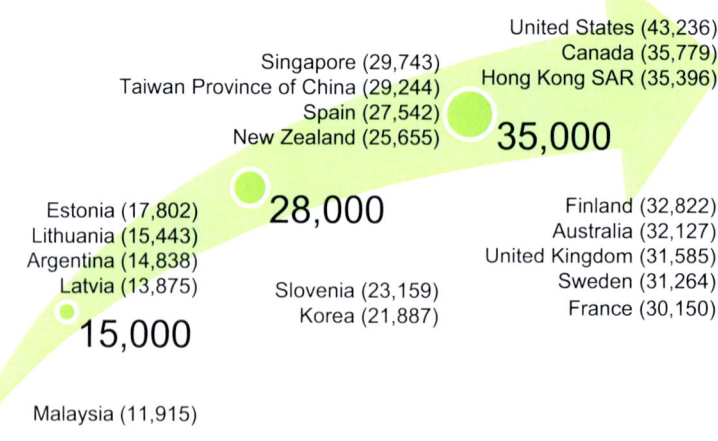

Figure 6.1　Country Ranking on GDP per Capita, 2011 (Purchasing power parity dollars)
Source: IMF, World Economic Outlook database.

helped double per capita incomes since 1960, most of the benefits have already been reaped. Comparing economic performance with the United States during 1960–2010, Latin American countries accumulated human and physical capital (12 percent and 16 percent gain, respectively, relative to the United States), but the GDP per capita gap relative to the United States (8 percent loss) has not closed. Again, it is inspiration (TFP growth) that is lacking (29 percent loss).

Moreover, even in countries with sound institutional settings that introduced major structural reforms during the 1980s and 1990s—especially by opening up economies to foreign competition and deregulating financial markets—TFP figures nonetheless suggest that the latter efforts are now showing diminishing returns.[2] For Chile, Fuentes, Gredig, and Larraín (2007) show that from 1986 until 1996 steady TFP growth prevailed (together with sound investment and employment rates). But as of 2000, it has stagnated, reaching near-zero average growth. The long duration of depressed TFP growth rates cannot be associated with a particular shock at a point in time. Slower TFP growth explains Chile's slower output growth, which fell from about 6 percent during the 1980s–1990s to 4.5 percent now. Argentina, Colombia, and Peru show similar patterns.

As Figure 6.2 shows, the TFP contribution to GDP growth is significantly lower in Latin American countries than in industrialized and East Asian countries during 1960–2010, a clear illustration of the perspiration strategy. Public policy should focus on improving TFP, and follow an inspiration strategy to increase long-term growth of income per capita.

Recent attention to stronger TFP growth has focused on export structure, especially for those countries with a highly concentrated export bundle, with

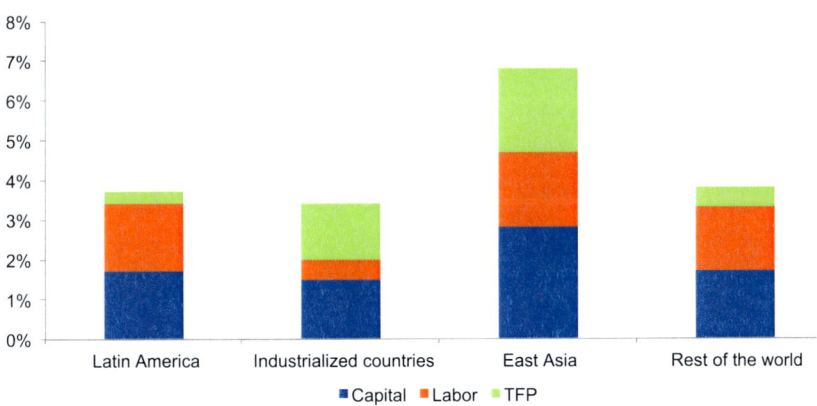

Figure 6.2 Sources of Real GDP Growth, 1960–2010 (Percent)

Sources: Bosworth and Collins (2003); and author's calculations.
Note: TFP = Total factor productivity.

---

[2] As shown by Pavcnik (2002) and Crespi (2006) in the case of Chile, and Roberts and Tybout (1996, 227–58) for Colombia.

exports representing the main source of recent growth improvements. While Korea's export matrix has been sophisticated in the 27 years through 2010, this has not been the case for any Latin American country. Today, chemicals, health-related products, and electronics represent a larger chunk of Korea's exports, while the share of garments, textiles, and fabrics has declined. The latter products have less value added, because they are less sophisticated in terms of knowledge than the former (Pavitt 1984; Hidalgo and Hausmann 2011). Analyzing a typical Latin American country, two fundamental characteristics emerge. The export pattern is, mostly, heavily biased toward less sophisticated products, such as commodities, agricultural products, and garments, and this pattern has not changed for nearly three decades through 2010.

Countries that have evolved from natural resource exploitation to more sophisticated and heterogeneous export patterns show better growth improvements, in particular in TFP. Thus the Latin American economies face the challenge of adding complexity to their production and export structure, implying less reliance on a few natural-resource-intensive products. Consistent with the previous evidence and based on the production complexity index of Hausmann and others (2011), the Latin American region is not on the frontline of the development race, which is currently led by the Asian tigers and Organisation for Economic Co-operation and Development countries. For instance, Colombia's production structure is heavily concentrated in a few products related to oil, while Chile's structure is focused on copper mining. The same pattern holds true for Peru.

Low diversification in product and export structure is related to the slow growth of TFP. According to the World Economic Forum (2013), Chile, for example, ranks quite well on most factors that compose the category of basic requirements for development, such as institutions, infrastructure, and macroeconomic environment. But it underperforms in those pillars related to innovation and business sophistication, which are key for growth in innovation-driven economies. Chile and the Latin American region in general are clearly lagging behind in terms of TFP growth.

In fact, leaving aside the "mean or average approach" and zooming in on the performance of the productive structure within a country, sector heterogeneities pop up swiftly. One can observe highly efficient and export-oriented sectors coexisting with unproductive ones, as can be inferred from the productivity statistics for Chile. Even when zooming in on one particular sector, one can observe different productivity levels among firms. Evidence suggests that this productivity heterogeneity could be represented by a hump-shaped distribution.

Firm and sector heterogeneities have important policy implications. A one-size-fits-all approach will not work when sectors and firms within the same region face dissimilar challenges. Some firms within a sector may be faced with financial constraints, especially the younger and smaller ones, while others may have problems with recruiting qualified human capital. This implies that when designing a new development strategy based on boosting firms' productivity, heterogeneities need to be taken into consideration. Nevertheless, given market failures, governments should always provide a sound basic institutional setting, which benefits all sectors, such as infrastructure, an educated labor force, and efficient regulation of markets.

PRODUCTION DIVERSIFICATION AND HOW INNOVATION MAY HELP

One of the main challenges the Latin American region faces in reaching the frontier of the development race is to reshape its productive structure, taking into consideration the highly heterogeneous performance across sectors and firms within each country (Crespi, Stein, and Fernandez-Aria 2014). The experience of the countries that started from a similar situation in income per capita, natural resource endowment, small domestic markets, and large distance from international markets, shows that more of the same is not enough. Inspiration-led growth could be part of the answer. None of them, for instance Australia, Finland, and New Zealand, pushed a development strategy based on concentrating efforts and productive structure in only a few natural resource products. On the contrary, they explicitly aimed for more diversified economies, increasing local value added in products and services as well as reducing the productivity heterogeneity in local firms.

Four specific country characteristics need to be taken into consideration in the design of a new development strategy:

1. *Size of the domestic markets*—One cannot compare a country like Brazil to a country like Peru, because the number of potential customers can make a huge difference for firm and sector development; it is a matter of scale.

2. *Natural resource abundance*—This is a fact that the region needs to internalize and to learn how to use wisely. There is clear evidence in some countries of the region showing that the adoption of an industrialization development strategy (and neglecting the comparative advantage of natural resource abundance) may not succeed, as the experience during the 1950s and the 1960s shows (import-substitution strategies). Most Latin American economies are nowadays attempting to build development strategies around their natural resources.

3. *Distance to international markets*—This implies a double challenge because transportation and logistics costs go up as distance increases, requiring extra efficiency in certain areas to ensure competitiveness. All sectors face this challenge, but it can get particularly critical for those that export fresh fruits and vegetables, for example.

4. *An enabling institutional setting*—This provides the environmental conditions for the productive sector and the society in general to flourish.

However, governments need to be aware that there is no silver-bullet intervention. To tackle these challenges, policymakers need to cope with the paramount task of building an all-encompassing development strategy.

Such a strategy requires the design of a robust conceptual framework that guides the direction of interventions, but always with the vision set on medium- and long-term targets. This framework should take into account the existence of market failures, mainly to ensure that the incentives of the private sector are properly aligned with the overall development strategy. Finally, the strategy should be able to properly balance vertical interventions (specific sectors) and horizontal ones (all sectors), avoiding the risk of government failures. These represent the damage the state can do to markets when trying to solve a market failure.

The introduction of new products and processes is a crucial mechanism to help countries diversify their production structures. It is not only the technical feasibility normally related with invention, but also a solution that creates value. If the production matrix needs to be expanded, by definition, new products should be produced either if they already exist in foreign markets or, as in the case of radical innovations, they are new to the world.

Innovation depends heavily on knowledge, and may need state intervention. Ideas, prototypes, pilot plants, scaling processes, beta versions, packing, patenting, technology transfers, among other activities, are knowledge intensive. This includes scientific, technological, productive, and marketing knowledge, which could be generated through either formal education or by experience (learning by doing). Moreover, knowledge has some economic properties, nonrivalry and nonexclusion, that classify it as a quasi-public good. As such, appropriation problems, asymmetric information, coordination, and other market failures could be raising obstacles when developing and applying knowledge in creating new products. Then, market forces may be insufficient to ensure critical mass for innovation to flourish. Public participation may help create the conditions for this to happen. Moreover, some argue that without state intervention, none of today's innovations would exist, or at least could have taken considerable time to arise (Mazzucato 2013).

But state interventions have their pitfalls. For a better characterization of state interventions in promoting innovation and production diversity, Crespi and others (2014) present a policy intervention taxonomy as a double-entry matrix (Table 6.1). The vertical axis captures the type of policy and the horizontal axis the scope of policy. The type may consist of the public provision of inputs aimed at solving specific market failures, for instance, setting up some rules of the game. Or policy may consist of a direct intervention in a market to influence the behavior of agents through the design of specific incentives. Scope is related to the pervasiveness of a policy within an economy, that is, if it affects all sectors (horizontal) or specific ones (vertical).

TABLE 6.1

		Policy Scope	
		Horizontal	Vertical
Type of Policy	Public Inputs	Property rights protection	Phytosanitary controls
	Market Interventions	R&D tax credits	Tourism tax exemptions

Different policy instruments are associated with each of the four quadrants of the policy intervention taxonomy. For instance, public inputs providing protection of property rights, particularly relevant for research and development (R&D) and innovation activities, affect all sectors of the economy and thus are considered a horizontal instrument. But specific laws affect particular sectors of the economy; phytosanitary controls, for example, are relevant for agriculture, but not for mining. These input policies are tailor-made for a specific sector and constitute a policy tool to tackle sector heterogeneities. The bottom-left quadrant of Table 6.1 shows policies that directly intervene in the markets with the aim of modifying the incentives of agents to influence their behavior. They can be horizontal or vertical. Under the former, for example, R&D tax credits change the cost that firms face when engaging in R&D, naturally modifying their assessment of expected returns on R&D projects. Other interventions may be aimed at specific sectors, such as tourism.

Vertical intervention policy tools have to be used carefully to avoid generating government failures. And under some circumstances, it is preferable to leave a market failure unattended than to intervene, because the costs may exceed the benefits.

Given the risks associated with policies of vertical scope, countries have preferred horizontal approaches to policymaking, focusing on enabling an institutional setting (rules of the game) that benefits all sectors of the economy. Once this is done, however, the specificities of each sector need to be dealt with, and then a vertical approach is required.

When doing so, policymakers need to avoid at least three types of state failure:

- *Time inconsistency*—This relates to policymakers' tendency to favor policies more visible to the citizenry in the short term, like building a bridge, because it may increase reelection possibilities. Because science, technology, and innovation policies, required to promote diversification of the production structure, are quite invisible compared with, say, a bridge, and yield benefits in the medium or long term, they are less likely to be implemented by policymakers focused on their political parties' reelection. This may be especially relevant within the short-term nature of the government settings. To avoid this, science, technology, and innovation and other production promotion policies should be implemented by state organizations with specific mandates to ensure time consistency.

- *Agency problems.* This occurs when the interest of the principal, say a president or prime minister, differs from the interest of a minister, such as the minister of industry. The problem is that the objectives of the principal and the agent may differ, introducing distortions between overall planning and implementation. Usually the agent that is closer to the implementation scene has more practical information about the beneficiary of a given policy or public instrument. Another derivative of the agency problem has to do with the absence of a clear responsibility for the policy implementation, which occurs given the interdisciplinary nature of the policy and tasks related to different ministries. Not having a clear definition of roles in science, technology, and innovation and production diversification policy intensifies the potential for dynamic inconsistency problems.

- *Public capture.* This occurs when the state is captured by the beneficiaries, who end up influencing the course and direction of some policies. A common case is the implementation of an intervention initially justified by a market failure. This intervention may take the shape of a subsidy aimed at a specific group. Once the failure has been resolved, however, the beneficiaries may lobby in favor of the continuation of the measure, in exchange for votes, for example.

Because of the threat of government failures, policies require a proper public institutional setting that minimizes their manifestation. This is what Latin American countries have been trying to do in the decade through 2014. The approach undertaken has consisted of dividing the strategy setting, policy design, and implementation tasks among different bodies of the public apparatus. The institutional setup for policy should be ideally composed of, at the first level, an advisory body in charge of defining the medium- and long-term objectives of policies, perhaps a chief executive officer of innovation or a state strategy agency properly insulated from political cycles. At the second level, a ministry, or a few ministries, would be in charge of policy design, based on the guidelines given by the advisory body; and finally, the third level would involve a public agency in charge of the direct implementation of the science, technology, and innovation and production diversification policy instruments.

WHAT SCIENCE, TECHNOLOGY, AND INNOVATION CAN DO

Latin American countries should learn three lessons about innovation. First, science and technology is not just a rich-country hobby. A large body of theoretical (Romer 1990; Aghion and Howitt 1992) and empirical (Grilliches 1995; Hall and Jones 1999; Rouvinen 2002) literature suggests that countries that have invested in R&D and related activities have achieved higher TFP growth rates and subsequent increases in income per capita.

The second lesson is that the effects of R&D efforts over TFP enhancement have a natural delay. That is, one may observe a drop in TFP in the short term, but it would eventually go up in the medium and long term (Goto and Suzuki 1989; Benavente, de Gregorio, and Nuñez 2006). This delay is associated with a natural learning process that goes hand in hand with the innovation process, as Schumpeter emphasized when he developed his idea of "creative destruction." This idea is quite intuitive for engineers who are aware that there is a natural adaptation process when a new machine is incorporated into the production process. But economists don't seem to have understood this very well. In fact, the data show that increases in TFP take about two years in the manufacturing sector and eight years in the biotechnology sector. Heterogeneity is unveiled in yet another dimension.

The third lesson is that competition problems are more prone to occur in a small market setting. Since competition is a necessary condition to promote innovation, smaller economies need to deal with this intrinsic limitation. A common strategy of smaller countries currently at the technological frontier has been to compete in global markets, not in domestic ones. The only way to keep up with fierce competition in international markets is to invest in R&D and innovation, which at the aggregate level will ultimately boost productivity growth (Bravo-Ortega, Benavente, and Gonzalez 2014). The latter implies a different innovation-TFP causality direction for small and large economies. The large ones, like Brazil or the United States, start increasing TFP and then become competitive within local markets, after which they begin exporting.

It is important to mention the side effects of the innovation process. Contrary to the common expectation that the innovation will decrease employment, evidence suggests that this is not the case (Harrison and others 2014; Mohnen and Hall 2013; Benavente and Lauterbach 2008). The introduction of innovations that involve incorporating machinery that may eventually substitute human capital for physical capital may affect employment. However, a more efficient firm may face higher demand for their product, triggering an increase in the demand for labor—and probably more qualified labor. Eventually, we observe a net increase in labor demand derived from the innovation process, especially for less-developed economies.

Finally, the innovation process may have important implications for income distribution issues so prevalent in Latin American economies. Because innovation goes hand in hand with learning, knowledge becomes of the utmost importance for these processes to occur. Because knowledge has public good characteristics, its rents tend to be dispersed more widely, as opposed to rents derived from land or physical capital. This has important implications when designing strategies to address income inequalities.

CONCLUSION

Recent events have shown that most Latin American countries remain vulnerable to the ups and downs of the global economy, especially commodity price fluctuations. Countries that elsewhere have succeeded in leapfrogging the middle-income trap have pushed inspiration-based policies. Those that put the different manifestations of knowledge at the center of their public policy goals have done well. They have focused on productivity enhancements, mission-oriented sciences, innovation, and entrepreneurship, among others. These countries have also introduced explicit mechanisms to diversify their production matrix, mostly based on the introduction of new products and more efficient processes.

Product diversification is not a goal in itself, but a means to leap into the frontline of the development race. The Latin American experience also tells us no single, silver-bullet policy can achieve this. On the contrary, a systemic and dynamic approach to policymaking needs to be adopted to successfully implement a development strategy that enables these economies to achieve their goals in the medium and long term.

In particular, the institutional setting under which the new strategies for development are implemented becomes of the utmost importance. Given that state failures can threaten the success of a well-designed development strategy, countries need to make an effort to design and establish an adequate institutional setting, no matter how difficult it is.

Policymakers, and citizens generally, must not forget that the results and benefits of science, technology, and product diversification policies may only become tangible in the medium and long term. Countries need to design institutions, explicitly and implicitly, that can help to avoid this anxiety, a characteristic that also explains the difference between developed economies and those that are lagging behind.

REFERENCES

Aghion, P., and P. Howitt. 1992. "A Model of Growth through Creative Destruction." *Econometrica* 60 (2): 323–51.

Benavente, J. M., J. de Gregorio, and M. Núñez. 2006. "Rates of Return for Industrial R&D in Chile." Working Paper No. 220, Department of Economics, University of Chile.

Benavente, J. M., and R. Lauterbach. 2008. "Technological Innovation and Employment: Complements or Substitutes?" *European Journal of Development Research* 20 (2): 318–29.

Bosworth, B., and S. Collins. 2003. "The Empirics of Growth: An Update." *Brookings Papers on Economic Activity* 34 (2): 113–206.

Bravo-Ortega, C., J. M. Benavente, and A. Gonzalez. 2014. "Innovation, Exports and Productivity: Learning and Self Selection in Chile." *Emerging Markets Finance and Trade.* 50 (1): 68–95.

Crespi, G. 2006. "Productivity and Firm Heterogeneity in Chile." PRUS Working Paper 36, Poverty Research Unit, University of Sussex.

Crespi, G., E. Stein, and E. Fernandez-Arias, eds. 2014. *Rethinking Productive Development: Sound Policies and Institutions for Economic Transformation.* London: Palgrave Macmillan.

Fuentes, R., F. Gredig, and M. Larraín. 2007. "Estimating the Output Gap for Chile." Working Papers Central Bank of Chile 455, Central Bank of Chile.

Goto, A., and K. Suzuki. 1989. "R&D Capital Rate of Return on R&D Investment and Spillover of R&D in Japanese Manufacturing Industries." *Review of Economics and Statistics.* 71 (4): 555–64.

Grilliches, Z. 1995. "R&D and Productivity." In *Handbook of the Economics of Innovation and Technological Change*, edited by P. Stoneman, 52–89. Oxford: Blackwell.

Hall, Robert E., and Charles I. Jones. 1999. "Why Do Some Countries Produce So Much More Output per Worker Than Others?" *Quarterly Journal of Economics.* 114 (1): 83–116.

Harrison, R., J. Jaumandreu, J. Mairesse, and B. Peters. 2014. "Does Innovation Stimulate Employment? A Firm-Level Analysis Using Comparable Micro-Data from Four European Countries." *International Journal of Industrial Organization* 35 (C): 29–43.

Hausmann, R., C. A. Hidalgo, S. Bustos, M. Coscia, A. Simoes, and M. Yildirim. 2011. *The Atlas of Economic Complexity.* Hollis, New Hampshire: Puritan Press.

Hidalgo, César A., and Ricardo Hausmann. 2011. "The Network Structure of Economic Output." *Journal of Economic Growth* 16: 309–42.

Mazzucato, M. 2013. *The Entrepreneurial State: Debunking Private vs. Public Sector Myths.* London: Anthem Press.

Mohnen, P., and B. Hall. 2013. "Innovation and Productivity: An Update." *Eurasian Business Review.* 3 (1): 47–65.

Pavcnick, N. 2002. "Trade Liberalization, Exit and Productivity Improvements: Evidence from Chilean Plants." *Review of Economic Studies* 69 (1): 245–76.

Pavitt, K. 1984. "Sectoral Patterns of Technical Change: Towards a Taxonomy and a Theory." *Research Policy* 13 (6): 343–73.

Roberts, M. J., and J. R. Tybout, eds. 1996. *Industrial Evolution in Developing Countries: Micro Patterns of Turnover, Productivity and Market Structure.* New York: Oxford University Press.

Romer, P. 1990. "Endogenous Technological Change." *Journal of Political Economy* 98 (5): 71–102.

Rouvinen, P. 2002. "R&D-Productivity Dynamics: Causality, Lags, and 'Dry Holes'." *Journal of Applied Economics* 5 (1): 123–56.

World Economic Forum. 2013. *Global Competitiveness Report, 2012–2013.* Geneva: World Economic Forum.

PART III

Key Policies to Support Diversification

CHAPTER 7

Growth Policy Design for Middle-Income Countries

PHILIPPE AGHION

How can middle-income countries enhance productivity growth, helping them to avoid the so-called middle-income trap? This chapter discusses potential determinants of firm-level productivity and productivity growth. It considers potential barriers to growth in firm size, and then revisits the role for vertical targeting (or sectoral policies). Drawing on this discussion, it proposes some elements of a new growth strategy for middle-income countries.

ENHANCING PRODUCTIVITY GROWTH

This section looks at the determinants of productivity growth, based on the following questions. How can it be enhanced in advanced countries versus emerging market economies? And is there anything to learn from observing the big technological waves and their diffusion patterns across countries? We first present a simple framework to discuss sources of productivity growth. We then look at the sources of this growth in advanced countries and emerging market economies. The section closes with an analysis of the technological waves and draws a few lessons from comparing the differences in their diffusion patterns across countries.

A Framework to Think about the Sources of Productivity Growth

Solow (1956) developed a model to show that in the absence of technical progress, there can be no long-term growth of GDP per capita. On the other hand, historical evidence suggests that productivity growth is an increasingly important component of growth (for example, see Helpman 2004). But what are the sources of productivity growth? A useful framework for thinking about productivity growth and its determinants is the so-called Schumpeterian paradigm, which revolves around four main ideas.

First, productivity growth relies on profit-motivated innovations. These can be process innovations to increase the productivity of production factors (for example, labor or capital); product innovations (introducing new products); or organizational innovations (to make the combination of production factors more efficient). Policies and institutions that increase the expected benefits should induce more innovation and thus faster productivity growth. In particular, this means better intellectual property rights protection, research and development (R&D) tax credits, more intense competition, and better-performing schools and universities.

Second is creative destruction. Here, new innovations tend to make old innovations, old technologies, and old skills obsolete. And this in turn underlies the importance of reallocation in the growth process.

Third, innovations may be either "frontier" innovations, pushing frontier technology forward in a particular sector, or "imitative" or "adaptive" innovations allowing a firm or sector to catch up with the existing technological frontier. The two forms require different types of policies and institutions.

Fourth is Schumpeterian waves. This is where technological history is shaped by the big technological waves that correspond to the diffusion of new "general-purpose technologies"—for example, the steam engine, electricity, and information and communication technologies (ICT)—to various sectors of the economy.

Enhancing Productivity Growth in Advanced Countries

To enhance productivity growth in advanced countries, where it relies more on frontier innovations, it helps to invest more in universities to maximize flexibility of product and labor markets and to develop financial systems that, importantly, rely on equity financing.

Aghion, Blundell, and others (2009) show how competition (measured here by the lagged foreign entry rate) affects productivity growth in domestic incumbent firms. We see that, on average, productivity growth in firms that are closer to the technological frontier worldwide in their sector (compared with the median) quickens amid more intense competition. This reflects an "escape competition effect" (such firms innovate more to escape more intense competition). In contrast, productivity growth in firms farther from the technological frontier in their sector worldwide than the median reacts negatively to more intense competition. This reflects a "discouragement effect." In sum, the closer a country is to the world's leading productivity level, the higher is the fraction of above-the-median firms, and therefore product market competition is more productivity enhancing. Similarly, one can show that more flexible labor markets, which facilitate creative destruction, foster productivity growth more in advanced economies.

Another lever of productivity growth in advanced economies is graduate education; indeed, frontier innovation requires frontier researchers. Aghion, Boustan, and others (2009) show that research education enhances productivity growth more in states that are relatively closer to the frontier in the United States; that is, those with higher GDP per capita, such as California and Massachusetts. Two years of college education, meanwhile, enhances productivity growth more in less advanced states, such as Alabama and Mississippi. The same is true across countries: higher education, especially graduate education, enhances productivity growth more in countries with higher GDP per capita.

The organization of the financial sector is also important for productivity growth. As Koch (2014) shows, choosing a bank-based financial system enhances productivity growth more in less advanced countries, whereas choosing a market-based financial system enhances productivity growth more in countries that are relatively closer to the frontier.

Aghion, Askenazy, and others (2009) conducted cross-country panel regressions of productivity growth on the share of ICT in total value added, and found a positive significant effect. But interestingly, once they control for product market regulation, the coefficient on ICT becomes nonsignificant. This in turn suggests that liberalizing product markets is key to enhancing productivity growth in developed countries, also because it facilitates the diffusion of the ICT wave through various sectors of the economy. Cette and Lopez (2012), who confirm this result, show that the euro area and Japan suffer from a lack of ICT diffusion compared with the United States.[1] Using an econometric analysis, they show that this is explained by institutional factors: a lower education level, on average, of the working-age population and more regulations on labor and product markets in the euro area and Japan. This result means that by implementing structural reforms, these countries could benefit from productivity acceleration linked to a catch-up of the U.S. ICT diffusion level.

Cette, Lopez, and Mairesse (2013) analyze the impact of anticompetitive regulations in upstream service industry sectors on productivity growth in downstream industries using inputs from upstream sectors. Using an unbalanced country-industry panel dataset covering 15 countries in the Organisation for Economic Co-operation and Development during 1987–2007, the authors find that anticompetitive upstream regulations have a significantly detrimental effect on productivity growth downstream, and that this effect operates in part (but not entirely) through R&D and ICT investments in downstream industries.

Productivity Growth in Emerging Market Economies

Hsieh and Klenow (2009), looking at the sources of productivity growth in emerging market economies where adaptive innovation and factor accumulation are the main sources of growth, emphasize the importance of input reallocation effects. In particular, if we compare the distribution of firm productivity in India and in the United States, the latter has a thinner tail of less productive plants and a fatter tail of more productive plants than India. In other words, it is harder for a more productive firm to grow, but also easier for a less productive firm to survive in India than in the United States. Thus, the creative destruction process operates more efficiently in the latter. This difference is attributable to various potential factors; in particular, more rigid capital markets and labor and product markets in India, the lower supply of skills in India compared to the United States, the poorer quality of infrastructure in India, and the lower quality of

---

[1] The euro area here is the aggregation of Austria, Finland, France, Germany, Italy, the Netherlands, and Spain. These seven countries together represented 88½ percent of the euro area's GDP in 2012. See Figure 4 in Cette and Lopez (2012).

institutions to protect property rights and to enforce contracts in India. These factors in turn operate on productivity growth through several potential channels. The management practices channel is particularly interesting. Recent work (for example, Bloom and Van Reenen 2010) shows that management practices are far worse in India than in the United States, and that the average management scores across countries are strongly correlated with the level of GDP per capita.

Obstacles to Growth in Firms

A large body of literature discusses firm dynamics and its impact on aggregate productivity growth. On the theory side, state-of-the-art work on the interplay between growth, reallocation, and firm dynamics are papers by Klette and Kortum (2004), Acemoglu and others (2013), and Akcigit, Alp, and Peters (2014). These papers build on the Schumpeterian growth paradigm (see Aghion and Howitt 1992, and Aghion, Akcigit, and Howitt 2013) to model firms as multi-line producers and innovators. Innovation improves a firm's productivity in producing a particular intermediate input, and it allows an incumbent firm to expand its scope (that is, the number of product lines it operates in). Successful innovation by an outsider on a product line covered by an incumbent firm eliminates that line from that firm's range of products, shrinking the number of product lines it covers. This framework generates an ergodic steady-state firm size distribution, which depends on the innovation technology, government policy toward incumbent firms and towards potential entrants, and regulatory or credit market characteristics, which will also affect the ability of firms to enter and grow after entry.

In particular, the Schumpeterian framework can account for various stylized facts about firm dynamics and firm size distribution. Some of these facts are:

1. The firm size distribution is highly skewed.

2. Firm size and age are highly correlated (in this framework, new firms are one-line firms, and to become large with sufficient lines they need to have innovated on all these lines and survived creative destruction on a sufficient number of lines that they used to operate on).

3. Small firms exit more frequently (it takes only one outside innovation to eliminate a one-line firm whereas it takes several successful outside innovations to eliminate an initially multi-line firm), but the ones that survive tend to grow faster than average (such a firm is more likely to be an efficient innovator, as well as being able to exploit R&D synergies across its multiple lines).

4. A large fraction of total R&D in the United States is done by incumbents.

5. The reallocation of inputs between entrants and incumbents is an important source of productivity growth.

This framework can also explain why factors that inhibit firm size growth in developing economies also inhibit aggregate productivity growth. For example,

Akcigit, Alp, and Peters (2014) argue that in developing economies contractual frictions become more dramatic as firms grow. It becomes increasingly hard to avoid hold-up by firm managers as the number of product lines controlled by a firm increases. This in turn inhibits the growth of the most efficient firms (that is, firms with higher innovation capabilities), and such firms have lower incentive to grow, because firm owners want to mitigate the hold-up problem with their managers. Less efficient firms thus remain active for longer before more efficient firms replace them.

Although contractual incompleteness and lack of trust are obvious obstacles to firm growth, previous studies have also emphasized adjustment costs induced by R&D and advertising of incumbent firms, administrative costs of creating a new firm, and labor market regulations.

Aghion, Fally, and Scarpetta (2007) present empirical evidence on the effect of financial development on the entry of new firms of different size and on the post-entry growth of successful entrants. They use harmonized firm-level data on entry and post-entry growth by industry, size class, and over time for a sample of industrialized, transitional, and Latin American countries as in Bartelsman, Haltiwanger, Scarpetta (2004). They consider two main indicators of financial development: the ratio of private credit and stock market capitalization. In their estimation, they use a detailed set of regulatory indicators that characterize the banking and securities markets as instruments for these financial development variables. Following Rajan and Zingales (1998), to minimize problems of omitted variable bias and other misspecification, they interact different indicators of financial development with the relative dependence on external financing of the corresponding sector in the United States.

The main results in Aghion, Fally, and Scarpetta (2007) are as follows. First, higher financial development enhances new firm entry in sectors that depend more heavily upon external finance. Second, the entry of the smallest firms benefits the most from higher financial development, whereas financial development has either no or negative effect on entry by larger firms. And third, financial development enhances the post-entry growth of firms in sectors that depend more upon external finance, even when controlling for labor market regulations.[2]

The effect of regulations on firm dynamics and size is itself a fascinating topic that has barely been touched. An interesting paper by Garicano, Lelarge, and Van Reenen (2013) analyzes the static welfare effects of the 50-employee regulatory threshold in France. They point to a significant source of allocative inefficiency (namely, an inefficient concentration of firm size just below the threshold).

---

[2] Previous work on the subject includes Beck and others (2008), who find that financial development is more growth enhancing for industries that rely more on small firms (measured by the share of small firms in the respective U.S. industry). In the same vein, Beck, Demirgüç-Kunt, and Maksimovic (2005) use a firm survey to assess firms' perceptions of financial constraints. They find that small firms tend to be more affected by financial as well as legal and corruption issues than larger firms.

DO WE STILL NEED VERTICALLY TARGETED POLICIES?

The Debate

The change of emphasis from industry-level to firm-level competitiveness, the evidence on the relationship between firm-level competitiveness and firm-level productivity, and the discussion on the determinants and policies to enhance productivity growth point toward giving priority to horizontal targeting, that is, to policies (be they competition, labor market liberalization, patent and R&D policies, among others) that enhance productivity growth in all sectors. This approach is the alternative to focusing on vertical targeting (policies aimed at promoting particular industries in the worldwide competition with similar industries in other countries).

Vertical targeting was popular in the aftermath of World War II. The World Bank and other international financial institutions welcomed import substitution policies in Latin American countries, whereby local industries would more fully benefit from domestic demand. Similarly, these institutions supported East Asian countries such as Japan or Korea that engaged in export promotion (for example, through tariffs and nontariff barriers, and partly through maintaining undervalued exchange rates). For some two or three decades after World War II, these policies, which belong to what is commonly referred to as "industrial policy," remained fairly noncontroversial, as both groups of countries were growing rapidly.

However, vertical targeting has come under increasing criticism since the early 1980s among academics and policy advisers in international financial institutions. In particular, it was criticized for allowing governments to pick winners and losers in a discretionary fashion, and consequently for increasing the scope for capture of government by local vested interests. Empirical studies by Frankel and Romer (1999) and Wacziarg (2001), pointing at a positive effect of trade liberalization on growth, reinforce the case against vertical targeting, as does recent work on competition and growth (for example, Aghion and others 2005, and Aghion and Howitt 2006).

However, three phenomena that have occurred since the 2000s invite us to rethink the issue. First, climate change and the increasing awareness that without government intervention to encourage clean production and innovation, global warming will intensify and generate negative externalities worldwide, such as drought, deforestation, migration, and conflicts. Second, the global financial crisis revealed the extent to which *laissez-faire* policies led several countries, in particular in southern Europe, to allow the uncontrolled development of nontradable sectors (particularly real estate) at the expense of tradable sectors that are more conducive to long-term convergence and innovation. And third, China has become so prominent on the world economic stage in large part because of its constant pursuit of industrial policy. An increasing number of scholars, particularly in the United States, are now denouncing the danger of the *laissez-faire* policies that lead developed economies to specialize in upstream R&D and in services, while outsourcing manufacturing tasks to developing economies with lower unskilled labor costs. These scholars point to the fact that countries like Germany and Japan have better managed to maintain intermediate manufacturing segments of their value chains by pursuing more active industrial policies, and that this in turn allowed them to benefit more from outsourcing other segments.

As noted, the most recurrent counterargument to industrial interventionism is the one on picking winners. True, industrial policy is always somewhat about picking winners, but as Vincent Cable, the United Kingdom's former Secretary of State for Business, Innovation, and Skills, points out, "the 'winners' in this sense are the skills we judge we will need for the future, and the sectors they support" (Cable 2010). However, this chapter argues that the picking-winners argument loses bite; first when a government chooses to pick sectors and not particular firms, and second when it uses sectoral interventions in a way that preserves or even enhances competition and Schumpeterian selection within the corresponding sectors.

Another criticism of traditional industrial policy is the risk of capture and rent-seeking behavior. But again, setting clear principles for the selection of sectors and for the governance of support to these sectors (competitiveness, exit mechanisms, and so on) should help address this criticism.

More fundamentally, knowledge spillovers are an important theoretical argument supporting growth-enhancing sectoral policies. For example, firms that choose to innovate in dirty technologies do not internalize the fact that current advances in such technologies tend also to make future innovations in them more profitable. More generally, when choosing where to produce and innovate, firms do not internalize the positive or negative externalities that these factors might have on other firms and sectors. Credit constraints are a reinforcing factor that may further limit or slow the reallocation of firms toward new, more growth-enhancing sectors. One can argue that the existence of market failures on their own is not sufficient to justify sectoral intervention. Even so, there are activities, typically in high-tech sectors, which generate knowledge spillovers on the rest of the economy, and where assets are highly intangible, making it more difficult for firms to borrow from private capital markets to finance their growth. As such, there might indeed be a case for subsidizing entry and innovation in these sectors, and to do so in a way that guarantees fair competition within the sector. Note that the sectors that typically come to mind are always the same four or five: notably, energy, biotech, ICT, and transportation.

Rethinking the Design and Governance of Industrial Policy

A convincing empirical study in support of properly designed industrial policy is Nunn and Trefler (2010). These authors use microdata on a set of countries to analyze whether, as suggested by the argument of "infant industry," productivity growth in a country is positively affected by the measure in which tariff protection is biased in favor of activities and sectors that are skill-intensive (that is, they use more intensively skilled workers). They find a significant positive correlation between productivity growth and the "skill bias" resulting from tariff protection.

Of course, such a correlation does not necessarily mean there is causality—the two variables may themselves be the result of a third factor such as the quality of a country's institutions. However, Nunn and Trefler (2010) do show that at least 25 percent of the correlation corresponds to a causal effect. Overall, their analysis suggests that adequately designed (meaning, in this instance, skill-intensive) targeting may actually enhance growth, not only in the sector being subsidized, but also in the country as a whole.

Aghion and others (2012) argue that sectoral policy should not be systematically opposed to competition policy. First, they develop a simple model showing that targeted subsidies can be used to induce several firms to operate in the same sector, and that the more competitive the sector is, the more firms will be induced to innovate to escape competition. Of course, a lot depends upon the design of industrial policy, which should target sectors and not particular firms (or "national champions"). This in turn suggests new empirical analyses in which productivity growth, patenting, or other measures of innovation and entrepreneurship would be regressed over some measures of sectoral intervention. These measures would be interacted with the degree of competition in a sector, and with the extent to which intervention in each sector is not concentrated on a single firm, but rather distributed over a number of firms.

To look at the interaction between state subsidies to a sector and the level of product market competition in that sector, Aghion and others (2012) use Chinese firm-level panel data[3] for all industrial firms in the Chinese National Business Survey (an annual survey of all firms with more than 5 million sales). The sample period is 1988–2007, and the survey contains information on inputs and outputs, firm-level state subsidies, and so on. Product market competition is measured by one minus the Lerner index, which in turn is calculated as the ratio of operating profits minus capital costs over sales. The authors show that total factor productivity (TFP), TFP growth, and product innovation (defined as the ratio between output value generated by new products to total output value) are all positively correlated with the interaction between state aid to a sector and market competition in that sector. Thus, the more competitive the recipient sector, the more positive the effects of targeted state subsidies to that sector on TFP, TFP growth, and product innovation. In fact, they show that for sectors with a low degree of competition the effects are negative, whereas the effects become positive in sectors with a sufficiently high degree of competition. They also show that the interaction between state aid and product market competition in a sector is more positive when state aid is less concentrated. In fact, if one restricts attention to the second quartile in the degree of concentration of state aid (this refers to sectors where state aid is not very concentrated), then state aid has a positive effect on TFP and product innovation in all sectors with more than a median level of product market competition.

---

[3] Data showing how much state aid each sector receives are not available for European Union countries.

Clean Innovations

Firms in a *laissez-faire* economy may innovate in the wrong direction, for example, in polluting energy activities, because they have acquired expertise on such activities and have not taken into account the environmental and the knowledge externalities that their choice entails. Aghion and others (2013) explore a cross-country panel data set of patents in the automotive industry. They distinguish between "dirty innovations," which affect combustion engines, and clean innovations, such as electric cars. They show that the larger the stock of past dirty innovations by a given entrepreneur, the dirtier are the current innovations by the same entrepreneur. This path-dependent phenomenon, together with the fact that innovations have been mostly dirty so far, implies that in the absence of government intervention, economies would generate too many dirty innovations. Hence, there is a role for government intervention to redirect technical change toward clean innovations.

As Acemoglu and others (2012) argue, delaying such directed intervention not only leads to further deterioration of the environment, but also longer delay in the introduction of clean innovations. The dirty innovation machine continues to strengthen its lead, making dirty technologies more productive and widening the productivity gap between dirty and clean technologies even further. This widened gap in turn requires a longer period for clean technologies to catch up and replace the dirty ones. Because this catching-up period is characterized by slower growth, the cost of delaying intervention in foregone growth will be higher. In other words, delaying action is costly.

Not surprisingly, the shorter the delay and the higher the discount rate (that is, the lower the value put on the future), the lower the cost will be. This is because the gains from delaying intervention are realized at the start in the form of higher consumption, while the loss occurs in the future through more environmental degradation and lower consumption. Moreover, because there are basically two problems to deal with—the environmental and innovation ones—using two instruments proves better than one. Here, the optimal policy involves using a carbon price to deal with the environmental externality, and, at the same time, direct subsidies to clean R&D (or a profit tax on dirty technologies) to deal with the knowledge externality. This approach, again, calls for vertical targeting.

One could always argue that a carbon price on its own deals with both environmental and knowledge externalities at the same time (discouraging the use of dirty technologies also discourages innovation in dirty technologies). However, relying on the carbon price alone leads to an excessive reduction in consumption in the short term. Because the two-instrument policy reduces the short-term cost in foregone short-term consumption, it reinforces the case for immediate implementation, even for values of the discount rate under which standard models would suggest delaying implementation.

In sum, the overall discussion in this section suggests that adequately targeted sectoral intervention—for example, to more skill-intensive or more competitive sectors—can be growth-enhancing. We have also argued against concentrating subsidies across firms in a sector. However, this is just the starting point for a much broader research program on how to govern industrial policy to make it more competition-friendly and more innovation-enhancing. In particular, how can industrial policy be designed to ensure that nonperforming projects will not be refinanced? And how should governments update their doctrine and practice of competition policy to factor in the latest thinking on how to design and implement industrial policy? The conjunction of the debate on climate change, the global financial crisis, and China's new dominance on the world market reinforces our conviction that although market competition is certainly the main engine of growth, specialization cannot be left entirely to the dynamics of *laissez-faire*. One increasingly realizes that the specialization model, whereby the most advanced economies focus on upstream R&D and services and outsource everything else to emerging market economies, may not be sustainable in the long term.

IMPLICATIONS FOR THE DESIGN OF A NEW GROWTH PACKAGE IN MIDDLE-INCOME COUNTRIES

Although improving management in existing firms can achieve more catch-up or reallocation-based growth (as just discussed), further liberalizing labor flows from rural to urban areas, developing the financial sector, and liberalizing capital flows will not be sustainable in the long term. There are several reasons for this; in particular, efficiency gains from reallocating resources from agriculture to industry and from absorption of imported technologies will be exhausted once the reallocation is completed. And wage increases will reduce an emerging market economy's comparative advantage in what it currently exports to the rest of the world.

Two questions thus naturally arise: How can an emerging market economy avoid the middle-income trap and make a successful transition from catch-up growth to innovation-led growth? And how can such a country achieve higher quality growth in this process? Our discussion on firm-level productivity growth as the ultimate source of competitiveness, as well as on the drivers of productivity growth, suggest four pillars of an innovation-based economy:

- *Competition and creative destruction*—Frontier innovation is fostered by competition and free entry to a much larger extent than imitation because incumbent firms at the technological frontier can escape competition and the threat of entry by innovating, and because most path-breaking innovations are made by new entrants. Checks and balances are therefore necessary to guarantee free entry and full competition, because this helps minimize the scope for collusion between local politicians and large incumbent firms.

- *Top research universities (that is, those with very high Shanghai rankings)*— Recent work on the subject suggests that to achieve such rankings more investment is needed in the university system, and that universities have autonomy on budget management, wage policy, hiring and firing decisions, and the design of academic programs. This autonomy must come hand in hand with more effective competition among universities as well as researchers. As for other sectors of the economy, upward accountability has to be replaced by more downward accountability and competitive pressure (Aghion and others 2010).

- *A dynamic labor market system*—This needs to combine (1) flexibility for firms to hire and fire; (2) a good training system to help workers move from one job to another; and (3) a social safety net with well-developed portable social security and pension rights, and with generous unemployment benefits (in turn conditional on the unemployed worker training and then accepting new jobs). Such a "flexicurity" system, incorporating both flexibility and security, makes creative destruction—and therefore innovation-led growth—work at full speed.

- *A financial system that relies more on venture capital, private equity, and stock markets*—Innovative investments are more risky and therefore investors need to get both a share of upside returns and control rights.

Consequently, which organizational and institutional changes (if any) does an emerging market economy need to introduce to move toward full-steam innovation-led growth? Obviously, we do not have the answer to this question, because we lack knowledge on how the current institutional system is organized and how it works in practice.

Yet, empirical and casual evidence suggests that a "smart" state can stimulate the innovation-led machinery by setting up a fiscal system that achieves the triple goal of (1) raising revenue to make innovation-enhancing investments in education, universities, and infrastructure; (2) being redistributive to avoid excessive inequality and poverty traps; and (3) encouraging innovation by not expropriating innovators. In addition, the smart state can achieve this by setting up adequate institutional mechanisms to strengthen checks and balances on the different levels of government to make sure that competition is fully enforced (as already argued), and that state investments aimed at enhancing innovation are properly targeted and monitored.

It would be somewhat paradoxical to recommend that an emerging market economy move from imitation-led to innovation-led growth by simply imitating the institutional arrangements of existing innovation-led economies. Instead, each country must find its own way to reform its state institutions to make the four pillars work fully. It must find its own answers to questions such as: How can they set up fully effective competition policy instruments and mechanisms starting from the current institutional context? Which contractual, organizational, or institutional changes should be introduced, in particular at the regional and local level for the country to gain full momentum in implementing sustainable and inclusive innovation-led growth? How can environmental and social (that is, inclusiveness) dimensions be factored in, in addition to GDP growth, when evaluating regional or local leaders and organizing the yardstick competition among them? How can the tax and welfare system be improved to reach best standards and practices among innovating countries, and, in particular, reconcile the need for redistribution and the need to finance good public infrastructure and services with innovation incentives?

CONCLUSION

In this chapter, we have taken on board modern trade economics, and, in particular, the idea that a country's competitiveness boils down to the competitiveness of its individual enterprises. We reported on recent empirical work showing that firm-level competitiveness is related to the productivity of firms and their ability to grow. We then looked at determinants of firm-level productivity and at potential obstacles that may inhibit growth in the size of firms. Finally, we have argued that while enhancing firm-level productivity growth calls first for horizontal policies (product and labor market liberalization, trade liberalization, higher education investments, and so on), there may be a case for vertically targeted (sectoral) policies provided these are properly designed and governed.

To conclude the discussion, we address the delicate issue of macroeconomic policy. Recent studies (Aghion, Hemous, and Kharroubi 2009 and Aghion, Farhi, and Kharroubi 2012) at the cross-country and cross-industry level show that more countercyclical fiscal and monetary policies enhance growth. Fiscal policy countercyclicality refers to countries increasing their public deficits and debt in recessions but reducing them in upturns. Monetary policy countercyclicality refers to central banks letting real short-term interest rates go down in recessions, and having them increase during upturns. Such policies can help credit-constrained or liquidity-constrained firms pursue innovative investments (R&D, skills and training, and so on) over the cycle despite credit tightening during recessions. It also helps maintain aggregate consumption and therefore the market size of firms over the cycle, as argued earlier (Aghion and Howitt 2009, Chapter 13). This in turn suggests that an innovation-based economy would benefit from more countercyclical macroeconomic policies, with higher deficits and lower real interest rates in recessions, and lower deficits and higher real interest rates in booms, to help credit-constrained innovative firms maintain their R&D and other types of growth-enhancing investments over the business cycle.

REFERENCES

Acemoglu, D., P. Aghion, L. Bursztyn, and D. Hemous. 2012. "The Environment and Directed Technical Change." *American Economic Review* 102 (1): 131–66.

Acemoglu, D., N. U. Akcigit, N. Bloom, and W. Kerr. (2013). "Innovation, Reallocation, and Growth." NBER Working Paper 18993, National Bureau of Economic Research, Cambridge, Massachusetts.

Aghion, P., and P. Howitt. 1992. "A Model of Growth through Creative Destruction." *Econometrica* 60: 323–51.

———. 2006. "Appropriate Growth Policy." *Journal of the European Economic Association* 4: 269–314.

———. 2009. *The Economics of Growth*. Cambridge, Massachusetts: MIT Press.

Aghion, P., U. Akcigit, and P. Howitt. 2013. "What Do We Learn From Schumpeterian Growth Theory?" Working Paper, Harvard University, Cambridge, Massachusetts.

Aghion, P., P. Askenazy, R. Bourles, G. Cette, and N. Dromel. 2009. "Education, Market Rigidities and Growth." *Economics Letters* 102 (1): 62–65.

Aghion, P., N. Bloom, R. Blundell, R. Griffith, and P. Howitt. 2005. "Competition and Innovation: An Inverted-U Relationship." *Quarterly Journal of Economics* 120: 701–28.

Aghion, P., R. Blundell, R. Griffith, P. Howitt, and S. Prantl. 2009. "The Effects of Entry on Incumbent Innovation and Productivity." *Review of Economics and Statistics* 91 (1): 20–32.

Aghion, P., L. Boustan, Hoxby, C., and J. Vandenbussche. 2009. "Exploiting States' Mistakes to Identify the Causal Effects of Higher Education on Growth." Unpublished, Harvard University, Cambridge, Massachusetts.

Aghion, P., A. Dechezlepretre, D. Hemous, R. Martin, and J. Van Reenen. 2013. "Carbon Taxes, Path Dependence and Directed Technical Change: Evidence from the Auto Industry." Unpublished, Harvard University, Cambridge, Massachusetts.

Aghion, P., M. Dewatripont, C. Hoxby, A. Mas-Colell, and A. Sapir. 2010. "The Governance and Performance of Universities: Evidence from Europe and the US." *Economic Policy* 25: 7–59.

Aghion, P., M. Dewatripont, L. Du, A. Harrison, and P. Legros. 2012. "Industrial Policy and Competition." Unpublished, Harvard University, Cambridge, Massachusetts.

Aghion, P., T. Fally, and S. Scarpetta. 2007. "Credit Constraints as a Barrier to the Entry and Post-Entry Growth of Firms." *Economic Policy* 22: 731–79.

Aghion, P., E. Farhi, and E. Kharroubi. 2012. "Monetary Policy, Liquidity and Growth." Unpublished, Harvard University, Cambridge, Massachusetts.

Aghion, P., D. Hemous, and E. Kharroubi. 2009. "Cyclical Fiscal Policy, Credit Constraints, and Industry Growth." *Journal of Monetary Economics* 62 (C): 41–58.

Akcigit, U., K. Alp, and M. Peters. 2014. "Lack of Selection and Imperfect Managerial Contracts: Firm Dynamics in Developing Countries." Unpublished, University of Pennsylvania, Philadelphia.

Bartelsman, E., J. Haltiwanger, and S. Scarpetta. 2004. "Microeconomic Evidence of Creative Destruction in Industrial and Developing Countries." IZA Discussion Papers 1374, Institute for the Study of Labor (IZA), Bonn, Germany.

Beck, T., A. Demirgüç-Kunt, L. Laeven, and R. Levine. 2008. "Finance, Firm Size, and Growth." *Journal of Money, Credit and Banking* 40 (7): 1379–1405.

Beck, T., A. Demirgüç-Kunt, and V. Maksimovic. 2005. "Financial and Legal Constraints to Firm Growth: Does Firm Size Matter?" *Journal of Finance* 60: 137–77.

Bloom, D., and J. Van Reenen. 2010. "Why Do Management Practices Differ Across Firms and Countries?" *Journal of Economic Perspectives* 24: 203–24.

Cable, Vince. 2010. "Vince Cable Speech." Speech at the Cass Business School, June 3, 2010. https://www.gov.uk/government/news/vince-cable-speech-cass-business-school-june-3-2010.

Cette, G., and J. Lopez. 2012. "ICT Demand Behavior: An International Comparison." *Economics of Innovation and New Technology* 21: 397–410.

Cette, G., J. Lopez, and J. Mairesse. 2013. "Upstream Product Market Regulations, ICT, R&D and Productivity." NBER Working Paper 19488, National Bureau of Economic Research, Cambridge, Massachusetts.

Frankel, J., and D. Romer. 1999. "Does Trade Cause Growth?" *American Economic Review* 89 (3): 379–99.

Garicano, L., Lelarge, C., and J. Van Reenen. 2013. "Firm Size Distortion and the Productivity Distribution: Evidence from France." NBER Working Paper 18841, National Bureau of Economic Research, Cambridge, Massachusetts.

Helpman, E. 2004. *The Mystery of Economic Growth*. Cambridge, Massachusetts: Belknap Press.

Hsieh, C.-T., and P. Klenow. 2009. "Misallocation and Manufacturing TFP in China and India." *Quarterly Journal of Economics* 124 (2): 771–807.

Klette, T., and S. Kortum. 2004. "Innovating Firms and Aggregate Innovation." *Journal of Political Economy* 112 (5): 986–1018.

Koch, W. 2014. "Bank-Based Versus Market-Based Finance as Appropriate Institution." Working Paper, Université du Québec à Montréal, Montreal, Canada.

Nunn, N., and D. Trefler. 2010. "The Structure of Tariffs and Long-Term Growth." *American Economic Journal: Macroeconomics* 2 (4): 158–94.

Rajan, R., and L. Zingales. 1998. "Financial Dependence and Growth." *American Economic Review* 88 (3): 559–86.

Solow, R. 1956. "A Contribution to the Theory of Economic Growth." *Quarterly Journal of Economics* 70 (1): 65–94.

Wacziarg, R. 2001. "Measuring the Dynamic Gains from Trade." *World Bank Economic Review*, 15 (3): 393–429.

CHAPTER 8

Diversification and the Economy: The Role of Government in Enhancing the Industrial Base

BILL FRANCIS, IFTEKHAR HASAN, AND YUN ZHU

An individual economy develops and evolves along various paths. How different paths lead to a variation in economic prosperity and stability has always been a matter of curiosity to economists and policymakers. In this chapter, we look at how industry-level sectoral diversification affects economic growth and other measures of economic output, and how policymakers could help deepen industrial diversification.

We investigate a matrix of the economic outcomes that are normally overlooked or overshadowed by the pure size or the growth of an economy. Specifically, we look at poverty alleviation, technological innovation, flow of foreign capital, empowerment of women, and entrepreneurship. In general, we find that industrial diversification greatly improves economic output for *all* of these nonconventional measures.

Given the empirical evidence that industrial diversification leads to stable and healthy growth, we discuss a number of cases in which governments have initiated and supported small business development through direct and indirect capital supply, tax incentives, equity guarantees, and so on. We emphasize the strategic importance of government initiatives in the enhancement of sectoral diversification, without which the economy may take much longer and more social resources to deliver a similar outcome.

For policymakers, this chapter sends a strong message that the effort spent in supporting and enhancing industry sectors, which countries fall short on, will result in more stable and balanced long-term economic growth.

DIVERSIFICATION, RISK, AND GROWTH

Any problem or debate on economic development starts with the measurement of GDP, which tracks annual growth, and by which the size of an economy can be compared across countries. However, policymakers and economists care more about the risk to growth and path of future development. As Lucas (1998) states, for advanced countries "growth rates tend to be very stable over long periods of time," while for poorer countries "there are many examples of sudden, large changes in growth rates, both up and down." Empirically, Ramey and

Ramey (1995) find a negative correlation between variability of growth rates and average growth for Organisation for Economic Co-operation and Development (OECD) countries. Quah (1993) finds that for higher-income countries, the probability of falling to low-income status is small, consistent with the general observation that highly developed economies experience lower volatility, and less-developed economies the opposite.

Industrial diversification has been shown to be a necessary path for development. It reduces idiosyncratic shocks from individual sectors, and enhances capital accumulation, capital allocation, and technology improvement. In the beginning of the development process, industrial concentration may support GDP growth. But it does not guarantee a stable growth pattern, and is vulnerable to long-term macroeconomic shocks (Koren and Tenreyro 2013). Thus, higher variance of GDP resulting from sectoral concentration may entail a welfare loss that outweighs the benefits (Kalemli-Ozcan, Sørensen, and Yosha 2003). Macroeconomic fluctuations also result from shocks at the micro level. The growth of the financial industry, for example, contributed to the surge of macroeconomic volatility in the past decades (Carvalho and Gabaix 2013).

Reducing variability through diversification is achieved by technology improvement and capital supply. At the early stage of development, technology advancement can be considerably limited by education level and the scarcity of necessary resources. It is only at a certain stage of economic development that capital can be reallocated into education, research and development, and government-sponsored technology-driven projects that would accelerate growth and expand traditional industrial sectors into new areas. It is crucial that this step be carried out. If left to the private sector, an economy has a higher chance of falling into the trap of idiosyncratic risk shocks.

Capital supply is the second driving force. At early stages, lack of capital makes countries exploit their natural resource endowments and invest in safe but less productive projects. The limited opportunity for diversification makes the earlier stages of development highly random and subject to abrupt shocks in growth rates. Therefore, a typical development pattern will consist of a lengthy period of "primitive accumulation" with highly variable output, followed by takeoff and financial deepening, and, finally, steady growth. "Lucky" countries will spend less time in the primitive accumulation stage and develop faster (Acemoglu and Zilibotti 1997).

Diversification is a key step in development. It reduces volatility and transforms a simple economy, focused on a few industries, into a diversified and comprehensive economy with stable future growth. Technology and capital supply (including the development of the finance sector) are the two major factors that determine whether and how quickly a simple economy can evolve into developed status.

INDUSTRIAL DEVELOPMENT AND THE ECONOMY

To provide an intuitive image of industrial development, we begin with a simple observation of the diversification patterns, and discuss a few important measures that capture various aspects of the development of an economy.

Diversification Patterns around the World

Figure 8.1 shows a plot of the time series diversification pattern of the United States, OECD countries, Gulf Cooperation Council (GCC) countries, and Middle East and North Africa countries.[1] We use the Herfindahl-Hirschman index (HHI) of sectoral output as a common measure of diversification.[2] We use industry and sectoral output data from the United Nations Industrial Development Organization, which has the most comprehensive coverage of the industrial output of 23 two-digit industrial sectors (127 in four-digit sectors) for 166 economies from 1963 onward.

Figure 8.1 shows that the United States and OECD countries had the highest and most stable diversification patterns in the past 50 years. The United States has the lowest concentration in our sample, with HHI of industrial concentration

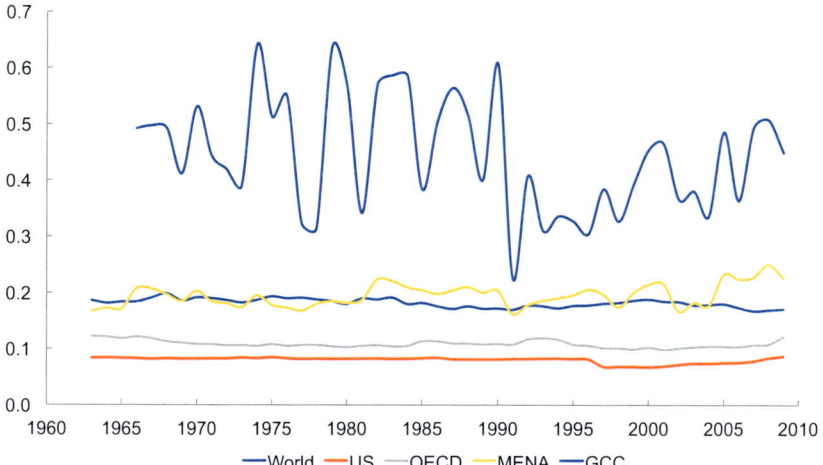

Figure 8.1 Global Diversification Model

Source: United Nations Industrial Development Organization.
Note: The Herfindahl-Hirschman index ranges between zero and one, with a larger number indicating higher concentration or less diversification. GCC = Gulf Cooperation Council; MENA = Middle East and North Africa; OECD = Organisation for Economic Co-operation and Development; US = United States.

---

[1] OECD includes Australia, Austria, Belgium, Canada, Chile, Czech Republic, Denmark, Estonia, Finland, France, Germany, Greece, Hungary, Iceland, Ireland, Israel, Italy, Japan, Korea, Luxembourg, Mexico, Netherlands, New Zealand, Norway, Poland, Portugal, Slovak Republic, Slovenia, Spain, Sweden, Switzerland, Turkey, United Kingdom, and United States; GCC includes Bahrain, Kuwait, Oman, Qatar, Saudi Arabia, and United Arab Emirates; Middle East and North Africa includes Algeria, Bahrain, Egypt, Iran, Iraq, Israel, Jordan, Kuwait, Lebanon, Yemen, United Arab Emirates, Libya, Morocco, Oman, Palestine, Qatar, Saudi Arabia, Syria, and Tunisia. The list varies over time as countries joined at various times.

[2] Specifically, in each country (or region) and each year, we first calculate the share of each industrial sector by dividing the sectoral output with the overall output of the economy. The HHI is then calculated by the sum of the squares of the shares of each industrial sector. The HHI ranges between zero and one, with a larger number indicating higher concentration or less diversification.

below 0.1. The HHI for OECD countries was just above 0.1 in 1963 and declined until the global financial crisis.

Middle East and North Africa countries experienced some fluctuations in their industrial concentration, partly coming from the GCC countries. The Middle East and North Africa countries together had an HHI of about 0.2, indicating reasonable diversification for developing or natural-resource-dependent entities. We also observed a slight increase in HHI since the early 2000s, partly due to the politics-induced change in economic environment post-2001 and partly due to the global financial crisis.

GCC countries have very low diversification and higher volatility. Their average HHI ranged from 0.4 to 0.5 over the past 50 years. Because of the limited number of industrial sectors and oil price volatility, the GCC experienced greater output volatility. Among all the countries in our sample, these have the lowest diversification.

For further insight into the industrial sectors in GCC countries, we plot the industrial output share of the top five industries of GCC countries in 2010. The results are shown in Figure 8.2. The sector coke, refined petroleum products, and nuclear industry dominates, with 73 percent of GCC industrial output. As shown in Figure 8.3, no single industry has a dominant share of worldwide industrial output, with the coke, refined petroleum products, and nuclear industry sector having an 8 percent share. This shows that a single-industry-dominated economy inevitably faces greater risk and external shocks.

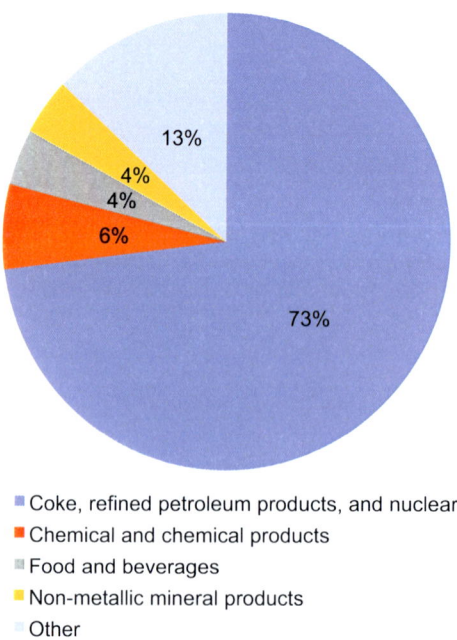

Figure 8.2 Shares of Top Industries in Total Output in GCC, 2010

Source: United Nations Industrial Development Organization.
Note: Percentages of industry output are in relation to total economic output. GCC = Gulf Cooperation Council.

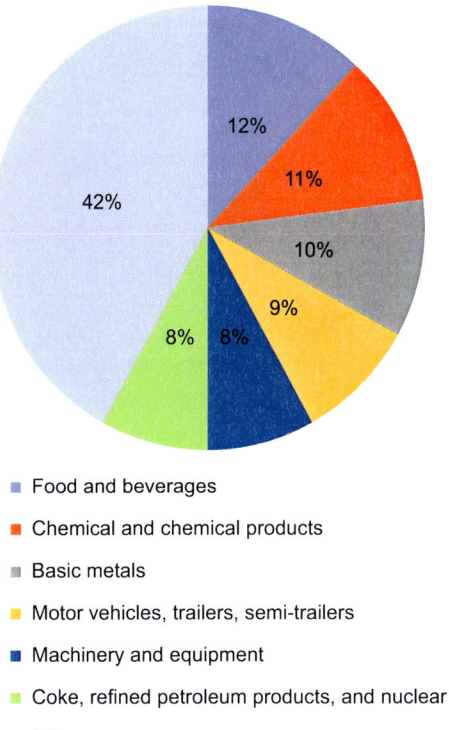

- Food and beverages
- Chemical and chemical products
- Basic metals
- Motor vehicles, trailers, semi-trailers
- Machinery and equipment
- Coke, refined petroleum products, and nuclear
- Other

Figure 8.3   Shares of Top Industries in Total Output Worldwide, 2010

Source: United Nations Industrial Development Organization.

Note: Percentages of industry output are in relation to total economic output. This figure also includes a segment for coke, refined petroleum products, and the nuclear industry.

The Effect of Diversification

Here, we study the impact of diversification on economic outcomes beyond GDP. We specifically explore income dispersion, technological innovation, the net flow of foreign capital, the empowerment of women, and entrepreneurship. We consider all of these as the key outcomes of a healthy economy.

Data

We use the industry and sectoral output data from the United Nations Industrial Development Organization to calculate diversification.[3] We collect country-level characteristics from the World Bank's World Development Indicators, and innovation information (patents) from EPO Worldwide Patent Statistical Database. The main variables of interests corresponding to the above economic outcomes are:

- The Gini index and income share held by the lowest 10 percent of earners, to capture income dispersion.

---

[3] We mainly use the output from the two-digit industry sectors, since a large number of countries do not have comprehensive information on four-digit industrial sectors.

- Patents (log), representing the country-level innovation output.
- Foreign direct investment (net, percent of total output) that proxies for the capital flow between a country and the rest of the world.
- The female-to-male employment ratio, which is used as an economic proxy for women's empowerment.
- New business registrations, a proxy for the entrepreneurial environment.

Figure 8.4 shows the time-series distribution of these variables. OECD countries have a lower level of income dispersion, more innovation output, a better environment for international capital flows, lower gender inequality, and a better environment for entrepreneurs. We also observe the improvement in almost all of the variables in the non-OECD countries.

Measurement of Industrial Diversification

To fully gauge a country's industrial diversification, we employ a number of measures for the concentration of output across industrial sectors: (1) the

Figure 8.4 Time-Series Distribution of Key Variables of Interest

Sources: EPO Worldwide Patent Statistical Database; and World Bank, World Development Indicators.

Note: OECD = Organisation for Economic Co-operation and Development.

HHI for sectoral output over a year, calculated as the sum of the squares of the shares of each industrial sector; (2) the maximum-minimum spread, calculated as the spread between the largest and smallest industrial sector shares; (3) the mean-median spread, calculated as the spread between the mean and median value of the industrial sector shares; and (4) the log-variance of sector shares, calculated as the log of variance of all the industrial sector shares.

Empirical Findings

The main results of the effects of diversification on various economic outcomes are presented in Table 8.1. We use ordinary least squares regressions, controlling for country characteristics such as GDP per capita, inflation rate, interest rate, and population (log), as well as year and country fixed effects. The main independent variables are four measures of industrial diversification; namely, the HHI for the sectoral output, the maximum-minimum spread, the mean-median spread, and the log-variance of sector shares. For simplicity, we suppress the control variables in the table.

The results are, in general, consistent with our main argument that diversification advances social welfare. The statistical significance varies among different measurements of diversification. Specifically, industrial diversification alleviates poverty by reducing income dispersion and increasing the income of the bottom 10 percent of a population.[4]

We also find that diversification improves country-level innovation (annual filings of patents). It has some positive but a generally weak effect on cross-border capital flow. Foreign direct investment can be affected by factors other than industrial diversification, but our results provide some evidence that with more industries—and more evenly distributed industrial pattern—an economy is able to attract more capital inflows.

The World Bank's World Development Indicators Database does not provide comprehensive coverage on the employment ratio of women in many countries. However, even within well-developed economies where the social status of women is relatively high, we still observe the positive influence of industrial diversification on women's empowerment. The new business registration improves with industrial diversification. As diversification promotes services sectors, more opportunities for small business are created.

Industrial diversification enhances economic and social welfare in multiple dimensions, and, in the next section, we discuss how government should facilitate diversification.

---

[4] The results may be driven by the natural gap between developed and developing countries, because more developed economies, mostly under democratic systems, had lower income dispersion throughout the sample period. However, the inclusion of fixed effects should mitigate this problem.

TABLE 8.1

Empirical Results of a Study of the Effects of Diversification on Select Economic Outcomes

Variables	Gini Index				Income Share Held by Lowest 10 Percent				Patent Number (Log)			
HHI	59.960*** (16.428)				-6.072*** (1.556)				-4.200 (2.646)			
Maximum-minimum spread		45.113*** (9.317)				-5.239*** (0.962)				-3.488** (1.556)		
Mean-median spread			301.383*** (79.153)				-21.048*** (7.783)				-42.400*** (10.570)	
Log variance				234.323*** (37.658)				-19.964*** (5.065)				-19.182*** (6.027)
Control	Yes	Yes	Yes	Yes	Yes	Yes	Yes	Yes	Yes	Yes	Yes	Yes
Country fixed effect	Yes	Yes	Yes	Yes	Yes	Yes	Yes	Yes	Yes	Yes	Yes	Yes
Constant	-22.551 (19.037)	-34.156* (18.504)	1.732 (17.795)	-41.802** (18.334)	9.179*** (2.091)	11.339*** (2.029)	5.598*** (1.967)	9.943*** (2.261)	-20.655*** (2.107)	-19.163*** (2.209)	-20.223*** (1.742)	-18.466*** (2.088)
Number of observations	496	496	496	496	525	525	525	525	2.254	2.249	2.249	2.249
Adjusted R^2	0.120	0.173	0.082	0.200	0.135	0.210	0.060	0.169	0.703	0.707	0.717	0.714

Variables	FDI (Net, % of Total Output)				Female-to-Male Employment Ratio				New Business Registration			
HHI	3.877 (2.440)				-0.187* (0.109)				-1.595** (0.655)			
Maximum-minimum spread		2.369 (1.675)				-0.103 (0.075)				-1.073** (0.484)		
Mean-median spread			19.407** (9.615)				-0.664* (0.336)				1.515 (3.560)	
Log variance				14.030* (7.179)				-0.486* (0.264)				-2.522 (2.439)
Control	Yes	Yes	Yes	Yes	Yes	Yes	Yes	Yes	Yes	Yes	Yes	Yes
Country fixed effect	Yes	Yes	Yes	Yes	Yes	Yes	Yes	Yes	Yes	Yes	Yes	Yes
Constant	10.832 (12.354)	13.022 (13.854)	1.853 (8.505)	10.756 (11.596)	-1.912 (1.169)	-1.855 (1.185)	-1.902 (1.155)	-1.869 (1.159)	-30.836** (11.994)	-31.241** (11.903)	-27.027** (12.421)	-29.036** (12.297)
Number of observations	443	443	443	443	1,145	1,145	1,145	1,145	425	425	425	425
Adjusted R^2	0.371	0.368	0.395	0.384	0.546	0.545	0.545	0.546	0.982	0.982	0.982	0.982

Note: FDI = foreign direct investment; HHI = Herfindahl-Hirschman index. Standard deviations are in parentheses.
* $p < .05$, ** $p < .01$, *** $p < .001$.

DIVERSIFICATION AND THE ROLE OF THE GOVERNMENT

Advantages of Government Support

Without going into the debate over whether a small or large government is better for economic development, government can take roles to subsidize education and research and development, and to provide venture capital with fiscal and regulatory frameworks. Governments in OECD countries have decades of experience in implementing direct programs to mobilize venture capital in support of small and technology-based firms and to produce public benefits through innovation and job creation. Government involvement aims to remedy deficiencies in private capital markets, to leverage private sector financing, and to reduce aggregate risk by diversifying the economy.

Evidence is ample that government involvement can provide greater social rates of return than the private sector. Various schemes can bring public benefits by targeting small firms with good job creation potential, or firms that can develop technologies important to long-term growth.

The government can fill funding gaps that prevent viable small businesses from obtaining funding on reasonable terms. Access to traditional venture capitalists is not available for many small firms, even in the United States and other OECD countries, where financial systems are highly developed (let alone in countries with lower levels of investor protection and capital liquidity).

By providing a small amount of financial support, governments can certify firms and reduce information asymmetry—and they do not have to completely close the funding gap. The certification effect involves bringing in other financial institutions, such as venture capitalists, private equity firms, banks, and so on. In many OECD countries, governments usually provide a small portion of seed funding, and, in doing so, greatly enhance the chance that funded firms will enjoy long-term growth.

Sponsoring nascent industries and technology helps diversify industrial sectors and further reduce aggregate shocks. And this is consistent with the chapter's argument that promoting new industries and supporting new technologies can be more effective with the help of government.

Governments therefore *can* and *should* play a pivotal role in industrial diversification. The next section looks at how this is done in OECD countries.

Financial Support for Industry Diversification in OECD Countries

There are two major types of support (shown in Table 8.2): to directly supply funding and to provide financial incentives, such as tax benefits, loans, and equity guarantees.

A number of governments choose tax incentives, particularly investor tax credits, to stimulate particular types of investment. Incentives may be available for investments made directly in qualifying small companies or for investments made

TABLE 8.2

Types of Financial Support in OECD Countries

Type	Purpose	Example
Direct Supply of Capital		
Research funding	Provide research and development funding for small-sized firms	United States: Small Business Innovation Research
Government equity investment	Make direct investments in venture capital firms or small firms	Belgium: Investment Company for Flanders
Government loans	Make low-interest, long-term and/or nonrefundable loans to venture capital firms or small firms	Denmark: VækstFonden (Business Development Finance) loan program
Financial Incentives		
Tax incentives	Provide tax incentives, particularly tax credits, for investing in small firms or venture capital funds	United Kingdom: Enterprise Investment Scheme and Venture Capital Trusts
Loan guarantees	Guarantee a proportion of bank loans to qualified small businesses	France: Société Française de Garantie des Financements des Petites et Moyennes Entreprises
Equity guarantees	Guarantee a proportion of the losses of high-risk venture capital investments	Finland: Finnish Guarantee Board

Source: Organisation for Economic Co-operation and Development (OECD).

in qualified pooled vehicles. An important decision in program design is whether the tax incentive should be given at the front or back end, which is tied to any capital gains realized at exit. The first approach rewards all investors, whereas the second rewards only winners.

Another difference between the two approaches is that front-end incentives may cause behavior motivated primarily by tax-shelter considerations. For example, Canada gives tax incentives to hybrid public and private funds as so-called Labor-Sponsored Venture Capital Corporations (LSVCCs), whose asset growth was particularly high in the 1990s. At the end of 1995, LSVCCs represented 49 percent of Canada's $6 billion of venture capital assets. In that year, hybrid funds raised $1.2 billion, whereas private funds raised only $0.3 billion. LSVCCs invest in Canadian small and medium-sized enterprises, and investments dedicated to early-stage deals, which represented 34 percent of their 1995 investments. The attraction of LSVCCs is that an investor receives a federal tax credit of 15 percent on up to $3,500 of an investment held for five years. In addition to the federal credit, investors in Ontario and Quebec, which account for the bulk of LSVCC funds, receive a 15 percent tax credit on these investments.

Most OECD countries offer some form of government-backed guarantee covering loans to small firms. Typically under these programs, the government guarantees a percentage of a qualified loan made by a financial institution. In the event of default, the loss incurred by the lender is only for the amount of the loan not covered by the guarantee. The aim of these programs is to encourage financial

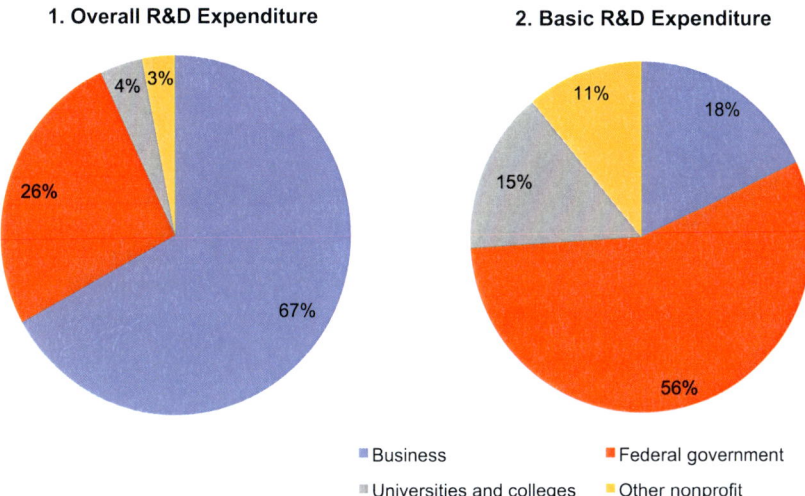

Figure 8.5 Financing Sources of Research and Development (R&D) in the United States, 2008
Source: National Science Foundation.

institutions, particularly commercial banks, to fund small firms that have viable projects but cannot meet collateral requirements.

The United States has strong support for research and development (R&D), especially for basic R&D (Figure 8.5). A major outlet of R&D funding is through financial support for small business.

Since 1953, the U.S. Small Business Administration (SBA) has run the 7(a) Guaranteed Business Loan Program that guarantees long-term loans to start-up and high-potential companies. These loans are then guaranteed by the SBA for up to 75 percent of the amount provided by the commercial lender. Interest rates are negotiated between the borrower and the lending bank. The maximum amount currently guaranteed by the SBA is $500,000. Between 1980 and 1991, the SBA guaranteed $31 billion in loans through the 7(a) program. Its default rate was 17 percent on loans guaranteed in 1995/96, and this varied over the life of the program; in 1983/84 it was 25 percent, but declined to 9.5 percent in 1992/93.

The Small Business Innovation Research (SBIR) Program was set up to promote the technological innovation in small-sized firms in the United States. The program has provided 20–25 percent of total funding for early-stage technology firms. In 2010 more than $1 billion in research funds were granted; over half the awards were given to firms with fewer than 25 people and a third to firms with fewer than 10. A fifth of these firms were minority or women-owned businesses. A quarter of these firms in 2009/10 were first-time recipients. Some of America's most dynamic companies have received support through federal programs, including Apple Computer, Compaq, FedEx, and Intel. In addition to funding firms, publicly sponsored funds provided early experience for many individuals who went on to lead independent venture organizations.

Empirically, Lerner (1999) shows that SBIR recipients enjoy substantially greater employment and sales growth, and were more likely to go on to receive private venture capital financing. The superior performance was confined to firms in regions with substantial venture capital activity, and was pronounced in high-technology industries.

Similar programs have been initiated in other OECD countries. For example, Germany's government equity investment program "Beteiligungskapital für junge Technologieunternehmen" (BJTU) reduced the failure rate of companies that it financed to 17 percent. The Netherlands' Technical Development Credits Scheme provides subordinated 10-year loans to firms for the development of new products, services, or processes. Here, repayment is based on firms' revenues and, in the event of technical or commercial failure, the loan is forgiven. The United Kingdom's Loan Guarantee Scheme has a repayment schedule of between 2 and 10 years. Companies less than two years old are eligible for a 70 percent guarantee on loans up to £100,000; older companies are eligible for an 85 percent guarantee on loans up to £250,000.

CONCLUSION

Economic development is not merely a matter of real GDP growth. It trickles down to other important aspects of society, such as inequality, innovation, and the empowerment of women. In this chapter, we demonstrate that industrial diversification is one of the most important economic variables.

By bringing supporting empirical evidence, we show that industrial diversification is correlated with poverty alleviation, technological innovation, the empowerment of women, capital supply, and entrepreneurship. All these are the common factors that we nowadays use to evaluate the prosperity of an economy and the health of a society.

Together with the empirical evidence, we review a number of practices in OECD countries in which government is involved in small business development through direct and indirect capital supply, tax incentives, equity guarantees, and so on. We argue that the strategic financing support of government is crucial for promoting small business and diversifying industrial sectors. Without this support, it may take much longer and more social resources to deliver a similar outcome, with a high possibility of falling into a slow and volatile growth pattern.

REFERENCES

Acemoglu, D., and F. Zilibotti. 1997. "Was Prometheus Unbound by Chance? Risk, Diversification, and Growth." *Journal of Political Economy* 105 (4): 709–51.

Carvalho, V., and X. Gabaix. 2013. "The Great Diversification and Its Undoing." *American Economic Review* 103 (5): 1697–1727.

Kalemli-Ozcan, S., B. E. Sørensen, and O. Yosha. 2003. "Risk Sharing and Industrial Specialization: Regional and International Evidence." *American Economic Review* 93 (3): 903–18.

Koren, M., and S. Tenreyro. 2013. "Technological Diversification." *American Economic Review* 103 (1): 378–414.

Lerner, J. 1999. "The Government as Venture Capitalist: The Long-Run Impact of the SBIR Program." *Journal of Business* 72 (3): 285–318.

Lucas, R. E. 1998. "On the Mechanics of Economic Development." *Journal of Monetary Economics* 29: 61–70.

Quah, D. 1993. "Empirical Cross-Section Dynamics in Economic Growth." *European Economic Review* 37 (2): 426–34.

Ramey, G., and V. A. Ramey. 1995. "Cross-Country Evidence on the Link between Volatility and Growth." *American Economic Review* 85 (5): 1138–51.

CHAPTER 9

A Practitioner's Narrative of Brazil's Industrialization and the Role of the Brazilian Development Bank

JULIO RAMUNDO

Development, as economists say, is path dependent. That is, it is based on the context of individual countries and is historically determined. This chapter adopts a very pragmatic approach to this issue—from the viewpoint of a practitioner—and takes a bird's eye view of Brazil's industrialization before focusing on the role the Brazilian Development Bank (Banco Nacional de Desenvolvimento Econômico e Social) has played in the country's growth since the 1950s.

The chapter reviews the successes and failures of the country's past industrial policies, as well as new industrial policies in the 2000s focused on innovation and competitiveness. It then discuss the policies and instruments the Brazilian Development Bank has implemented as a development-oriented venture capitalist.

BRAZIL'S INDUSTRIALIZATION AND NEW INDUSTRIAL POLICY

Industrialization during 1950–2000

The Brazilian Development Bank has played an important role in Brazil's substantial economic structural transformation and diversification. Founded as a joint effort between the American and the Brazilian governments in the early 1950s to industrialize and transform the country, the development bank has ingrained into its operations the idea of structural change. Development is also a process of structural change, and this is what Brazil has witnessed. A more dynamic economy has emerged, as the country has risen from lower-productivity to higher-productivity activities with linkages within and outside product value chains.

More important, structural change has created domestic competencies. National institutions are being built and firms are focusing on innovation. At the same time, in recent years, the emphasis has shifted toward an inclusive and environmentally sustainable development path.

In the past, Brazilian policymakers did not attach much importance to innovation, and had they read Schumpeter[1] when they were implementing the first stage of industrial policy, the country could have set the stage earlier for innovation-driven growth.

That said, even though a military regime controlled the country during the 1950s, consistent and convergent policies provided a favorable environment for implementing industrial policy. Supportive macroeconomic policies, a high level of coordination, and an intense use of classic instruments such as tariff protection, financial support through the Brazilian Development Bank, and fiscal incentives helped the transformation process. State-owned enterprises were deployed to overcome coordination problems common in the implementation of development strategies.

Industrial policy helped transform the country from what was a huge plantation into an industrialized country; without this change in the 1950s to 1970s, Brazil would probably have remained primarily an agricultural economy. Instead, with its high growth, it was the China of the time. High productivity growth fueled industry, the seeds of a national science and technology system were sown, and most of the current economic structure and institutions were founded.

Manufacturing increased steadily, reaching more than 20 percent of GDP (in constant prices) by the late 1980s from about 10 percent in the early 1950s (Figure 9.1). New sectors, such as petrochemicals, pulp and paper, and capital

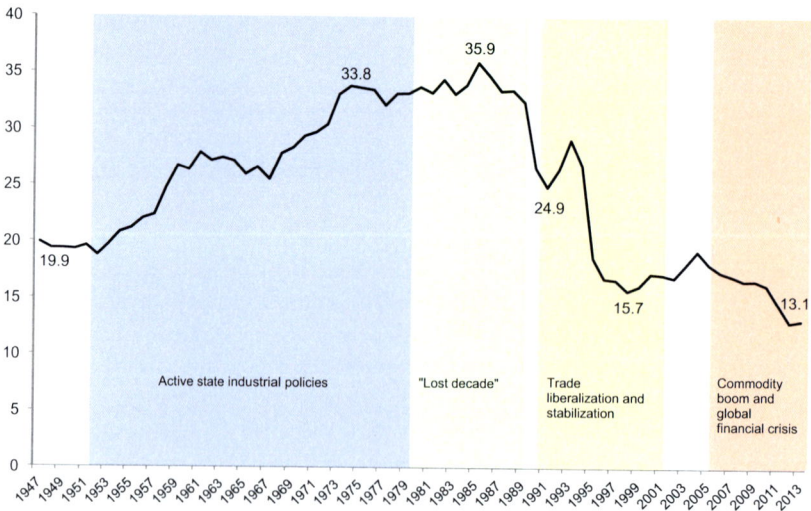

Figure 9.1 Manufacturing Share of GDP (Percent)
Source: Brazilian Institute of Geography and Statistics (data obtained from IPEADATA).

---

[1] Joseph Schumpeter, an early twentieth-century Austrian-American economist, emphasized the importance of innovation and entrepreneurship and the process of "creative destruction" in sustaining economic growth. Also see Chapter 7 for more details.

goods, were established. Exports of agricultural commodities, such as soybeans, were developed substantially after considerable technological advancement from Empresa Brasileira de Pesquisa Agropecuária, a government agency devoted to agricultural research. Mineral commodities were developed, driven by another state-owned enterprise established in the 1940s, which received considerable support during the industrialization period. In the pulp and paper sector, the state supported the building of competencies, while in high-technology sectors, such as aircraft making, state-owned Embraer Air beat all odds to carve out a global niche.

But Brazil was less successful at spurring innovation and technology development. Other dynamic industries that emerged in the 1960s–1970s, such as computers, failed to take off. The country was also ineffective in regulating existing sectors such as textiles and the automotive sector, and nonselective trade protection of these areas was used for far too long. In contrast to Asian countries, the country did not push export promotion much and gave little importance to education-oriented policies.

From the late 1980s until recently, macroeconomic policies and the reform of the state took center stage in the debate, with no industrial policy as such during this time, despite some stop and go in that area. The focus was instead on reforming the country's state governments, including through privatization, a fiscal responsibility law, deregulation, and so on. From the 1990s until the early 2000s, economic stabilization was on the agenda in the form of the *Realo Plano.*[2]

But industrial policy made a comeback from the early 2000s, in three different waves, with the common elements of innovation and competitiveness. Innovation was especially important as the private sector had invested too little in research and development (R&D) and was inward looking, an approach that was in place from past development strategies.

The three waves were designed and implemented within the context of the time, each with its specific sectoral concentrations. The first wave, the Industrial, Technology, and Trade Policy (2004–07), was launched at the time of trade balance constraints, with the aim to reduce the trade deficit and spur technology-based innovation. It focused on sectors such as software, semiconductors, pharmaceuticals, and capital goods.

The second wave, the Productive Development Policy (2008–10), started during the commodities boom, a strong domestic market, and income redistribution policies to innovate and invest for sustainable growth. The sectoral concentration policy focused on strategic areas, strengthening competitiveness, and promoting national champions.

Finally, the *Brasil Maior* Plan (2011–14) was initiated after the global financial crisis in an environment of slow growth and loose monetary policies to innovate, compete, and add value. It had a sectoral focus on innovation diffusion, agro-business, and services, and was scale- and labor-intensive.

---

[2] The "Real Plan" was instituted to fight inflation, and one of the basic features was the introduction of a new currency, the *real*, that was allowed to float against the U.S. dollar.

Shifting Economic Landscape and the Focus on Innovation

Since the early 2000s income distribution in Brazil has undergone a major shift. More than 30 million people were lifted from the poor class to low-middle-income class, significantly transforming the domestic market. Yet, as the economy has developed, infrastructure bottlenecks have become apparent, with the last major investments seen in the 1970s. Naturally, a large pipeline of investments is directed toward infrastructure and industry. In this, however, the focus on innovation and competiveness cannot be cast aside.

Brazil has also done well in commodities and minerals, part of an evolution of trade that underpins the economy. Yet the dynamism of its export basket and innovative industries has substantially lagged behind other emerging markets, despite the importance of manufacturing in exports such as aircraft making. And even in traditional, labor-intensive industries, the country has been losing competitive ground. At the same time, its exchange rate has appreciated compared with other countries such as Korea and Mexico over 1994–2014, constraining the types of initiatives and projects it can pursue to remedy the problems.

As noted, innovation is crucial for Brazil's development strategy. But the country has not done well in this area, in keeping with the record of other Latin American countries. More important, many firms report innovation primarily through acquisition of machinery, which is different from implementing R&D activities. The reported innovation is in fact imported machinery, and Brazil lags behind other countries on private R&D, both as a share of GDP and in the growth rate of expenditures (shown in Figures 9.2 and 9.3 and Table 9.1).

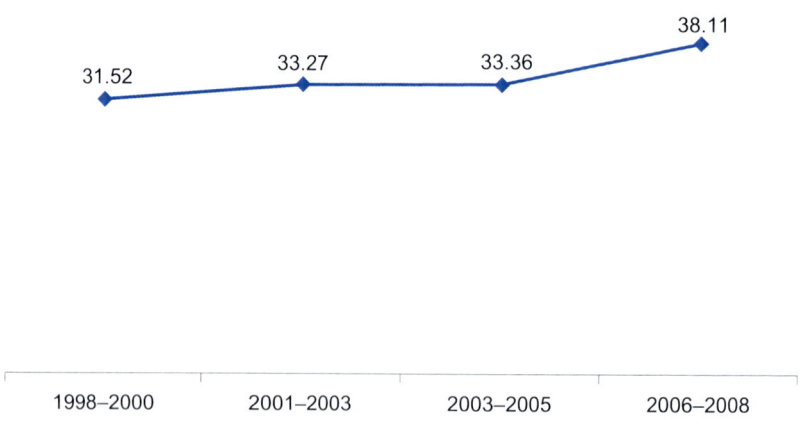

Figure 9.2 Innovation Rate (Percent of companies)

Source: Brazilian Institute of Geography and Statistics, Survey of Technological Innovation 2008.

Figure 9.3 Brazil Lags Other Countries on Innovation

Source: Cavalcante and De Negri (2011).

Note: OECD = Organisation for Economic Co-operation and Development; R&D = research and development.

TABLE 9.1

Expenditure on Innovation in Manufacturing (Percent)	
Item	**Expenditures**
Machinery and equipment	49.2
Internal R&D	24.5
Industrial projects	9.1
Introducing innovation in the market	5.7
External R&D	4.0
Other external know-how	2.7
Software	2.6
Training	2.1
Total	100

Source: Brazilian Institute of Geography and Statistics, Survey of Technological Innovation 2008.

Note: R&D = Research and development.

Brazilian Development Bank and Innovation—Three Short Tales of the New Industrial Policy

With the changing economic landscape in Brazil and the need for sustainable growth, the Brazilian Development Bank has focused much of its activity and agenda on innovation. Money lent to companies for this purpose has been growing, both in equity investments and loans and grants, increasing from 332 million reals (R$) in 2007 to R$5.2 billion in 2013, a remarkable increase in the R&D disbursement. We now look at the pharmaceutical, sugarcane, and software industries to illustrate the new drive for innovation.

The Pharmaceuticals Industry

Brazil's pharmaceutical market has been growing substantially since the early 2000s. As in many countries, the population is aging, with the share of the population 60 and above expected to overtake the under-15 group by 2030. As a result, the health care market has also shifted alongside changes in prevalent disease. Noncommunicable diseases such as cancer and heart disease are becoming more commonplace and already represent about two-thirds of the disease burden, replacing communicable diseases as the main concern demanding resources.

The growing middle class further changes the nature of the health care market, and Brazil has been rising in the global rankings of pharmaceutical market size (by sales in constant U.S. dollars), from 10th in 2005 to a projected sixth in 2015, according to IMS Health reports.

Development of the pharmaceutical industry was one of the first initiatives undertaken after the return of industrial policy in the early 2000s. Emphasis was put on best manufacturing practices and incremental innovation. More recently, however, the country has attempted to leapfrog and catch up with the technology frontier to produce "biosimilars"[3] in the biotech industry. The pharmaceutical industry is the most R&D intensive in the country, with a ratio of R&D to sales of about 2.5 percent compared with just over 0.5 percent for the total industry in 2011. Crucially, local companies' share of the Brazilian pharmaceuticals market has been growing, reaching about 60 percent in 2013, from about 35 percent in 2003. Companies receiving support from the Brazilian Development Bank have been doing better than the industry average on growth, revenues, and R&D.

The Sugarcane Industry

Sugarcane, an important crop in Brazil since colonial times, provides a traditional agro-industrial asset base. And in recent years, the country's high land availability and the low cost of feedstock has supported the development of flex fuel, based on the crop. More than 60 percent of the Brazilian vehicle fleet runs on both ethanol and gasoline, and sugarcane biomass now not only provides all the energy needed for the industry, but also adds its energy surplus to the electric grid. The sugarcane industry creates possibilities for

---

[3] Biosimilars are pharmaceutical products that are almost identical to the original products but manufactured by a different company after the original product's patent expires.

building a green economy and developing economies of scope from biofuels to biochemicals.

The Brazilian Development Bank has therefore focused on developing the industry. The Plan to Support Technological Innovation in the Sugar and Ethanol Industries—with good preliminary results—was set up to develop new technologies and facilitate partnerships of Brazilian companies with foreign firms, supporting a transfer of technology. The industry has begun to show tangible results, with the productivity yield of second-generation ethanol expected to increase from about 7,000 liters per hectare in the mid-2000s to more than 10,000 liters by 2020. With a $57 million portfolio invested in new technologies in 2010, the development bank grew its portfolio to more than $1.5 billion, by early 2014, in biofuels and renewable chemicals.

The Software Industry

Until 1994, the Brazilian Development Bank had very little involvement in the software industry, with its focus instead on brick-and-mortar-type industries. In its shift in focus to innovation, it implemented a program that grew to more than $2.5 billion investment in the segment (Figure 9.4). The three software companies listed on the Brazilian stock market received funds from the development bank before going public. One of these is now an internationally renowned company in enterprise resource planning.

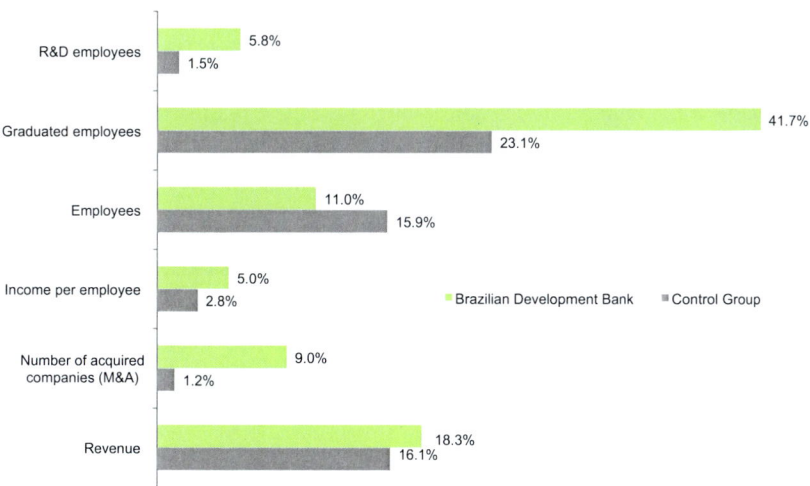

Figure 9.4 Brazilian Development Bank Support for Software Companies, 2006 and 2010 (Annual growth rate)

Source: Brazilian Development Bank.
Note: M&A = mergers and acquisitions; R&D = research and development.

THE BRAZILIAN DEVELOPMENT BANK AS A VENTURE CAPITALIST

The Brazilian Development Bank's venture capitalist role as a development-oriented equity investor is a typical one. In the 1970s it set up a specific arm devoted to equity investments, BNDES Participações (BNDESPAR)—doing so at the same time as the inception of the Brazilian corporation law—which provides equity funding and fosters domestic capital markets. The equity arm has shared decision processes through independent committees, the same executive board as Brazilian Development Bank, and specific policies and procedures to comply with when investing in a company. The agency is compliant with the Brazilian Security and Exchange Commission.

The total portfolio of the equity arm has grown substantially since the 1970s, investing in more than 300 companies and, since the mid-2000s, most of its companies have received funds through seed venture capital and private equity funds. In 2013, total market value exceeded R$80 billion. Equity shares are bought and sold every year, and the agency has generated stable dividends and profits.

The activities of the equity arm have also evolved. Initially, in the 1970s, the agency only engaged in direct equity investments, but instruments now include convertible bonds, private equity, and venture capital funds, as well as seed capital investments.

The equity arm is the biggest venture capital and seed investor in Brazil, and the equity portfolio through venture capital and private equity funds comprises 34 funds, 162 companies, R$2.5 billion invested, 15 different sectors, and 3-to-1 leverage from the private sector for each real invested. The agency aims to build institutional capacity, and because of this mandate in developing the Brazilian capital markets, it constantly introduces new funds. It established the country's first seed capital fund and is building a small and medium-sized enterprise access fund, and corporate venture funds, in addition to public-private partnership funds.

The agency's strategy is to focus on long-term company fundamentals and total portfolio performance. Benefiting from the portfolio approach, rather than focusing on the losses of specific ventures, the equity arm invests in leapfrog and risky ventures.

It does not do buyouts, however, and no longer practices debt-to-equity balance sheet restructurings, such as debt-to-equity swaps, because of many failed deals in the 1980s. The agency backs companies and their market dynamics rather than stock market trends. And there is a thorough review process with the companies on performance and other firm activities.

The development bank used to take control of companies, but it no longer follows this micromanaging approach. It does not appoint any managers, but encourages the best corporate governance practices. In fact, the involvement of Brazilian Development Bank implies a stamp of approval, and as a result, it is an influential and a key shareholder in most companies that it invests in.

CONCLUSION

A broader view of development requires a review of its historical aspects and implementation of policies to lift constraints. Building professional state institutions is crucial, and the Brazilian Development Bank is one of these. Despite some of its failures, it has been relatively successful overall in promoting Brazilian development, including in the industrialization of recent decades and in the focus on innovation today.

To promote innovation and the growth that follows it, it is important to support firms in strategic industries, engage in risky and leapfrog investments, focus on the long term, and integrate best governance practices and performance measures, among other things. Brazil's experience makes clear that the state can play an important role in implementing development strategies and attaining a sustainable growth path.

REFERENCE

Cavalcante, L. R., and F. De Negri. 2011. "Recent Innovation Indicators in Brazil" [Trajetória Recente dos Indicadores de Inovação no Brasil]. Discussion Paper 1659, Institute of Applied Economic Research (IPEA), Brazil.

CHAPTER 10

Implications of Korea's *Saemaul Undong* for Development Policy: A Structural Perspective

HUCK-JU KWON

Although quality of life is higher than ever before, a billion people still live in absolute poverty. To fight it, it is necessary for the developing economies, where the majority of poor people live, to achieve both economic and social development. Nevertheless, it is clear that developing economies cannot tackle poverty by themselves. Governments, civil society organizations, and citizens of developed economies must participate in this fight. One way to help developing economies reduce poverty is to provide financial assistance. Another is to share the development experience of once-poor countries that have made a successful transition to industrialized economies by offering development policy options.

It is in this context that this chapter examines the *Saemaul Undong* movement (New Village Movement) in Korea from a structural perspective; that is, what socioeconomic conditions made the movement successful, and what role did it play in the country's transition from a predominantly rural economy to a modern, industrialized one? The chapter seeks policy implications for the international development debate.

The government initiated Saemaul Undong in 1971 as a rural community movement. Through it, the government provided small startup subventions for projects to develop local communities economically. For example, it allocated material for constructing village roads, bridges, electrification infrastructure, and storage sheds crucial for these communities' economic development. Villagers provided free labor for these projects. Government subventions accounted for 20–30 percent of community expenditures, local residents' labor and other contributions constituted another 30–60 percent, and private donations and bank loans provided the rest (Kim 1991).

The government spent on average 2.5 percent of gross national product per year on Saemaul Undong projects—an immense amount of social spending, given that there was only a strict, means-tested public assistance program in place

This chapter was initially published in the *Korean Journal of Policy Studies* in 2010 and substantially revised, drawing on new research.

in the early 1970s. These policies were combined with a nationwide campaign to mobilize human resources and change the attitudes of ordinary people about socioeconomic development. Saemaul Undong was a social endeavor that combined aspects of a social fund program and a community movement.

APPROACHES TO DEVELOPMENT POLICY

During the early 2000s, international development policy emphasized good governance as a development strategy, arguing that poor performance in economic development and poverty reduction in many developing economies stemmed from inadequate governance (Grindle 2004). The good governance approach was a response to failures in past state- and market-centered development policy paradigms. Gough and Wood (2004, 15) point out that the lack of effective and efficient state and market institutions in many developing economies is the main obstacle to development. In many of these countries, market institutions are not working well in producing goods, and the state is captured by special interests instead of functioning as a neutral actor to manage different social interests. The authors maintain that good governance in market institutions is necessary for overcoming such difficulties and achieving development.

Good governance requires trust between people, among other things. The simple fact that there are institutions in place does not automatically mean that they are working effectively. It is necessary for public and private actors to work together. This involves rational discussion, persuasion, and coordination. Development strategy based on governance theory is an effort to synthesize state- and market-centered paradigms of development, which are often seen as competing.

The Millennium Development Declaration, in which 189 heads of state and leaders of government pledged support in September 2000, aimed to reduce global poverty by half, based on a strategy of good governance. The World Bank and the United Nations Millennium Project, headed by Jeffrey Sachs, emphasized the importance of good governance as a way to achieve the Millennium Development Goals (MDGs) in general and poverty reduction in particular (UNDP 2005). This led to an emerging consensus among global institutions and policy commentators that good governance would reduce poverty. Some commentators, however, argue that good governance does not necessarily lead to poverty reduction and economic development (Coelho and Favareto 2008; Kwon and Kwak 2008).

After 15 years of implementation, however, the MDGs show a mixed outcome. The goal of reducing the number of people living in poverty by half by 2015 is expected to have been met on a global basis (World Bank 2005). Clearly, this is good news for the MDGs, but progress has been unequal among regions of the world and within nation-states. China's economic growth accounts for a great deal of poverty reduction in the world, while sub-Saharan Africa, Latin America, and parts of Southeast Asia have not made significant progress (UNDP 2005). Therefore, it is hard to say that we are on track to success in achieving MDG 1, to eradicate extreme poverty and hunger.

As a result, the effectiveness of current anti-poverty strategies in developing countries has been questioned. If market solutions are not enough, and good governance does not reduce poverty as intended, what is the missing link? This chapter argues that a program like Saemaul Undong could link state, market, and civil society efforts for poverty reduction.

Indeed, among the many successful community movements, Saemaul Undong deserves close examination because it shows that a community movement and the state can work together for poverty reduction. Saemaul Undong was able to bring about people's active participation, which is often missing in development projects. The following sections examine the historical conditions for the movement's success, and its role in linking state, civil society, and grassroots participation in development. This is followed by examining the land reform that took place in Korea in the late 1940s and 1950s, and the conditions that were instrumental in that success. The chapter then shows that Saemaul Undong was not only a community movement, but also a multifunctional link for development policy that the state could implement for economic development and poverty reduction. Finally, it explains how Saemaul Undong contributed to Korea's social and economic development through multiple functions, such as social inclusion and the income-generation mechanism.

HISTORICAL BACKGROUND: LAND REFORM IN KOREA

Land reform has been a controversial issue in the development debate.[1] Some argue that it is a prerequisite to successful economic development, while others hold that it inevitably brings about political turmoil, which disrupts economic development. A body of literature has pointed out that successful land reform in the late 1940s in Japan, Korea, and Taiwan Province of China was strongly related to economic development and poverty reduction (for example, World Bank 2006). Access to even a small amount of land can provide farmers a source of self-employment and an important safety net for the economic contingencies that occur over a lifetime (Dasgupta and Ray 1987; Deininger and Binswanger 1999). Land ownership also affects economic growth through investment in soil improvement and farming tools—an effort that owners are much more likely to make than tenants, because it improves their assets.

Despite this positive relationship between equitable landownership and agricultural productivity, it is not necessarily true that there has been a direct positive relationship between land reform and economic development in Korea. The country's economic development was not mainly based on the growth of the agricultural sector (Adelman 1997), and some scholars see its land reform as a failure because it did not create an agricultural sector that was dominated by middle-class farmers (Hwang 1985). The mechanism by which land reform

---

[1] This section draws extensively on the author's previous work in Kwon and Yi (2009).

contributed to economic development has been discussed in depth elsewhere; this chapter focuses on the link between the land reform and Saemaul Undong.

Korea's land reform, which took place in three waves from 1946 to 1955, gave people who had been tenants of Korean and Japanese landlords under Japanese rule (1910–45) the opportunity to become independent farmers. After World War II, the American military government (1945–48) took the first step toward land reform in 1946. It limited peasants' rental payments for land to one-third of the value of the land's annual harvest, a drastic reduction. In 1948 the American military government sold land that belonged to the Japanese Oriental Development Company (later the New Korea Public Company) to tenants for prices equivalent to three years of harvests.

Concerned by the socialist land reform in North Korea, the sovereign Korean government, established in 1948, promulgated a series of land reform laws, implementing them from 1949 to 1955. These included three basic principles that put more emphasis on equality than growth: (1) only farmers could own farm land, (2) land could be owned up to a maximum of three hectares, and (3) farmers could not contract out their land to others for farming (Sin 1988). Based on these principles, the government bought land from those who owned more than the maximum or did not farm it themselves, and sold it to those who had farmed the same land as tenants.[2]

Although some landowners sold their land before the implementation of land reform, more than 60 percent of the farmland was bought by government. Landowners were paid with government bonds, while tenant farmers were able to buy the land from the government at a price equivalent to one and a half times the annual harvest, which they could pay over a three-year period (Kim 1997, 307). In 1945, 65 percent of farmers were tenant farmers; by 1951, after the land reform, the figure was 8.1 percent.

It would be fair to say that land reform in Korea was successful in that it helped farmers own their own land, and therefore the inequality of land ownership was reduced sharply. For example, in Yongmun village in Chungnam Province, the Gini index of land ownership declined from more than 0.63 to less than 0.50 as a result of land reform (Cho 2003, 297). Furthermore, the productivity of farming increased.

Land reform provided two vital conditions for the success of Saemaul Undong. It created farmers who owned their own land and whose economic interest was in line with community development in rural areas. Saemaul Undong's core program was the construction and renovation of community infrastructure. For independent farmers, modernizing the infrastructure of their community would

---

[2] There are three main explanations of the political rationale for the land reform. The first stresses that peasants suffered the most from Japanese rule while many landlords were seen as collaborators. The second is that former president Syngman Rhee wanted to undermine the economic basis of the conservative political elite, many of whom were landlords. The third was that land reform was a U.S. counter-revolution against the communist threat. The United States urged land reform not only to the Korean government, but also to the government of Taiwan Province of China (Kim 1976).

directly lead to the increased productivity of their agricultural land. But tenant farmers would not necessarily see the direct benefits of such efforts.

Saemaul Undong was launched in April 1970 when former president Park Chung Hee addressed rural residents and local officials during a visit to the southeast region. He said, "We need to support ourselves to develop our villages. With aspirations of self-help, self-reliance and cooperation, we can make our village rich and turn it into a good place to live" (Oh 2002).

Park's statement emphasizes that people in rural communities should not expect the state to help them, but should help themselves. Therefore, the key idea of Saemaul Undong was self-help, which was then extended to self-reliance and cooperation. Citizens who participated in the Saemaul Undong movement needed to contribute their labor and other resources to community projects. Government support, mostly in the form of raw materials and occasionally financial subsidies, accounted for only a small part of what was needed to complete the accomplished projects.

According to newspaper reports in the early 1970s, there was significant support for Saemaul Undong in rural villages (Kim 2004). Such energetic voluntary participation at the grassroots level was made possible not only by government mobilization, but also by the genuine prospect of a better quality of life. Local officials, who were catalytic in this process, enthusiastically supported Saemaul Undong (Table 10.1).

Land reform boosted the expansion of education, becoming a catalyst of Saemaul Undong. The movement's community leaders, who were educated, were able to organize the movement effectively. And families in rural areas who now owned land and experienced higher productivity were able to send their children to school instead of the paddy fields (Cho 2003).

Education was the biggest item in the government budget after defense in the late 1950s and 1960s. This resulted in an astonishing record of educational expansion compared with other developing economies, which reinforced the effect of the land reform on education. In Korea, the number of students from both rural and urban backgrounds increased 370 percent for liberal arts secondary schools, 299 percent for vocational high schools, and 1,292 percent for higher education from 1945 to 1959; and the literacy rate reached almost 90 percent in the late 1950s (USAID 1959; Cho and Oh 2003, 283). Land reform not only

TABLE 10.1

Growth of Saemaul Undong								
Participants and Projects	**1971**	**1972**	**1973**	**1974**	**1975**	**1976**	**1977**	**1978**
Participants in rural areas[1]	72	320	675	373	489	351	451	1,336
Total participants[1]	72	320	693	1,069	1,169	1,175	1,372	2,709
Projects in rural areas[2]	385	320	1,093	415	696	630	2,200	
Total projects[2]	385	320	1,093	1,099	1,598	887	2,463	2,667

Source: Oh (2002).

[1] Hundred thousands.

[2] Thousands

sharply reduced the inequality of land ownership, but also played a powerful role in reducing poverty and increasing the level of education in the rural population.

SAEMAUL UNDONG AS A MECHANISM FOR SOCIAL INCLUSION

Another important aspect of Saemaul Undong was its role in promoting social integration during Korea's rapid industrialization. A large body of literature on Saemaul Undong agrees that it contributed to economic development during the 1970s. While this is certainly true, it is also necessary to take a balanced point of view on this issue. Economic development in Korea in the 1970s and 1980s was mainly driven by industrialization, with a smaller contribution by the agricultural sector (Adelman 1997), where the number of workers decreased steadily (Table 10.2). This suggests that the success of Saemaul Undong, which took place mainly in rural agricultural communities, had only limited impact on overall economic development.

Indeed, some have argued that Saemaul Undong was not a success in that more people left rural communities for cities in the 1970s (3.7 percent of rural dwellers) than in the 1960s (1.3 percent) (Oh 2002). Even so, it is also necessary to look at Saemaul Undong from the perspective of the changing structure of Korean society.

Korea's economic development has been primarily industrial: first in the form of import substitution, second through exports, and third through heavy and chemical industries. After the 1990s, the economic strategy shifted to advanced technology-based industries such as information technology, electronics, and automobiles. Because this development was not based primarily on agricultural or raw materials, any assessment of Saemaul Undong must take Korea's industrialization into consideration. In this context, the movement needs to be looked at from a structural viewpoint to examine how it contributed to the structural transition of Korean society, from predominantly rural to modern and industrialized.

Many developing economies that were initially successful in industrialization were not able to sustain this process, as in the cases of Argentina, Brazil, and the Philippines, for example. One of the main reasons for the failure of such countries to achieve sustainable growth through industrialization was their extreme

TABLE 10.2

Year	Agriculture and Forestry	Manufacturing and Mining	Service
Employees by Industry in Korea *(Percentage)*			
1966	57.89	10.48	31.27
1971	48.44	14.19	37.37
1978	38.41	23.15	38.44
1985	24.94	24.44	50.62
1990	18.25	27.32	54.42

Source: National Statistical Office 1966, 1986, 1990.

social inequality and inability to tap the huge reservoir of human resources in the rural areas (Kohli 2004; Kwon and Yi 2009).

Underlying Korea's successful and sustained industrialization was the fact that rural areas were not left behind. On the contrary, people in rural areas supported a vital core of industrialization by supplying young and educated workers for industrializing urban areas—and this was made possible by mass education and land reform from 1946 to 1955. The latter also seriously weakened the landowner class, who might have hindered the structural changes of industrialization, and provided a vital source of income to families in the agricultural sector.

In 1961, the government adopted poverty-reduction policies that included eliminating usurious loans in rural areas. Usury had been widespread, embedded in an economy based on subsistence agriculture. Shortly after taking power in 1961, the military government enacted measures to ensure that loans were registered. Farmers with high-interest debts could transfer them to agricultural cooperatives—nationwide farmers' organizations—that offered a longer grace period and lower interest, while lenders received a bond from the cooperatives. Furthermore, usurious practices were made illegal. Agricultural cooperatives then began to play the role of formal rural credit institutions where loans were traded competitively and effectively. These cooperatives were able to respond to the credit needs of specific crop growers or in specific regions with their diversified loan portfolios.

Saemaul Undong developed after these efforts had already brought major social changes to the agricultural sector. Through this movement, farmers renovated their houses, repaired village roads, built community halls, and established cooperatives. These projects in turn raised living standards and drastically reduced poverty (Table 10.3). And, crucially, rural communities kept pace with the changes brought about by economic development.

By contrast, public projects to improve rural infrastructure from the 1960s did not produce effective outcomes. Saemaul Undong's project frameworks were superior to those used to improve infrastructure: government provided public resources for the start-up of local projects and residents contributed their labor. Such a combination eased the difficulties which community movements often face at the initial stage. Furthermore, Saemaul Undong was not only about improving infrastructure, but also about raising the levels of income of the rural households (Lee 2013). In the early 1970s, the government was able to supply

TABLE 10.3

Incidence of Absolute Poverty (Percentage)					
Households	1965	1970	1976	1980	1991
Urban households	54.9	16.2	18.1	10.4	8.7
Rural households	35.8	27.9	11.7	9.0	2.8
All households	40.9	23.4	14.8	9.8	7.6

Source: Kwon (1998, 34).
Note: The absolute poverty line was 121,000 won per month (at 1981 prices) for a five-person household.

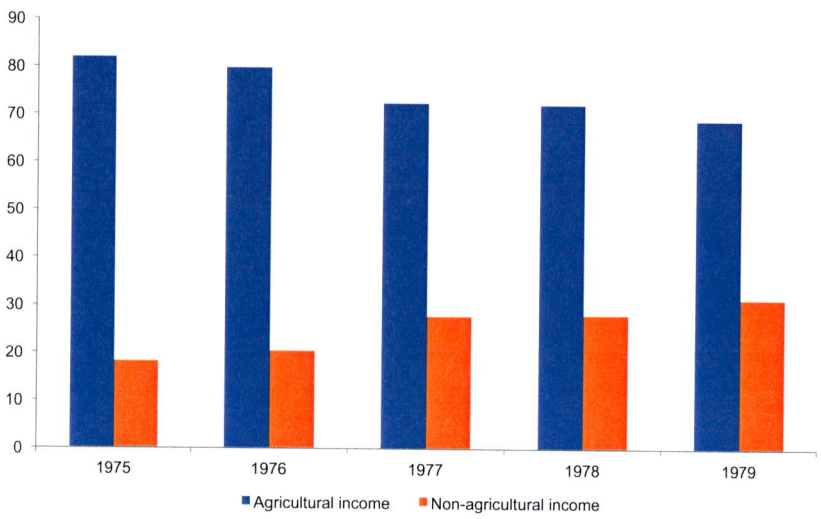

Figure 10.1 Diversification of Income Sources of Rural Households in Korea (Percent)
Source: Lee (2013).

fertilizers, chemical pesticides, and other chemicals to raise agricultural productivity. These were produced locally and were hence much cheaper than imports. The government also encouraged local businesses to establish food processing plants to diversify rural income sources, which bought locally produced agricultural products. At the same time, new rice strains developed by government research laboratories were introduced to improve yields. Saemaul Undong combined these various efforts in the early 1970s.

Saemaul Undong did not simply come out of the blue, and if it had, it would not have received such an enthusiastic reception. It was part of an historical effort that made Korea's economic development broad-based, marked by effective poverty reduction and a more equal distribution of income. Koh (2006), despite being a critic of of Saemaul Undong, nevertheless recognized that it brought small farmers and their families into the fold of a modern citizenry. In this sense, it was an important factor in Korea's economic success, although it did not reverse the decline of the rural sector (Figure 10.1).

SAEMAUL UNDONG AS A FORM OF AUTHORITARIAN MOBILIZATION

A key idea of Saemaul Undong is self-help, which is extended to self-reliance and cooperation. As mentioned earlier, citizens who participated in the movement contributed their labor and other resources to community projects. The government's contribution of raw materials and, occasionally, funds accounted for only a small part of the movement's support. Furthermore, people came together and discussed what projects their communities needed. In other words, this was a quintessential community movement, and one, as already noted, that had enthusiastic grassroots support (Kim 2004). One of the local officials who was involved in Saemaul Undong explained: "We were doing for ourselves not for President Park Chung Hee. We are renovating the road to our village to relieve our hardship. When I explained this to people, they all understood very well." (Eom 2011) This energetic voluntary participation was the linchpin that linked economic development to poverty reduction. This could be a vital lesson for many other developing economies.

Nevertheless, critics have pointed out, and it would be difficult to deny, that Saemaul Undong was also a political mobilization tool for an authoritarian government (Lim 2004). Although people voluntarily participated in the movement, they were also expected to support the Park Chung Hee regime. To understand this, it is necessary to understand the political context of the early 1970s in Korea.

Park Chung-Hee led the 1961 military coup that crushed a democratic political system. After the coup he first served as vice-chairman and later as chairman of the temporary Supreme Council for National Reconstruction until he had himself elected president in 1963. The new regime had an urgent need to give itself legitimacy. In its first year it published a five-year economic plan (building on planning that had been started under the Second Republic[3]), in which it presented the coup as a revolution. In its economic policy, the Park government shifted from import-substitution industrialization to export-led development in the mid-1960s, during which the economy grew impressively and poverty fell.

During this period, gross national product increased rapidly and unemployment fell sharply (Table 10.4). Import-substitution industrialization absorbed labor effectively, with employment rising 10 percent despite an increase of the economically active population by 12 percent (Adelman 1997, 514). From 1967 to 1971, labor-intensive industries continued to absorb labor, together with a growing services sector, raising the income of the working population and, in particular, reducing poverty in urban areas. Rising incomes in urban households widened the income gap with rural ones, which on average were 62.6 percent of

TABLE 10.4

Major Economic Indicators in Korea						
Indicator	1961	1966	1972	1981	1987	1993
GNP per capita (dollars)	90	125	306	1,741	3,218	7,513
Growth rate (percent)	1.6	6.8	16.1	21.3	10.7	15.2
Unemployment rate (percent)[1]	17[2]	15	10	10	5	4
	(7)	(6)	(4)	(4)	(3)	(3)

Source: Adelman (1997, 535).
Note: GNP = gross national product.
[1] This includes both the unemployed and those working fewer than 18 hours a week. Figures in parentheses represent the completely unemployed.
[2] This figure is for 1963.

---

[3] The Second Republic was the government in charge for eight months in 1960–61 under the parliamentary system.

urban households (Oh 2002, 163). Saemaul Undong was one of the responses intended to correct this gap.

Nevertheless, politics played a role in the voluntary community movement. Park Chung-Hee, serving his second term as president, was supposed to retire from politics in 1971. But he stood for a third term in 1971 after the constitution was changed. He changed the constitution again in 1972 so that he could remain in office for as long as he wanted. Considering that the Saemaul Undong was started in 1970 by Park, it is difficult to tell the difference between voluntary participation in the movement and political mobilization by an authoritarian government (Koh 2006).

Scholars and commentators have long debated the political nature of Saemaul Undong. It is clear that the movement had both strengths and weaknesses in its political nature. Although people participated voluntarily and with great enthusiasm, it is also important to recognize that the movement could be taken advantage of politically.

POLICY IMPLICATIONS

Much attention has been paid to the policy implications of Saemaul Undong's micro-level characteristics. Such an approach is useful for community activists who can learn directly from the experiences of Saemaul Undong. It is also necessary to view Saemaul Undong from a structural perspective, and investigate what socioeconomic conditions allowed it to be so successful and the role it played in facilitating Korea's transition from a rural economy to a modern industrialized one.

Given that the core features of Saemaul Undong are self-help and self-reliance for community development, I argued that the land reform that created independent farmers in Korea in the 1950s was critical for the movement's success. Because better community infrastructure improved the productivity of land-owning farmers, Saemaul Undong was able to attract their active participation. Furthermore, despite political mobilization by the government, it is fair to say that Saemaul Undong was organized by local community leaders who knew best what their communities needed. Thus, a community movement for economic development should have a social structure that allows people to participate voluntarily, not only for community development, but also for the improvement of their own well-being.

In terms of the structural role of Saemaul Undong, it contributed to the social inclusion of rural community members in industrialization. Not only did it improve the quality of life in rural areas, but it also brought rural communities into the mainstream of social change. This is a key reason that Korea's experience of development has been strong and sustainable.

The most critical weakness of Saemaul Undong today is that it seems to remain in its old form. Its present image and perspectives are still set in the context of the Korean society of 30 years ago. Its antiquated form of understanding is becoming irrelevant. The challenge is to transform Saemaul Undong so that it can continue to provide useful guidelines for community movements.

It is also important for scholars and community movement activists to understand developing societies and their social challenges. Attempting to transfer the Korean experience to other societies without understanding those societies would be futile. International collaboration is essential, for example, in the form of academic workshops and common community projects. And the role of the government is critical to ensuring that this collaboration takes place.

REFERENCES

Adelman, I. 1997. "Social Development in Korea, 1953–1993." In *The Korean Economy 1945–1995*, edited by D. Cha, K. Kim, and D. Perkins, 509–40. Seoul: Korea Development Institute.

Cho, S. 2003. "Land Reform and Capitalism in Korea." In *The History of the Korean Development Model and Its Crisis*, edited by C. Yoo. Seoul: Cobook.

Cho, S., and Y. Oh. 2003. "The Formation of Some Preconditions for the Condensed Growth in the 1950s." *Donghyanggwa Chonmang* 59: 258–302 (in Korean).

Coelho, V. S. P., and A. Favareto. 2008. "Participatory Governance and Development: In Search of a Causal Nexus." Paper presented at the RC19 Annual Conference on the Future of Social Citizenship, Stockholm, September.

Dasgupta, P., and D. Ray. 1987. "Inequality as a Determinant of Malnutrition and Unemployment Policy." *Economic Journal* 97 (385): 177–88.

Deininger, K., and H. Binswanger. 1999. "The Evolution of the World Bank's Land Policy: Principles, Experience and Future Challenges." *World Bank Research Observer* 14 (2): 247–76.

Eom, Sek-Jin. 2011. "Between Mobilization and Participation: A Study on the Roles of Public Officials in Local Administration during the Rural Saemaul Undong in the 1970s." *Korean Public Administration Review* 45 (3): 97–122 (in Korean).

Gough, I., and G. Wood. 2004. *Insecurity and Welfare Regimes in Asia, Africa and Latin America: Social Policy in Development Contexts*. Cambridge: Cambridge University Press.

Grindle, M. S. 2004. Good Enough Governance: Poverty Reduction and Reform in Developing Countries. *Governance* 17 (4): 525–48.

Hwang, H. 1985. "A Study on Land Reform in Korea." In *The Modern History of Korea*, edited by J. Choi. Seoul: Yeoleum (in Korean).

Kim, D. 2004. "A Study on Park Chun-Hee's National Mobilization: Focusing on the New Community Movement." *Economy and Society* (Spring) (in Korean).

Kim, I. 1991. "Saemaul Movements and Changes in Rural Communities in the 1970s in Korea. Urban Growth and Regional Change after the 1940s." Academy of Korean Studies. Seongnam, (in Korean).

Kim, J. 1976. *Divided Korea: The Politics of Development 1945–1972*. Cambridge, Massachusetts: Harvard University Press.

Kim, S. 1997. "A Study of Land Reform in Korea. In *Essays on Korean Economic History*, edited by K. Kim. Seoul: Areum.

Koh, W. 2006. The New Community Movement in the President Park Era and the Making of Modern Citizens. *Economy and Society* (Spring) (in Korean).

Kohli, A. 2004. *State-Directed Development: Political Power and Industrialization in the Global Periphery*. New York: Cambridge University Press.

Kwon, H. J. 1998. "Democracy and the Politics of Social Welfare: A Comparative Analysis of Welfare Systems in East Asia." In *East Asian Welfare Model: Welfare Orientalism and the State*, edited by R. Goodman, G. White, and H.-J. Kwon. London: Routledge.

———. 2010. "Implications of Korea's Saemaul Undong for International Development Policy: A Structural Perspective." *Korean Journal of Policy Studies* 25 (3): 87–100.

Kwon, H. J., and H. K. Kwak. 2008. "Global Governance and the Possibility of Global Social Policy: Why Is It Difficult to Achieve MDGs?" Paper presented at the International Conference on Globalization and Reframing the Public Sector, Seoul, October.

Kwon, H. J., and I. Yi. 2009. "Economic Development and Poverty Reduction in Korea: Governing Multifunctional Institutions." *Development and Change* 40 (4): 769–92.

Lee, H. B. 2013. "The Development of the Project to Increase Income during the Saemaul Movement." *DongKook Sahak* 55 (in Korean).

Lim, J. 2004. "Mapping out Mass-Authoritarianism." In *Mass-Authoritarianism: Between Oppression and Consent*, edited by J. Lim and Y. Kim. Seoul: Book World (in Korean).

National Statistical Office. 1966, 1986, 1990. *National Statistical Yearbook.* Seoul: National Statistical Office.

Oh, Y. 2002. "Park Chung-Hee's Modernization Strategy and Rural Saemaul Movement." *Trends and Prospects* 55: 157–77 (in Korean).

Sin, P. 1988. "Comparative Research on Land Reform in Korea and Taiwan." *Korea and World Politics* 4 (2): 29–91 (in Korean).

United Nations Development Programme (UNDP). 2005. *Investing in Development: A Practical Plan to Achieve the UN Millennium Development Goals.* New York: UNDP.

United States Agency for International Development (USAID). 1959. *Country Program Book Aid Level Section.* Washington: USAID.

World Bank. 2005. *Global Monitoring Reports 2005: Millennium Development Goals: From Consensus to Momentum.* Washington: World Bank.

———. 2006. *World Development Report 2006.* Washington: World Bank.

CHAPTER 11

Lessons for Today and the Way Forward

Reda Cherif, Fuad Hasanov, and Alfred Kammer

Will Singapore be around in 100 years? I am not so sure. Whatever the choices are, I am absolutely sure that if Singapore gets a dumb government, we are done for. This country will sink into nothingness.

Lee Kuan Yew, the late founder of Singapore

This volume makes a case for the importance of the "leading hand" of the state in the development process. Whether we call it the "developmental state" or the "entrepreneurial state," the growth miracles of the Asian Tigers, in particular Singapore and Korea, illustrate the "leading hand" principle in practice. The Asian experiences show how the state successfully led the development process, whereas in Latin America and more recently in most of Africa and the Middle East, by and large, the "leading hand" of the state has given way to the "grabbing hand" or retreated to market-centered development and private interests.

Following this chapter we have included the transcript of a conversation between His Excellency Minister Muhammad Al Jasser of Saudi Arabia and IMF Deputy Managing Director Min Zhu, which makes it clear that the way the state intervenes is important, and both incentives and market forces have their role. His Excellency Minister Anas Al Saleh of Kuwait, at the beginning of this volume argued that a large public sector providing comfortable jobs acts as a strong deterrent to the investment in skills and industry development, and a change in incentives, practices, and societies is needed. These discussions shed light on the state's role in promoting sustainable growth and they raise an important question: How should the state intervene; that is, which key goals and policies should the state focus on?

Building a dynamic and sophisticated tradable sector to support sustainable growth is the prevailing theme of this volume. It discusses at length the state's role in creating industries, promoting innovation, and investing in human capital, from East Asia to Latin America. Whether the missing ingredients are human capital, infrastructure, or innovative firms, the state needs to devise policies to remedy them. Engaging public agencies, the private sector, and citizens to achieve this goal would increase the odds of success.

Oil exporters, especially in the Cooperation Council for the Arab States of the Gulf (GCC), provide stark examples of the market failures preventing the development of sophisticated tradables, given their highly risky nature. These countries are plagued by Dutch disease—the crowding-out of the non-oil tradable sector by oil-export income—which exacerbates the failures and produces a growth model that relies on oil as the major export and the recycling of petrodollars through government spending, imports of most tradable goods, and a high level of production and consumption of nontradables. For the past decades this model has yielded sizable achievements for human and infrastructure development. However, the model has led to income and productivity stagnation, as the GCC countries and oil exporters in general have been outperformed by many other countries. Similarly, many Latin American countries, including "high performers" and natural resource exporters, have experienced dismal productivity growth compared with East Asian countries (Chapter 6). In essence, productivity growth is at the heart of the development process and its engine lies in the development of sophisticated tradables (Chapter 7).

To correct market failures and spur the development of the sophisticated tradable sector to sustain productivity growth, the state needs to change the incentive structure for workers and firms (Chapter 1). The main hurdles facing diversification efforts in the GCC stem from market failures rather than government failures. Although there is room for improving the business environment, infrastructure, skill sets, and institutions, these are unlikely to be enough to develop non-oil exports on their own. The government needs to encourage individuals to develop skills and work in the private sector, and help firms to look beyond the confines of domestic markets and seek new export opportunities. Improving the quality of education, especially in early childhood, and implementing a social development program are important elements of changing incentives.

Experiences in other countries discussed in this volume show that diversification policy often followed a mix of vertical diversification in existing export industries and horizontal diversification in suppliers' clusters for those industries and in industrial beachheads into high-value-added and innovation sectors. Policy instruments included subsidies to support exporters and taxes on firms in the nontradables, access to financing and business support services through venture capital funds, development banks, and export promotion agencies, and the creation of special economic zones, industry clusters, research-and-development centers, and start-up incubators. This support was combined with skill development, the emphasis on technological upgrading and competition in international markets, and accountability frameworks for the firms receiving support.

Developing skills and human capital is among common elements that underlie the development experiences of the countries discussed in this volume. The experiences of Algeria and Saudi Arabia (Chapter 2) indicate that achieving a high level of human capital, although important, is not a prerequisite for industrialization. Algeria has created many skilled workers, who have remained underemployed in the economy without much tradable production. In contrast, Saudi Arabia has developed heavy industries but human capital has not caught up.

Developing tradables needs to go hand in hand with improvements in primary and secondary education (for example, in math and basic skills proficiency), technical degrees, and teacher quality. Faced with a shortage of skilled professionals, Singapore not only made it easier to bring in foreign skilled workers, but also created training institutes and technical and business schools to upgrade the skills of the local labor force (Chapter 3). Korea's Saemaul Undong movement has paved the way for rural households to get educated and provide the needed labor for the industrialization of the country (Chapter 10). Malaysia has also put an emphasis on science, technology, and innovation skills in its five-year development plans, but has yet to succeed in achieving a high ratio of science graduates in the local workforce (Chapter 4).

Building a strong work ethic, trust, and social capital—that is, transforming society—is key to development, if not the ultimate societal goal. A social development program should be another important component of the development strategy. Korea's Saemaul Undong program shows how the state can combine the social fund program on various projects (for example, in local infrastructure) with a community movement to mobilize human resources and change social attitudes (Chapter 10). Community leaders and local officials engaged the population in a grassroots movement to participate in local infrastructure projects by providing labor services with the goal to improve quality of life and instill self-reliance and cooperation among community members. The state provided start-up resources and later supported efforts for businesses to diversify their sources of income (such as establishing food processing plants instead of relying only on raw agricultural products). Designed to alleviate citizens' concerns, the movement attracted participation and encouraged social integration as the society was transforming from rural poverty-stricken communities to an urban industrialized nation. Singapore also engaged in social development with the provision of low-cost housing development programs, environmental cleanups, and urban planning and development (Chapter 3).

The promotion of industries provides the final piece of the development puzzle. Singapore promoted manufacturing to build factories in place of swamps and provide employment for its population, moving to higher-value-added industries, value chains, clusters, and research and development. Integrating public and private sectors, relevant infrastructure such as urban planning and high-tech zones, and human capital development, Singapore expects to move forward as an innovation- and knowledge-driven economy (Chapter 3). Malaysia has used its natural resources such as oil, palm oil, and rubber to create value added and build around the value chains (Chapter 4). Specific tasks, such as promoting rural development or improving urban public transport, assigned to relevant public agencies promote accountability and efficiency. Malaysia has also embarked on the path of science, technology, and innovation, which are integral to high-value-added production and export sophistication.

Korea's relatively recent path to industrialization in the 1960s to 1970s was strongly driven by the state, with officially targeted industries such as steel, chemicals, metals, machine building, shipbuilding, and electronics (Chapter 5). Large economies of scale were targeted and the products had to be of high quality not only for import substitution but mostly to gain market shares for exports from the beginning. With resources spent and various forms of support given to *chaebols*, the Korean state nevertheless used strict disciplinary actions if targets were not met.

The choice of industries is not particularly straightforward, but a focus on exports and high-value-added production with spillover potential and productivity gains is clear. Dubai used its locational advantage and business-friendly environment to set up free trade zones and attract foreign investment, but its exports are yet to expand much beyond gold and jewelry. Further, in the GCC, some degree of coordination of industry promotions may be needed to ensure that countries do not all develop in the same area (tourism, logistics, or finance hubs, for example) and thereby risk crowding each other out. Moreover, cross-country competition in the tradable sectors and intrasector trade, as is the case among advanced economies, could be helpful. In contrast, Singapore established various manufacturing, science, and high-tech parks to promote industry clusters and research and development, and it was much more successful in export diversification. After the return of industrial policy in the 2000s, Brazil decided to develop pharmaceuticals, sugarcane, and software industries and, with the support of the Brazilian Development Bank, has made substantial progress (Chapter 9).

Innovation with the help of an adapted innovation policy can make it possible to compete in high-value-added goods on international markets. Research and development activities ignite higher productivity growth as the innovation and learning-by-doing processes take hold (Chapter 6). International markets provide the discipline for firms from developing economies to compete and improve productivity. Investment in research and development, knowledge, and innovation would level the playing field of fierce global competition. The introduction of new goods and efficient processes would require public inputs and market interventions across both horizontal and vertical (sectoral) spheres. For instance, for the past decade, Brazil has focused on innovation policy to support industry growth (Chapter 9). Properly designed targeted sectoral policies could improve innovation, the growth of firms, and productivity. The state intervention should focus on developing specific sectors rather than picking firms, and should preserve competition and "creative destruction" (Chapter 7). In other words, "picking winners" should be about picking sectors rather than picking firms. Government failures such as short-term focus, agency problems, and public capture would require proper institutions, clear assignment of responsibilities across public agencies, and transparent rules for selecting sectors and providing and terminating support to these sectors.

To finance innovation, the state and the private sector, including the financial system, would need to collaborate as a venture capitalist for the country as a whole. Venture capital, private equity, stock markets, and other risk-sharing financial arrangements such as Islamic finance can support risky innovation activities. The state can further provide financial support through fiscal policy instruments such as tax credits and research spending and other programs such as loan guarantees and equity investments (Chapter 8). The Small Business Innovation Research program to promote technology and innovation in small firms in the United States has worked well.

In conclusion, as Meredith Woo stressed in Chapter 5, learning "piecemeal" from each other, from people's interactions and books, country experiences, theories and empirics, is an important way forward on the path of understanding development. "Creative destruction," as argued by Philippe Aghion, one of the pioneers of the Schumpeterian paradigm in growth theory, fuels the development lift-off that a developing country seeks. Each country's path is unique, but the collective history of nations offers patterns to uncover for the seeker of the grail of economic development.

Postscript

This is an edited and abridged version of a conversation between His Excellency Minister Muhammad Al Jasser, then Minister of Economy and Planning of Saudi Arabia, and Min Zhu, IMF Deputy Managing Director, following the diversification conference that took place in Kuwait on April 30–May 1, 2014. The discussion was moderated by Alfred Kammer.

A CONVERSATION ON DIVERSIFICATION CHALLENGES

MR. KAMMER: We had a very rich discussion over the last one-and-a-half days, setting out a number of elements that are important for oil exporters to diversify their economies and to create sustainable non-oil growth. We heard from academics about the important elements of a development strategy. We heard from policymakers about case studies of what worked and what did not work in particular countries.

It is now a great opportunity to hear from a policymaker from the region, who has been designing and implementing development strategies and diversification agendas, Minister Al Jasser, and from Min Zhu on the IMF's global perspective on these issues.

We heard that the GCC region has made great progress in terms of human development. But we also heard that its relative economic performance fell. The non-oil sector expanded and became more diverse within the nontradable sector, but at the same time, total productivity growth declined and became negative. One of the main elements coming out of the conference was a strong drive in successful countries to develop the tradable sector. Why is the tradable sector so important for a successful diversification strategy? What does it actually bring to sustainable growth in the long term?

MR. ZHU: Diversification is very much a process, and the tradable sector plays a very important role in this process. When we talk about diversification, we talk about industrialization, and there are a few important elements. First, we have to stick to a market-based approach where market signals are not ignored. This approach allows us to introduce competition in international markets. The tradable sector plays a very important role in bringing international competition to the local market. We need to let the local economy and local companies compete with international companies. The tradable sector transforms skills and experience, and drives the process of climbing the "quality ladder" in the local economy.

It is also very important to facilitate improvements in productivity. When we talk about diversification, the key issue we learn from the global experience is that sustainable growth is very much driven by a sustainable increase in productivity. The tradable sector contributes most to the sustainable productivity increase. Many studies show that in the tradable sector the productivity increase is much larger than in the nontradable sector. I think one explanation has to do with introducing international competition.

When we talk about diversification, we need to think about opening up the economy, using a market-driven approach, introducing international competition, and expanding the tradable sector.

MR. KAMMER: So open up and the tradables will come. From the experiences that seem to have worked in some countries, there is a role for the government to come in to support vertical and horizontal diversification and to create clusters of knowledge.

The GCC, including Saudi Arabia, have worked along these lines to jump-start the tradable sectors. Economic cities were created; certain industries were targeted and supported; and entrepreneurship through the establishment of small and medium enterprises was given full support. Yet, the tradable sector has not emerged in full force.

What is your experience in Saudi Arabia? What is working? What are the lessons to take away and the obstacles you are running into in developing the tradable sector?

MR. AL JASSER: Let me take a step back and look at this issue from an historical perspective. The initial conditions and the cultural setting cannot be overlooked. Otherwise, the development strategy and processes will invariably face significant obstacles.

Before the 1970s, the GCC countries were very underdeveloped. In the early 1970s, life expectancy in Saudi Arabia—and I think probably for the GCC as a whole it was not much different—was about 53 years. Now, it is 75 years. We have come a long way, and that is a product of education, health care, awareness, better food, and many other developments.

We were totally dependent on the export of crude oil, and people started saying, well, that is not enough value-added. We moved into refining and extracting. As a result, other ingredients of the development process came along—training, expertise, knowledge transfer and accumulation, and sophistication of the labor force and a large share of local workers in these industries. For example, Aramco has about 85 percent to 90 percent local workers.

We continued in our approach of expanding value-added activities. We were flaring associated gas that was coming out of the ground during the oil extraction. The government, out of its own budget, initiated a gas-gathering project, which was implemented by the government rather than the oil company. The gas was gathered, and that is how SABIC [the Saudi Basic Industries Corporation] and the petrochemical industry were born. This is another stage of development, and with all the associated activities, learning and the transfer of knowledge were made possible. Yet, as SABIC was created in 1976, we did not start very early on to take the production process further down the value chain as much as we could have. The secondary industries that could have sprung out of this venture decades ago did not. Now we are catching up. The government established a new corporation for industrialization. Its task is to take the products, the basic products of SABIC and others, and see how to go further down the value chain.

Over the years, diversification has taken place but of course, it is not enough. Leaving oil exports aside and looking at non-oil exports, even though there are petrochemicals in there (which is still manufacturing industry), the growth rate of non-oil exports has been about 17 percent per year since 2001, growing from 31 billion riyals to 204 billion riyals at end-2013. This is an important achievement.

Coming back to the main question, why do we want tradables and exports? Take our non-oil exports as a ratio of our imports. How much of my imports can I finance through my non-oil exports? It has risen to 34 percent of our imports from about 25 percent in 2001, even though our imports have increased substantially.

In a way, the governments in the GCC have tried to emulate *The Entrepreneurial State*, the title of the recently published book.[1] I think this is a concept that has been applied in the GCC. The governments have felt that one way to deploy large revenues from oil, or from the other extractive industries, and how to use them more effectively, was to push the development process much faster. We are trying to build the downstream industries, where there are higher value added, employment opportunities, and diversity of knowledge, expertise, and management skills that can be transferred.

I will mention another example of the entrepreneurial state. In Saudi Arabia, we did not develop our mineral resources except oil. Now, the Saudi Mining Company, created only about 10 years ago, is developing huge deposits of phosphates in northern Saudi Arabia, and bauxite for aluminum in the central region of the country. We have built, for the first time, a huge railroad network to transfer the ore from the mines to a new seaport on the east coast to refine those products—phosphoric acid fertilizers, and aluminum with all of its varieties—and ship them to markets, particularly in Asia. Out of this initiative, we see a potential development of the auto industry cluster. Why do we think so? We will produce a special type of aluminum that can be used for the car body at a very reasonable cost.

We are now riding this wave of industrialization and the development of tradables. We are trying to bring in foreign direct investment, not because we need capital, which is the case in many other countries, but because for us, it is the transfer of knowledge and expertise.

One final point I will say on the challenge we have faced all along—and this may be peculiar to the GCC countries—is that we have relied, particularly in

---

[1] *The Entrepreneurial State: Debunking Public vs. Private Sector Myths* by Mariana Mazzucato (Anthem Press, 2013).

the private sector industries, on foreign labor. My concern is not remittances but the brain drain that leaves the country as the accumulation of knowledge that occurred in our lands is gone after the contract expires. We go back to square zero. It is critical that we start accumulating knowledge. It is not the leakage of money that is significant but the leakage of expertise and the accumulation of knowledge. This is where we need to concentrate.

Diversification is not an end in itself; it is really the accumulation of knowledge that will make us, as societies, more self-reliant, with time, on our local labor force. Nothing can happen overnight. In order to ensure that we become knowledge-based societies, all the knowledge that we acquire, or that passes through our countries, our institutions, and our factories, does get accumulated in the country.

Tying this point to productivity, to my mind, the most important element of productivity is the knowledge content. The knowledge content is not only technical skills, but also is the work ethic, the discipline, and all of the elements that make a person and the labor force productive. Only through our own labor force can we achieve this productivity growth. If we achieve it, then diversification will become a by-product of this process.

MR. KAMMER: I think this is a very important point—accumulating knowledge, improving skills, and building up human capital—and we will come back to it. On the role of the state, usually we see that the role of the state is to create a climate to let the private sector flourish and correct market failures. How much should the state be a venture capitalist?

MR. ZHU: What we learned from the examples of Algeria, Brazil, Malaysia, South Korea, and Singapore, we see there is a role for the state to play. Yet this role of the state has also been evolving over time. I feel, today, it may play a slightly different role.

The typical prescriptions we give is to provide the enabling environment for the market—physical infrastructure, the legal framework, tax policies, incentives, education, etc. These elements are important. Yet I would say that in addition to this list, since we are not starting from scratch, other issues have also become relevant.

With the role of the state to promote diversification and sustainable growth, the first issue is reform, that is, to clean the house. For example, whether the government is able to manage the wage bill for the public sector is absolutely important. If the public sector wage bill is very high, it will be very difficult to attract workers into the private sector and to attract the foreign investors in the industries because the best people prefer to go to the public sector. Other issues such as accountability and transparency are important, too. By leveling the playing field, companies can move in to compete with each other.

As to how much the government should play a role of a venture capitalist, it is important for the states to be careful as to what to choose. I would still emphasize the first point is to open the door, let foreign companies into the market, and encourage them to compete with each other. The second point is that even if governments do the planning, the governments could pick the sector or the industry, but not winners. The government is not in a good position to sort out winners.

In addition, talking about this role of a venture capitalist, it is not about funding the industry; rather, it is about funding entrepreneurship. If the government can spend resources and design policies to facilitate and promote entrepreneurship rather than pick a sector, it will make the development process even better.

In today's world of the Internet and globalization, countries can tap the world markets, access the global knowledge, and attach to the supply and value chains. The government has to be careful in picking sectors and should let the market play a role.

MR. KAMMER: So pick a sector, but be careful. Did Saudi Arabia go further as a venture capitalist?

MR. AL JASSER: I mentioned the examples such as the Saudi Mining Company, SABIC, the new industrialization company, the clusters program we have initiated, and the auto industry. The government is playing an entrepreneurial role, particularly since many of these companies will be IPOed and privatized. In fact, this is what happened—for instance, SABIC has been IPOed.

We claim in the GCC that our economies are market economies, even though there is a role for the entrepreneurial state. One of the most significant roles of the state is setting and enforcing regulations. Regulations need to be transparent, understood, and anti-monopolistic. In Saudi Arabia, we have a competitiveness council that has been reorganized, and now it is pushing the issues of anti-competition and anti-monopoly practices. It should evolve, with time, to become a significant landmark in the regulatory framework of the country.

The government has also started shifting, at least in terms of discourse, away from the employer of the first resort, and we now hear more about entrepreneurship. Every one of our sons or daughters should not think first of having a government job, or just even a job. They should be thinking, "Can I create a job for myself? And, if I do, can I create jobs for others?" This change in the state of mind is very significant.

The role of the state is significant in many ways, not just in picking winners or sectors, but also creating clusters. The clusters program does not comprise only basic industries or petrochemicals, mining from bauxite and phosphates or fertilizers and the like, but also the auto industry. Its linkages—let's say, spare parts and the other components that go into this industry—are very much needed in other industries. Until there is the connectivity with other industries within a society, there is no cascade effect that is going to push the economy to higher levels of productivity, of competitiveness, and hence—not as a target but as an outcome—of diversification.

MR. KAMMER: You mentioned the importance of changing the mindset, of bringing out the importance of entrepreneurship. One of the issues the GCC countries are struggling with is that wages in the public sector are very high, and therefore they make it very difficult for nationals to go to the private sector and participate in this tradable sector revolution. What can we do about it?

MR. AL JASSER: In fact, if you ask those that are very educated and very skilled, they no longer want to be in the government. We have problems attracting very qualified citizens to work in the government. In a way, it is a positive development because many of them want to be entrepreneurs or work in the private sector. At the lower level of qualification, the attractiveness of the public sector is still high. The new labor ministry is going to examine how to rationalize the labor market on a market-based methodology. For instance, the Nitaqat system is a market-based system. Every sector was examined for local versus foreign labor, and a line was drawn, below which companies would need to catch up to increase the share of local workers. This has resulted in a lot of catching up and even the average Saudization ratio has started rising. In the next round, we are going to start looking at wages. The more productive the worker is, then the higher will be the premium paid by the employer and by the government, and workers will have market-based incentives to be more productive and to be more engaged in the labor market.

MR. KAMMER: A recurring theme is building up human capital. The theme of the tradable sector, the knowledge gained, and keeping the knowledge in the country comes from the production side. On the education side, it is about the importance of good and broad primary education, open and competitive education at the university level, and perhaps even sending people abroad to get the knowledge. Saudi Arabia has been doing a lot on this front. About 180,000 students have been sent outside the country to study. What have your experiences been?

MR. AL JASSER: We reached 185,000 students all over the world, in the United States, Canada, China, Korea, and Europe. But there was also a push on the other front, universities within the country. Now we have 30 public universities. All of the new universities emphasize basic sciences, medicine, engineering, IT, and business administration.

The discourse on education within our society is changing. It is no longer, "Oh, my son or daughter knows how to read and write." Rather, parents are asking schools: What problem-solving skills and critical-thinking concepts do you teach our kids? I recall Paulo Freire in his book, *The Pedagogy of the Oppressed*, talking about how dialogical education is very important. This is what we need. Modern education should help our kids develop skills that will make them proud of themselves and also make them productive in the society. We have a very young population (61 percent of the population between ages 15 and 64 and 35 percent below age 15). We have a national labor force that is entering the market that needs to be accommodated. We as the government cannot fall into the trap of trying to create jobs to take them in instead of giving them all the skills they deserve and need to be productive citizens.

MR. ZHU: To add a point on education, on one hand, education needs to start early and be broad, and it is the main conduit to train and nurture the generation of tomorrow. It should be more open-minded, more creative, and more widely available. I think this has become even more important now. Meanwhile, on the other hand, training is also important to provide the current generation with the skills for today. The two approaches have to go in parallel. We need new generations to become more open and more creative. We also need training for the specific skills and needs of the industries.

MR. AL JASSER: Our work to transition to a knowledge-based society and a knowledge-based economy is far from done, and we need to domicile the knowledge content. The 185,000 students we have overseas, the 30 universities concentrating on basic sciences, the King Abdullah City for Atomic and Renewable Energy, the King Abdulaziz City for Science and Technology, King Abdullah University for Science and Technology, King Fahd University of Petroleum and Minerals, and the Tech Valley next to it, will help us in this transition. In the Tech Valley, foreign companies are setting up shop to develop research, hiring graduates from the Saudi universities, and building up those cadres of basic and applied research. For example, GE is building generating turbines in Saudi Arabia, and we have some of the advanced electronics built by the Saudi Advanced Electronics Company.

All of these efforts are just starting to snowball. We are building up our capabilities to make what we need instead of relying totally on foreign expertise. We are accumulating knowledge. Engineers and other specialists working in the advanced sectors would support this process and even if they leave their companies, they will start new industries or join other industries that are on the cutting edge of technology. The knowledge accumulation process and the process of domiciling the knowledge is taking place. We should work harder on getting there.

Contributors

EDITORS

Reda Cherif is an Economist at the IMF, at the Institute for Capacity Development. He previously worked in the Fiscal Affairs and the Middle-East and Central Asia Departments of the IMF. He has written and published papers on development economics, fiscal policy, and international trade. He holds a PhD in Economics from the University of Chicago and an MSc in Economics from the London School of Economics.

Fuad Hasanov is an Economist at the IMF and an Adjunct Professor of Economics at Georgetown University. He joined the IMF in 2007 and worked on Kazakhstan, Romania, Ukraine, Kuwait, Bahrain, and Oman, the IMF's *Fiscal Monitor* publication, and economic training of staff and country officials. Before joining the IMF, Mr. Hasanov was an Assistant Professor of Economics at Oakland University in Rochester, Michigan in 2004–2007. He has written and published articles on consumption and saving, real estate returns, growth and inequality, fiscal policy and debt, and natural resources. He received a PhD, an MS, and a BA in Economics from the University of Texas at Austin.

Min Zhu assumed the position of Deputy Managing Director of the IMF on July 26, 2011. Previously he served as Special Advisor to the Managing Director of the IMF from May 3, 2010 to July 25, 2011. Mr. Zhu, a native of China, was a Deputy Governor of the People's Bank of China. He was responsible for international affairs, policy research, and credit information. Prior to his service at China's central bank, he held various positions at the Bank of China where he served as Group Executive Vice President, responsible for finance and treasury, risk management, internal control, legal and compliance, and strategy and research. Mr. Zhu also worked at the World Bank and taught economics at both Johns Hopkins University and Fudan University. Mr. Zhu received a PhD and an MA in Economics from Johns Hopkins University, an MPA from the Woodrow Wilson School of Public and International Affairs at Princeton University, and a BA in Economics from Fudan University.

CONTRIBUTORS

Philippe Aghion has been a Professor at College de France and at the London School of Economics since 2015. Previously, he was the Robert C. Waggoner Professor of Economics at Harvard University, and taught at the Massachusetts Institute of Technology, Nuffield College (Oxford), and University College London. He is a fellow of the Econometric Society and of the American Academy of Arts and Sciences. Mr. Aghion's main research areas are growth economics and the theory of contracts and organizations. With Peter Howitt, he pioneered the so-called Schumpeterian Growth paradigm, which was subsequently used to analyze the design of growth policies and the role of the state in the growth process. He is managing editor of the journal *The Economics of Transition*, which he launched in 1992. He holds a PhD in Economics from Harvard University.

His Excellency Muhammad Al Jasser is a Minister at the Royal Court of Saudi Arabia. He was the Minister of Economy and Planning from 2011 to 2015, Governor of the Saudi Arabian Monetary Agency (SAMA) from 2009 to 2011, and Vice-Governor from 1995 to 2009. He held the position of the Saudi Executive Director at the IMF from 1988 to 1995. He started his career at the Ministry of Finance. He holds a PhD in Economics from the University of California.

Jose Miguel Benavente spent more than fifteen years as a Professor in the Department of Economics at the University of Chile, and is currently a Professor (on leave) at the Business School at the University Adolfo Ibanez. He is the Chief of the Competitiveness and Innovation Division at the Inter-American Development Bank. His areas of research include innovation, entrepreneurship, small- and medium-enterprise finance, and economic development, and he has many publications in these areas. He has been Vice President of the Chilean National Innovation Council for about ten years, and has been a consultant for the World Bank, the Organisation for Economic Co-operation and Development, and several Latin American governments. He is an industrial engineer and has a PhD in Economics from the University of Oxford.

Tim Callen is Assistant Director in the IMF's Middle East and Central Asia Department. He is the IMF's Mission Chief for Saudi Arabia and is the Chief of the Gulf Cooperation Council (GCC) Countries' Division. In these roles, he is responsible for the IMF's published reports on Saudi Arabia and the GCC. Mr. Callen joined the IMF in 1993, and has also worked in the Asia and Pacific, Communications, Research, and Western Hemisphere Departments. He was the IMF Mission Chief to Kazakhstan during 2008–09, led the production of the IMF's *World Economic Outlook* publication from 2004 to 2007, and worked extensively on Japan, India, Korea, and Australia prior to these assignments. Before joining the IMF, he worked in the Economic Departments at the Bank of England and the Reserve Bank of Australia on monetary and economic forecasting issues, and at Hambros Bank, where he was responsible for bond and currency analysis for the G-7 countries. He holds a bachelor's degree in Economics from the University of Essex and a master's degree in Economics from the University of Warwick.

Bill Francis is the Bruggeman Professor of Finance at the Lally School of Management at Rensselaer Polytechnic Institute, a position he has held since 2005. He is also the Director of the PhD program and the head of the Finance and Accounting Department at the Lally School of Management. Professor Francis is the author of more than 60 articles and book chapters on financial markets, exchange rates, and managerial decision making. His work has been published in the top finance journals and he is on the editorial board of several finance journals. Prior to joining the Lally School of Management, he held appointments at the University of South Florida and at the University of North Carolina at Charlotte. Professor Francis holds a PhD in Financial Economics from the University of Toronto.

Iftekhar Hasan is the E. Gerald Corrigan Chair in International Business and Finance at Fordham University's Gabelli School of Business and Co-director of the Center for Research in Contemporary Finance. Professor Hasan has served as a scientific advisor at the Central Bank of Finland. He is the managing editor of the *Journal of Financial Stability*. Professor Hasan's research interests are in the areas of financial institutions, corporate finance, capital markets, and entrepreneurial finance, and he has published numerous articles and books on finance, economics, accounting, and management. He has consulted for international organizations, including the World Bank, the IMF, the United Nations, the Federal Reserve Bank of Atlanta, the Banque de France, and the Italian Deposit Insurance Corporation. He holds a PhD from the University of Houston.

Clement M. Henry is Visiting Research Professor at the Middle East Institute of the National University of Singapore and Emeritus Professor of Government and Middle East Studies from the University of Texas at Austin. From 2011 to 2014 he served as Chair of the Political Science Department at the American University of Cairo, where he had previously taught from 1969 to 1973. He has spent an additional five years of teaching and research in the Maghrib and written extensively on North African politics and political economy. In addition to collecting and editing the memoirs of former Algerian student leaders, his most recent research has focused on Islamic finance and the evolution of states and civil societies in the aftermath of the Arab uprisings. He holds a PhD in Political Science from Harvard University and an MBA from the University of Michigan.

Alfred Kammer is Deputy Director of the Strategy, Policy, and Review Department of the IMF, and oversees the work on strategy and surveillance. Previously, he was Deputy Director of the Middle East and Central Asia Department, overseeing regional economic developments and financial sector issues; Director of the Office of Technical Assistance Management, advising management on technical assistance operations and overseeing global partnerships for capacity building; and Advisor to the Deputy Managing Director, advising on a wide range of country, policy, and strategic issues. In the late 1990s, Mr. Kammer served as the IMF's Resident Representative in Russia and was advisor to the First Deputy Chairman of the Central Bank of Russia. Since joining the IMF in 1992, Mr. Kammer has also worked on countries in Europe, central Asia, and Africa, and on a wide range of policy and strategic issues. He obtained his graduate degree in Economics from the State University of New York at Albany and postgraduate degrees from the Kiel Institute of World Economics in Germany and the University of Southern California in Los Angeles.

Huck-ju Kwon is a Professor at the Graduate School of Public Administration and Deputy Director of the Asia Development Institute at Seoul National University.

He was Visiting Scholar at the Harvard-Yenching Institute, and worked as Director of the Global Research Network on Social Protection in East Asia, funded by the Korea Research Council (2010–2013). He is Co-Editor of *Global Social Policy* and has served as Vice-President of the RC19, International Sociological Association since 2010. He served on a number of government committees in the Republic of Korea, including the Ministerial Commission on the Civil Service Pension Reform. He holds a PhD in Politics from the University of Oxford.

Julio Ramundo has been the Managing Director at the Brazilian Development Bank (BNDES) since May 2011. Previously, he was a Deputy Managing Director in the Social Inclusion Division, responsible for operations with the public sector, urban infrastructure, sanitation, health, and education, as well as in the Industrial Division, responsible for operations in automotive, consumer goods, biofuels, trade and services, creative industries, and pharmaceuticals sectors. He was Executive Manager of the Trade and Services Department (2001–2002) and Head of the Electronic Industry Department (2003–2006), when he headed the redesign of the Bank's operations in the software industry. He was the BNDES representative on a number of councils and interministerial groups in the areas of information technology and innovation. Over the past few years, Mr. Ramundo has been the Bank's representative on several boards of directors and the Chairman of the Board of FAPES, BNDES's Assistance Foundation and Social Security. He holds an MBA from the London Business School.

Ahmad Tajuddin Ali is Chairman of the UEM Group Berhad, a Malaysian infrastructure conglomerate involved in property development, toll highways ownership and operation, engineering and construction, asset and facilities management, and cement manufacturing. He also serves as the President of The Academy of Sciences Malaysia and Joint Chairman of the Malaysian Industry-Government Group for High Technology (MIGHT). He was Chairman of the Energy Commission until the end of March 2014. Earlier in his career, Dr. Tajuddin Ali served as the Director-General of Standards and Industrial Research Institute of Malaysia (SIRIM), and the Executive Chairman of Tenaga Nasional Berhad (TNB), Malaysia's national power company. He holds degrees in Mechanical Engineering and a doctorate in Nuclear Engineering from the University of London.

Meredith Woo is the Director of the International Higher Education Support Program at the Open Society Foundation in London. She previously was a professor and the Buckner W. Clay Dean of Arts and Sciences at the University of Virginia. She also taught at the University of Michigan and Northwestern University, where she helped rebuild the Department of Political Science and co-founded the Center for International and Comparative Studies. An expert on international political economy and East Asian politics, she has written and edited seven books in these areas. She holds master's and doctoral degrees in International Affairs, Latin American Studies, and Political Science from Columbia University.

Philip Yeo is Chairman of SPRING Singapore (Standards, Productivity, and Innovation for Growth), the Singaporean government's development agency with the mission to enable growth of small and medium enterprises, and Chairman of EDIS, an economic development management services company, whose mission is to plan, develop, and manage overseas technology parks and eco-cities. He was Chairman of A*STAR, Agency for Science, Technology, and Research, from 2001 to 2007 and served as Chairman of the Economic Development Board from 1986 to 2006. He also served as a member of the United Nations Committee of Experts in Public Administration and a chairman on the boards of a number of private companies. Mr. Yeo was also Senior Advisor for Science and Technology to the Ministry of Trade and Industry and Special Adviser for Economic Development in the Prime Minister's Office. He has a Master of Science degree in Systems Engineering from the University of Singapore and an MBA from Harvard University.

Yun Zhu is an Assistant Professor of Finance at St. John's University, New York. He has research interests in corporate governance, political economy, financial intermediation, and international finance. His current research focuses on the relationship between political environment and firms' investment and financing decisions at various political entities. His recent work has been published in leading finance journals. He received his PhD from Rensselaer Polytechnic University.

Index

THE WINNERS

GILLIAN JACKSON

BLOODHOUND
— BOOKS —